C++ Game Development By Example

Learn to build games and graphics with SFML, OpenGL, and Vulkan using C++ programming

Siddharth Shekar

BIRMINGHAM - MUMBAI

C++ Game Development By Example

Copyright © 2019 Packt Publishing

Every effort has been made in the preparation of this book to ensure the accuracy of the information presented. However, the information contained in this book is sold without warranty, either express or implied. Neither the author, nor Packt Publishing or its dealers and distributors, will be held liable for any damages caused or alleged to have been caused directly or indirectly by this book.

Packt Publishing has endeavored to provide trademark information about all of the companies and products mentioned in this book by the appropriate use of capitals. However, Packt Publishing cannot guarantee the accuracy of this information.

Commissioning Editor: Kunal Choudhari
Acquisition Editor: Trusha Shriyan
Content Development Editor: Keagan Carneiro
Technical Editor: Leena Patil
Copy Editor: Safis Editing
Language Support Editor: Storm Mann
Project Coordinator: Kinjal Bari
Proofreader: Safis Editing
Indexer: Pratik Shirodkar
Graphics: Alishon Mendonsa
Production Coordinator: Shraddha Falebhai

First published: May 2019

Production reference: 2131219

Published by Packt Publishing Ltd.
Livery Place
35 Livery Street
Birmingham
B3 2PB, UK.

ISBN 978-1-78953-530-3

www.packtpub.com

To my loving mother, Shanti Shekar, and my caring father, Shekar Rangarajan, for their sacrifices and for exemplifying the power of determination.

— Siddharth Shekar

`Packt.com`

Subscribe to our online digital library for full access to over 7,000 books and videos, as well as industry leading tools to help you plan your personal development and advance your career. For more information, please visit our website.

Why subscribe?

- Spend less time learning and more time coding with practical eBooks and Videos from over 4,000 industry professionals

- Improve your learning with Skill Plans built especially for you

- Get a free eBook or video every month

- Fully searchable for easy access to vital information

- Copy and paste, print, and bookmark content

Did you know that Packt offers eBook versions of every book published, with PDF and ePub files available? You can upgrade to the eBook version at `www.packt.com` and as a print book customer, you are entitled to a discount on the eBook copy. Get in touch with us at `customercare@packtpub.com` for more details.

At `www.packt.com`, you can also read a collection of free technical articles, sign up for a range of free newsletters, and receive exclusive discounts and offers on Packt books and eBooks.

Contributors

About the author

Siddharth Shekar is a game developer and teacher with over 6 years' industry experience and 12 years' experience in C++ and other programming languages. He is adept at graphics libraries such as OpenGL and Vulkan, and game engines such as Unity and Unreal.

He has published games on the iOS and Android app stores. He has also authored books including *Swift Game Development, Mastering Android Game Development with Unity*, and *Learning iOS 8 Game Development Using Swift*, all published by Packt Publishing.

He currently lives in Auckland, New Zealand, and is a lecturer in the games department at Media Design School. He teaches advanced computer graphics programming, PlayStation 4 native game development, and mentors final year production students.

About the reviewers

Simone Angeloni is a software engineer with over 14 years' experience in C/C++. His skill set includes cross-platform development, network communications, embedded systems, multithreading, databases, web applications, low-latency architectures, user interfaces, game development, and visual design. At present, he is the principal software engineer of the R&D department of MRMC, a subsidiary company of Nikon Corporation, where he develops robotic motion control solutions used for live broadcasts, film productions, and photography.

Andreas Oehlke is a professional full-stack software engineer. He holds a bachelor's degree in computer science and loves to experiment with software and hardware. His trademark has always been his enthusiasm and affinity for electronics and computers. His hobbies include game development, building embedded systems, sports, and making music. He currently works full-time as a senior software engineer for a German financial institution. Furthermore, he has worked as a consultant and game developer in San Francisco, CA. He is also the author of *Learning LibGDX Game Development*, published by Packt Publishing.

Packt is searching for authors like you

If you're interested in becoming an author for Packt, please visit authors.packtpub.com and apply today. We have worked with thousands of developers and tech professionals, just like you, to help them share their insight with the global tech community. You can make a general application, apply for a specific hot topic that we are recruiting an author for, or submit your own idea.

Table of Contents

Preface

Computer graphics programming is considered to be one of the hardest subjects to cover, as it involves complex mathematics, programming, and graphics concepts that are intimidating to the average developer. Also, with alternative game engines available, such as Unity and Unreal, it is important to understand graphics programming, as it is a lot easier to make 2D or 3D games using these more sophisticated game engines. These engines also use some rendering APIs, such as OpenGL, Vulkan, Direct3D, and Metal, to draw objects in a scene, and the graphics engine in a game engine constitutes more than 50% of it. Therefore, it is imperative to have some knowledge about graphics programming and graphics APIs.

The objective of this book is to break down this complex subject into bite-sized chunks to make it easy to understand. So, we will start with the basic concepts that are required to understand the math, programming, and graphics basics.

In the next section of the book, we will create a 2D game, initially with **Simple and Fast Multimedia Library (SFML)**, which covers the basics that are required to create any game, and with which you can make any game with the utmost ease, without worrying about how a game object is drawn. We will be using SFML just to draw our game objects.

In the next part of the book, we will see how game objects get presented onscreen using OpenGL. OpenGL is a high-level Graphics API that enables us to get something rendered to a scene quickly. A simple sprite created in SFML goes through a lot of steps before actually getting drawn on the screen. We will see how a simple image gets loaded and gets displayed on the screen and what steps are required to do so. But that is just the start. We will see how to add 3D physics to the game and develop a physics-based game from the ground up. Finally, we will add some lighting to make the scene a little more interesting.

With that knowledge of OpenGL, we will dive further into graphics programming and see how Vulkan works. Vulkan is the successor to OpenGL and is a low-level, verbose graphics API. OpenGL is a high-level graphics API that hides a lot of inner workings. With Vulkan, you have complete access to the GPU, and with the Vulkan graphics API, we will learn how to render our game objects.

Who this book is for

This book is targeted at game developers keen to learn game development with C++ and graphics programming using OpenGL or the Vulkan graphics API. This book is also for those looking to update their existing knowledge of those subjects. Some prior knowledge of C++ programming is assumed.

What this book covers

Chapter 1, *C++ Concepts*, covers the basics of C++ programming, which are essential to understand and code the chapters in this book.

Chapter 2, *Mathematics and Graphics Concepts*, In this chapter we cover the basic topics of maths such as vector calculations and knowledge on matrices. These are essential for graphics programming and basic physics programming. We then move on to the basics of graphics programming, starting with how a bunch of vertices is sent to the graphics pipeline and how they are converted into shapes and rendered on the screen.

Chapter 3, *Setting Up Your Game*, introduces the SFML framework, its uses, and its limitations. It also covers creating a Visual Studio project and adding SFML to it, creating a basic window with the basic framework of the game to initialize, update, render, and close it. We will also learn how to draw different shapes and learn how to add a textured sprite to the scene and add keyboard input.

Chapter 4, *Creating Your Game*, covers the creation of the character class and adding functionality to a character to make them move and jump. We will also create the enemy class to populate enemies for the game. We will add a rockets class so the player can spawn rockets when they fire. Finally, we will add collision detection to detect collisions between two sprites.

Chapter 5, *Finalizing Your Game*, covers finishing the game and adding some polishing touches by adding scoring, text, and audio. We'll also add some animation to the player character to make the game more lively.

Chapter 6, *Getting Started with OpenGL*, looks at what OpenGL is, its advantages, and its shortcomings. We'll integrate OpenGL into the Visual Studio project and use GLFW to create a window. We'll create a basic game loop and render our first 3D object using Vertex and fragment shaders.

Chapter 7, *Building on the Game Objects*, covers adding textures to an object. We'll include the Bullet Physics library in the project to add physics to the scene. We will see how to integrate physics with our 3D OpenGL rendered object. Finally, we will create a basic level to test out the physics.

Chapter 8, *Enhancing Your Game with Collision, Loop, and Lighting*, covers adding a game-over condition and finishing the game loop. We will add some finishing touches to the game by adding some basic 3D lighting and text to display the score and game-over condition.

Chapter 9, *Getting Started with Vulkan*, looks at the need for Vulkan and how it is different from OpenGL. We'll look at the advantages and disadvantages of Vulkan, integrate it into the Visual Studio project, and add GLFW to create a window for the project. We will create an app and a Vulkan instance, and add validation layers to check whether Vulkan is running as required. We'll also get physical device properties and create a logical device.

Chapter 10, *Preparing the Clear Screen*, covers the creation of a window surface to which we can render the scene. We also need to create a swap chain so that we can ping-pong between the front buffer and back buffer, and create image views and frame buffers to which the views are attached. We will create the draw command buffer to record and submit graphics commands and create a renderpass clear screen.

Chapter 11, *Creating Object Resources*, covers creating the resources required to draw the geometry. This includes adding a mesh class that has all the geometry information, including vertex and index data. We'll create object buffers to store the vertex, index, and uniform buffers. We'll also create DescriptorSetLayout and Descriptor Sets, and finally, we'll create shaders and convert them to SPIR-V binary format.

Chapter 12, *Drawing Vulkan Objects*, covers creating the graphics pipeline, in which we set the vertices and enable viewports, multisampling, and depth and stencil testing. We'll also create an object class, which will help create the object buffers, descriptor set, and graphics pipeline for the object. We will create a camera class to view the world through, and then finally render the object. At the end of the chapter, we will also see how to synchronize information being sent.

To get the most out of this book

The book is designed to be read from the start, chapter by chapter. If you have prior knowledge of the contents of a chapter, then please feel free to skip ahead instead.

It is good to have some prior programming experience with C++, but if not, then there is a chapter on C++ programming, which covers the basics. No prior knowledge of graphics programming is assumed.

To run OpenGL and Vulkan projects, make sure your hardware supports the current version of the API. The book uses OpenGL 4.5 and Vulkan 1.1. Most GPU vendors support OpenGL and Vulkan, but for a full list of supported GPUs, please refer to the GPU manufacturer or to the wiki, at https://en.wikipedia.org/wiki/Vulkan_(API).

Download the example code files

You can download the example code files for this book from your account at www.packt.com. If you purchased this book elsewhere, you can visit www.packtpub.com/support and register to have the files emailed directly to you.

You can download the code files by following these steps:

1. Log in or register at www.packt.com.
2. Select the **Support** tab.
3. Click on **Code Downloads**.
4. Enter the name of the book in the **Search** box and follow the onscreen instructions.

Once the file is downloaded, please make sure that you unzip or extract the folder using the latest version of:

- WinRAR/7-Zip for Windows
- Zipeg/iZip/UnRarX for Mac
- 7-Zip/PeaZip for Linux

The code bundle for the book is also hosted on GitHub at https://github.com/PacktPublishing/CPP-Game-Development-By-Example. In case there's an update to the code, it will be updated on the existing GitHub repository.

We also have other code bundles from our rich catalog of books and videos available at https://github.com/PacktPublishing/. Check them out!

Download the color images

We also provide a PDF file that has color images of the screenshots/diagrams used in this book. You can download it here:

https://www.packtpub.com/sites/default/files/downloads/9781789535303_ColorImages.pdf.

Conventions used

There are a number of text conventions used throughout this book.

CodeInText: Indicates code words in text, database table names, folder names, filenames, file extensions, pathnames, dummy URLs, user input, and Twitter handles. Here is an example: "Here, the printing of Hello, World is tasked to the main function."

A block of code is set as follows:

```
#include <iostream>
// Program prints out "Hello, World" to screen
int main()
{
std::cout<< "Hello, World."<<std::endl;
return 0;
}
```

When we wish to draw your attention to a particular part of a code block, the relevant lines or items are set in bold:

```
int main() {
    //init game objects
        while (window.isOpen()) {
            // Handle Keyboard events
            // Update Game Objects in the scene
        window.clear(sf::Color::Red);
        // Render Game Objects
        window.display();
        }
        return 0;
    }
```

Bold: Indicates a new term, an important word, or words that you see onscreen. For example, words in menus or dialog boxes appear in the text like this. Here is an example: "In **Input** and under **Linker**, type the following `.lib` files."

 Warnings or important notes appear like this.

 Tips and tricks appear like this.

Get in touch

Feedback from our readers is always welcome.

General feedback: If you have questions about any aspect of this book, mention the book title in the subject of your message and email us at customercare@packtpub.com.

Errata: Although we have taken every care to ensure the accuracy of our content, mistakes do happen. If you have found a mistake in this book, we would be grateful if you would report this to us. Please visit www.packtpub.com/support/errata, selecting your book, clicking on the Errata Submission Form link, and entering the details.

Piracy: If you come across any illegal copies of our works in any form on the Internet, we would be grateful if you would provide us with the location address or website name. Please contact us at copyright@packt.com with a link to the material.

If you are interested in becoming an author: If there is a topic that you have expertise in and you are interested in either writing or contributing to a book, please visit authors.packtpub.com.

Reviews

Please leave a review. Once you have read and used this book, why not leave a review on the site that you purchased it from? Potential readers can then see and use your unbiased opinion to make purchase decisions, we at Packt can understand what you think about our products, and our authors can see your feedback on their book. Thank you!

For more information about Packt, please visit `packt.com`.

Section 1: Basic Concepts

This section covers some basic concepts of C++ game development. We need to have a good understanding of math, programming, and computer graphics to get ready for the later sections in the book.

The following chapters are in this section:

Chapter 1, *C++ Concepts*

Chapter 2, *Mathematics and Graphics Concepts*

C++ Concepts 1

In this chapter, we will explore the basics of writing a C++ program. Here, we will cover just enough to wrap our heads around the capabilities of the C++ programming language. This will be required to understand the code used in this book.

To run the examples, use Visual Studio 2017. You can download the community version for free at `https://visualstudio.microsoft.com/vs/`:

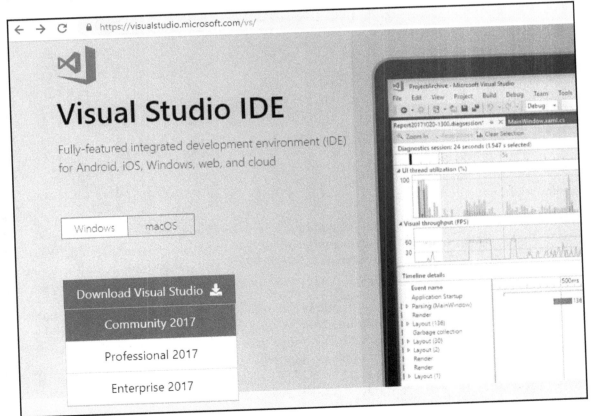

The topics covered in this chapter are as follows:

- Program basics
- Variables
- Operators
- Statements
- Iteration
- Functions
- Arrays and pointers
- `Struct` and `Enum`
- Classes and inheritance

Program basics

C++ is a programming language, but what exactly is a program? A program is a set of instructions executed in sequence to give a desired output.

Let's look at our first program:

```
#include <iostream>
// Program prints out "Hello, World" to screen
int main()
{
    std::cout<< "Hello, World."<<std::endl;
    return 0;
}
```

We can look at this code line by line.

The hash (#) include is used when we want to include anything that is using valid C++ syntax. In this case, we are including a standard C++ library in our program. The file we want to include is then specified inside the <> angle brackets. Here, we are including a file called iostream.h. This file handles the input and output of data to the console/screen.

On the second line, the // double slash marks the initiation of a code comment. Comments in code are not executed by the program. They are mainly to tell the person looking at the code what the code is currently doing. It is good practice to comment your code so that when you look at code you wrote a year ago, you will know what the code does.

Basically, `main()` is a function. We will cover functions shortly, but a `main` function is the first function that is executed in a program, also called the entry point. A function is used to perform a certain task. Here, the printing of `Hello, World` is tasked to the `main` function. The contents that need to be executed must be enclosed in the curly brackets of the function. The `int` preceding the `main()` keyword suggests that the function will return an integer. This is why we have returned 0 at the end of the main function, suggesting that the program can be executed and can terminate without errors.

When we want to print out something to the console/screen, we use the `std::cout` (console out) C++ command to send something to the screen. Whatever we want to send out should start and end with the output operator, `<<`. Furthermore, `<<std::endl` is another C++ command, which specifies the end of a era line and that nothing else should be printed on the line afterward. We have to use the prefix before `std::` to tell C++ that we are using the standard namespace with the `std` namespace. But why are namespaces necessary? We need namespaces because anyone can declare a variable name with `std`. How would the compiler differentiate between the two types of `std`? For this, we have namespaces to differentiate between the two.

Note that the two lines of code we have written in the main function have a semicolon (`;`) at the end of each line. The semicolon tells the compiler that this is the end of the instructions for that line of code so that the program can stop reading when it gets to the semicolon and go to the next line of instruction. Consequently, it is important to add a semicolon at the end of each line of instruction as it is mandatory.

The two lines of code we wrote before can be written in one line as follows:

```
std::cout<< "Hello, World."<<std::endl;return 0;
```

Even though it is written in a single line, for the compiler, there are two instructions with both instructions ending with a semicolon.

The first instruction is to print out `Hello, World` to the console, and the second instruction is to terminate the program without any errors.

It is a very common mistake to forget semicolons, and it happens to beginners as well as experienced programmers every now and then. So it's good to keep this in mind, for when you encounter your first set of compiler errors.

Let's run this code in Visual Studio using the following steps:

1. Open up Visual Studio and create a new project by going to **File | New | Project**.
2. On the left-hand side, select **Visual C++** and then **Other**. For the **Project Type**, select **Empty Project**. Give this project a **Name**. Visual Studio automatically names the first project `MyFirstProject`. You can name it whatever you like.
3. Select the **Location** that you want the project to be saved in:

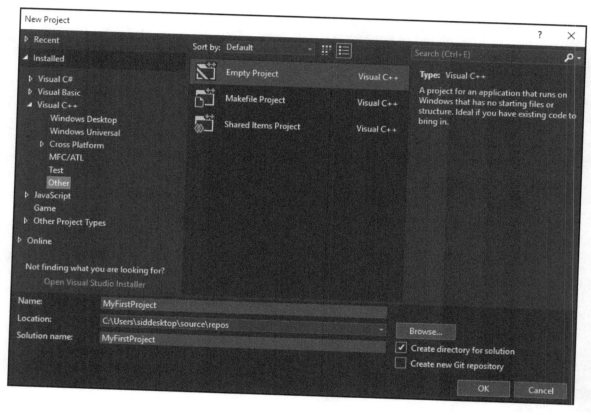

4. Once the project is created, in **Solution Explorer**, right-click and select **Add | New Item**:

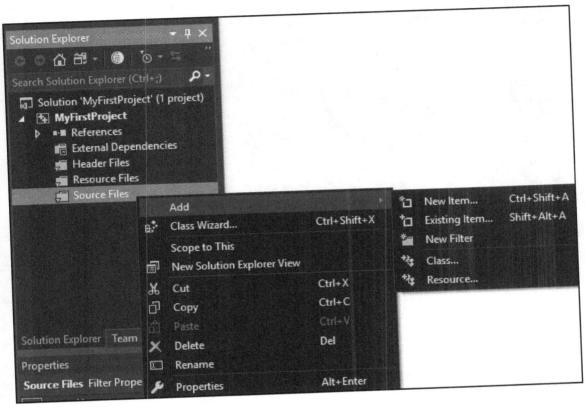

5. Create a new `.cpp` file, called the `Source` file:

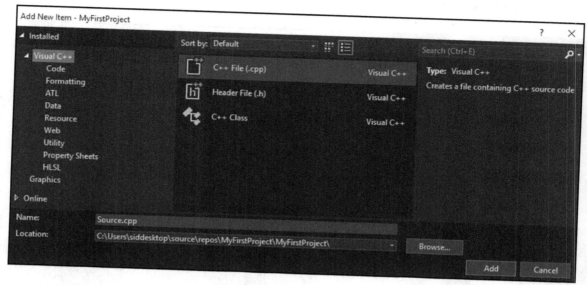

6. Copy the code at the start of the section into the `Source.cpp` file.
7. Now press the *F5* key on the keyboard or press the **Local Window Debugger** button at the top of the window to run the application.
8. A popup of the console should appear upon running the program. To make the console stay so that we can see what is happening, add the following highlighted lines to the code:

```
#include <iostream>
#include <conio.h>
// Program prints out "Hello, World" to screen
int main()
{
    std::cout << "Hello, World." << std::endl;
    _getch();
    return 0;
}
```

What `_getch()` does is it stalls the program and waits for a character input to the console without printing the character to the console. So, the program will wait for some input and then close the console.

To see what is printed to the console, we just add it for convenience. To use this function, we need to include the `conio.h` header.

9. When you run the project again, you will see the following output:

Now that we know how to run a basic program, let's look at the different data types that are included in C++.

Variables

A variable is used to store a value. Whatever value you store in a variable is stored in the memory location associated with that memory location. You assign a value to a variable with the following syntax.

We can first declare a variable type by specifying a type and then the variable name:

```
Type variable;
```

Here, `type` is the variable type and `variable` is the name of the variable.

Next, we can assign a value to a variable:

```
Variable = value;
```

Now that value is assigned to the variable.

Or, you can both declare the variable and assign a value to it in a single line, as follows:

```
type variable = value;
```

Before you set a variable, you have to specify the variable type. You can then use the equals sign (=) to assign a value to a variable.

Let's look at some example code:

```cpp
#include <iostream>
#include <conio.h>
// Program prints out value of n to screen
int main()
{
    int n = 42;
std::cout <<"Value of n is: "<< n << std::endl;
    _getch();
    return 0;
}
```

Replace the previous code with this code in `Source.cpp` and run the application. This is the output you should get:

C:\Users\siddesktop\source\repos\MyFirstProject\Debug\MyFirstProject.exe

Value of n is: 42

In this program, we specify the data type as `int`. An `int` is a C++ data type that can store integers. So, it cannot store decimal values. We declare a variable called n, and then we assign a value of 42 to it. Do not forget to add the semicolon at the end of the line.

In the next line, we print the value to the console. Note that to print the value of n, we just pass in n in `cout` and don't have to add quotation marks.

On a 32-bit system, an int variable uses 4 bytes (which is equal to 32 bits) of memory. This basically means the int data type can hold values between 0 and 2^{32}-1 (4,294,967,295). However, one bit is needed to describe the sign for the value (positive or negative), which leaves 31 bits remaining to express the actual value. Therefore, a signed int can hold values between -2^{31} (-2,147,483,648) and 2^{31}-1 (2,147,483,647).

Let's look at some other data types:

- `bool`: A bool can have only two values. It can either store `true` or `false`.
- `char`: These stores integers ranging between *-128* and *127*. Note that `char` or character variables are used to store ASCII characters such as single characters—letters, for example.
- `short` and `long`: These are also integer types, but they are able to store more information than just int. The size of int is system-dependent and `long` and `short` have fixed sizes irrespective of the system used.
- `float`: This is a floating point type. This means that it can store values with decimal spaces such as 3.14, 0.000875, and -9.875. It can store data with up to seven decimal places.
- `double`: This is a `float` with more precision. It can store decimal values up to 15 decimal places.

Data type	Minimum	Maximum	Size (bytes)
bool	false	true	1
char	-128	127	1
short	-32768	327677	2
int	-2,147,483,648	2,147,483,647	4
long	-2,147,483,648	2,147,483,647	4
float	$3.4 \times 10\text{-}38$	3.4×1038	4
double	$1.7 \times 10\text{-}308$	1.7×10308	8

You also have unsigned data types of the same data type used to maximize the range of values they can store. Unsigned data types are used to store positive values. Consequently, all unsigned values start at 0.

So, `char` and unsigned `char` can store positive values from *0* to *255*. Similar to unsigned char, we have unsigned `short`, `int`, and `long`.

You can assign values to `bool`, `char`, and `float`, as follows:

```
#include <iostream>
#include <conio.h>
// Program prints out value of bool, char and float to screen
int main()
{
    bool a = false;
    char b = 'b';
    float c = 3.1416f;
    unsigned int d = -82;
```

```
std::cout << "Value of a is : " << a << std::endl;
std::cout << "Value of b is : " << b << std::endl;
std::cout << "Value of c is : " << c << std::endl;
std::cout << "Value of d is : " << d << std::endl;

_getch();
return 0;
}
```

This is the output when you run the application:

Everything is printing fine except d, which was assigned -82. What happened here? Well that's because d can store only unsigned values, so if we assign it -82, it gives a garbage value. Change it to just 82 without the negative sign and it will print the correct value:

Unlike int, bool stores a binary value where false is 0 and true is 1. So, when you print out the values of true and false, the output will be 1 and 0, respectively.

Basically, char stores characters specified with single quotation marks, and values with decimals are printed just how you stored the values in the floats. An f is added at the end of the value when assigning a float, to tell the system that it is a float and not a double.

Strings

Variables that are non-numerical are either a single character or a series of characters called strings. In C++, a series of characters can be stored in a special variable called a string. A string is provided through a standard string class.

To declare and use `string` objects, we have to include the string header file. After `#include <conio.h>`, also add `#include <string>` at the top of the file.

A string variable is declared in the same way as other variable types, except before the string type you have to use the `std` namespace.

If you don't like adding the `std::` namespace prefix, you can also add the line using the `std` namespace after `#include`. This way, you won't have to add the `std::` prefix, as the program will understand well enough without it. However, it can be printed out just like other variables:

```cpp
#include <iostream>
#include <conio.h>
#include <string>

// Program prints out values to screen

int main()
{

    std::string name = "The Dude";

    std::cout << "My name is: " << name << std::endl;

    _getch();
    return 0;
}
```

Here is the output:

Operators

An operator is a symbol that performs a certain operation on a variable or expression. So far, we have used the = sign, which calls an assignment operator that assigns a value or expression from the right-hand side of the equals sign to a variable on the left-hand side.

The simplest form of other kinds of operators are arithmetic operators such as +, −, *, /, and %. These operators operate on a variable such as `int` and `float`. Let's look at some of the use cases of these operators:

```cpp
#include <iostream>
#include <conio.h>
// Program prints out value of a + b and x + y to screen
int main()
{
    int a = 8;
    int b = 12;
    std::cout << "Value of a + b is : " << a + b << std::endl;
    float x = 7.345f;
    float y = 12.8354;
    std::cout << "Value of x + y is : " << x + y << std::endl;

    _getch();
    return 0;
}
```

The output of this is as follows:

```
C:\Users\siddesktop\source\repos\MyFirstProject\Debug\MyFirstProject.exe
Value of a + b is : 20
Value of x + y is : 20.1804
```

Let's look at examples for other operations as well:

```cpp
#include <iostream>
#include <conio.h>

// Program prints out values to screen

int main()
{
    int a = 36;
    int b = 5;

    std::cout << "Value of a + b is : " << a + b << std::endl;
    std::cout << "Value of a - b is : " << a - b << std::endl;
    std::cout << "Value of a * b is : " << a * b << std::endl;
    std::cout << "Value of a / b is : " << a / b << std::endl;
    std::cout << "Value of a % b is : " << a % b << std::endl;
```

```
    _getch();
    return 0;
}
```

The output is as follows:

```
C:\Users\siddesktop\source\repos\MyFirstProject\Debug\MyFirstProject.exe

Value of a + b is : 41
Value of a - b is : 31
Value of a * b is : 180
Value of a / b is : 7
Value of a % b is : 1
```

The +, −, *, and / signs are self-explanatory. However, there is one more arithmetic operator: %, which is called the modulus operator. It returns the remainder of a division.

How many times is 5 contained in 36? The answer is 7 times with a remainder of 1. That's why the result is 1.

Apart from the arithmetic operators, we also have an increment/decrement operator.

In programming, we increment variables often. You can do a=a+1; to increment and a=a-1; to decrement a variable value. Alternatively, you can even do a+=1; and a-=1; to increment and decrement, but in C++ programming there is an even shorter way of doing that, which is by using the ++ and -- signs to increment and decrement the value of a variable by 1.

Let's look at an example of how to use it to increment and decrement a value by 1:

```cpp
#include <iostream>
#include <conio.h>

// Program prints out values to screen

int main()
{
    int a = 36;
    int b = 5;

    std::cout << "Value of ++a is : " << ++a << std::endl;
    std::cout << "Value of --b is : " << --b << std::endl;
```

```
    std::cout << "Value of a is : " << a << std::endl;
    std::cout << "Value of b is : " << b << std::endl;

    _getch();
    return 0;
}
```

The output of this is as follows:

```
C:\Users\siddesktop\source\repos\MyFirstProject\Debug\MyFirstProject.exe
Value of ++a is : 37
Value of --b is : 4
Value of a is : 37
Value of b is : 4
```

Consequently, the ++ or -- operator increments the value permanently. If the ++ operator is to the left of the variable, it is called a pre-increment operator. If it is put afterward, it is called a post-increment operator. There is a slight difference between the two. If we put ++ on the other side, we get the following output:

```
C:\Users\siddesktop\source\repos\MyFirstProject\Debug\MyFirstProject.exe
Value of a++ is : 36
Value of b-- is : 5
Value of a is : 37
Value of b is : 4
```

In this case, a and b are incremented and decremented in the next line. So, when you print the values, it prints out the correct result.

It doesn't make a difference here, as it is a simple example, but overall it does make a difference, and it is good to understand this difference. In this book, we will mostly be using post-increment operators.

In fact, this is how C++ got its name; it is an increment of C.

Apart from arithmetic, increment, and decrement operators, you also have logical and comparison operators.

The logical operators are shown in the following table:

Operator	Operation
!	NOT
&&	AND
| |	OR

Here are the comparison operators:

Operator	Comparison
==	Equal to
!=	Not equal to
<	Less than
>	Greater than
<=	Less than equal to
>=	Greater than equal to

We will cover these operators in the next section.

Statements

A program may not always be linear. Depending on your requirements, you might have to branch out or bifurcate, repeat a set of code, or take a decision. For this, there are conditional statements and loops.

In a conditional statement, you check whether a condition is true. If it is, you will go ahead and execute the statement.

The first of the conditional statements is the `if` statement. The syntax for this looks as follows:

```
If (condition) statement;
```

Let's look at how to use this in the following code. Let's use one of the comparison operators here:

```cpp
#include <iostream>
#include <conio.h>

// Program prints out values to screen

int main()
{
    int a = 36;
    int b = 5;

    if (a > b)
    std::cout << a << " is greater than " << b << std::endl;

    _getch();
    return 0;
}
```

The output is as follows:

```
C:\Users\siddesktop\source\repos\MyFirstProject\Debug\MyFirstProject.exe
36 is greater than 5
```

We check the whether `a` is greater than `b`, and if the condition is true, then we print out the statement.

But what if the opposite is true? For this, we have the `if...else` statement, which is a statement that basically executes the alternate statement. The syntax looks like this:

```cpp
if (condition) statement1;
else statement2;
```

Let's look at it in code:

```cpp
#include <iostream>
#include <conio.h>

// Program prints out values to screen

int main()
{

    int a = 2;
```

```
int b = 28;

if (a > b)
std::cout << a << " is greater than " << b << std::endl;
else
std::cout << b << " is greater than " << a << std::endl;

_getch();
return 0;
}
```

Here, the values of a and b are changed so that b is greater than a:

```
 C:\Users\siddesktop\source\repos\MyFirstProject\Debug\MyFirstProject.exe

28 is greater than 2
```

One thing to note is that after the if and else conditions, C++ will execute a single line of statement. If there are multiple statements after if or else, then the statements need to be in curly brackets, as shown:

```
if (a > b)
{
        std::cout << a << " is greater than " << b << std::endl;
}
else
{
        std::cout << b << " is greater than " << a << std::endl;
}
```

You can also have the if statements after using else if:

```
#include <iostream>
#include <conio.h>

// Program prints out values to screen

int main()
{
    int a = 28;
    int b = 28;

    if (a > b)
```

```
        {
                std::cout << a << " is greater than " << b << std::endl;
        }
        else if (a == b)
    {
                std::cout << a << " is equal to " << b << std::endl;
        }
        else
        {
                std::cout << b << " is greater than " << a << std::endl;
        }

        _getch();
        return 0;
}
```

The output is as follows:

```
C:\Users\siddesktop\source\repos\MyFirstProject\Debug\MyFirstProject.exe
28 is equal to 28
```

Iteration

Iteration is the process of calling the same statement repeatedly. C++ has three iteration statements: the `while`, `do...while`, and `for` statements. Iteration is also commonly referred to as loops.

The `while` loop syntax looks like the following:

```
while (condition) statement;
```

Let's look at it in action:

```
#include <iostream>
#include <conio.h>
// Program prints out values to screen
int main()
{
    int a = 10;
    int n = 0;
    while (n < a) {
            std::cout << "value of n is: " << n << std::endl;
            n++;
```

```
    }
    _getch();
    return 0;
}
```

Here is the output of this code:

```
■ C:\Users\siddesktop\source\repos\MyFirstProject\Debug\MyFirstProject.exe
value of n is: 0
value of n is: 1
value of n is: 2
value of n is: 3
value of n is: 4
value of n is: 5
value of n is: 6
value of n is: 7
value of n is: 8
value of n is: 9
```

Here, the value of n is printed to the console until the condition is met.

The do while statement is almost the same as a while statement except, in this case, the statement is executed first and then the condition is tested. The syntax is as follows:

```
do statement
while (condition);
```

You can give it a go yourself and see the result.

The loop that is most commonly used in programming is the for loop. The syntax for this looks as follows:

```
for (initialization; continuing condition; update) statement;
```

The for loop is very self-contained. In while loops, we have to initialize n outside the while loop, but in the for loop, the initialization is done in the declaration of the for loop itself.

Here is the same example as the while loop but with the for loop:

```
#include <iostream>
#include <conio.h>
// Program prints out values to screen
int main()
```

```
{
    for (int n = 0; n < 10; n++)
        std::cout << "value of n is: " << n << std::endl;
    _getch();
    return 0;
}
```

The output is the same as the `while` loop but at look how compact the code is compared to the `while` loop. Also, n is scoped locally to the `for` loop body.

We can also increment n by 2 instead of 1, as shown:

```
#include <iostream>
#include <conio.h>

// Program prints out values to screen
int main()
{
    for (int n = 0; n < 10; n+=2)
        std::cout << "value of n is: " << n << std::endl;
    _getch();
    return 0;
}
```

Here is the output of this code:

Select C:\Users\siddesktop\source\repos\MyFirstProject\Debug\MyFirstProject.exe
```
value of n is: 0
value of n is: 2
value of n is: 4
value of n is: 6
value of n is: 8
```

Jump statements

As well as condition and iteration statements, you also have the `break` and `continue` statements.

The `break` statement is used to break out of an iteration. We can leave a loop and force it to quit if a certain condition is met.

Let's look at the break statement in use:

```cpp
#include <iostream>
#include <conio.h>
// Program prints out values to screen
int main()
{
    for (int n = 0; n < 10; n++)
    {
        if (n == 5) {
            std::cout << "break" << std::endl;
            break;
        }
        std::cout << "value of n is: " << n << std::endl;
    }
    _getch();
    return 0;
}
```

The output of this is as follows:

The continue statement will skip the current iteration and continue the execution of the statement until the end of the loop. In the break code, replace break with continue to see the difference:

```cpp
#include <iostream>
#include <conio.h>

// Program prints out values to screen

int main()
{

    for (int n = 0; n < 10; n++)
    {
```

```
        if (n == 5) {
            std::cout << "continue" << std::endl;

            continue;
        }
        std::cout << "value of n is: " << n << std::endl;
    }
    _getch();
    return 0;
}
```

Here is the output when break is replaced with continue:

Switch statement

The last of the statements is the switch statement. A switch statement checks for several cases of values, and if a value matches the expression, then it executes the corresponding statement and breaks out of the switch statement. If it doesn't find any of the values, then it will output a default statement.

The syntax for it looks as follows:

```
switch( expression){

case constant1:   statement1; break;
case constant2:   statement2; break;
.
.
.
default: default statement; break;

}
```

This looks very familiar to the `else if` statements, but this is more sophisticated. Here is an example:

```cpp
#include <iostream>
#include <conio.h>

// Program prints out values to screen

int main()
{
    int a = 28;

    switch (a)
    {
    case 1: std::cout << " value of a is " << a << std::endl; break;
    case 2: std::cout << " value of a is " << a << std::endl; break;
    case 3: std::cout << " value of a is " << a << std::endl; break;
    case 4: std::cout << " value of a is " << a << std::endl; break;
    case 5: std::cout << " value of a is " << a << std::endl; break;
    default: std::cout << " value a is out of range " << std::endl; break;
    }

    _getch();
    return 0;
}
```

The output is as follows:

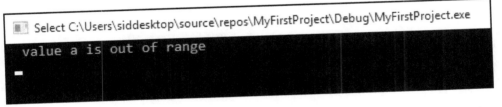

Change the value of `a` to equal 2 and you will see that it prints out the statement when the 2 case is correct.

Also note that it is important to add the `break` statement. If you forget to add it, then the program will not break out of the statement.

Functions

So far, we have written all of our code in the main function. This is fine if you are doing a single task, but once you start doing more with a program, the code will become bigger and over a period of time everything will be in the main function, which will look very confusing.

With functions, you can break your code up into smaller, manageable chunks. This will enable you to structure your program better.

A function has the following syntax:

```
type function name (parameter1, parameter2) {statements;}
```

Going from left to right, `type` here is the return type. After performing a statement, a function is capable of returning a value. This value could be of any type, so we specify a type here. A function has only one variable at a time.

The function name is the name of the function itself.

Then, inside brackets, you will pass in parameters. These parameters are variables of a certain type that are passed into the function to perform a certain function.

Here is an example: two parameters are passed in but you can pass as many parameters you want. You can pass in more than one parameter per function, and each parameter is separated by a comma.

Let's look at this example:

```cpp
#include <iostream>
#include <conio.h>

// Program prints out values to screen

void add(int a, int b)
{
    int c = a + b;

    std::cout << "Sum of " << a << " and " << b << " is " << c <<
    std::endl;
}
int main()
{
    int x = 28;
    int y = 12;
```

```
    add(x, y);

    _getch();
    return 0;
}
```

Here, we create a new function called `add`. For now, make sure the functions are added before the `main` function; otherwise, `main` will not know that the function exists.

The `add` function doesn't return anything so we use the `void` keyword at the start of the function. Not all functions have to return a value. Next, we name the function `add` and then pass in two parameters, which are `a` and `b` of the `int` type.

In the function, we create a new variable called `c` of the `int` type, add the values of the arguments passed in, and assign it to `c`. The new `add` function finally prints out the value of `c`.

Furthermore, in the `main` function, we create two variables called `x` and `y` of the `int` type, call the `add` function, and pass in `x` and `y` as arguments.

When we call the function, we pass the value of `x` to `a` and the value of `y` to `b`, which is added and stored in `c` to get the following output:

When you create new functions, make sure they are written above the main function; otherwise, it will not be able to see the functions and the compiler will throw errors.

Now let's write one more function. This time, we will make sure the function returns a value. Create a new function called `multiply`, as follows:

```
int multiply(int a, int b) {

    return a * b;

}
```

In the `main` function, after we've called the `add` function, add the following lines:

```
add(x, y);

int c = multiply(12, 32);

std::cout << "Value returned by multiply function is: " << c <<
std::endl;
```

In the `multiply` function, we have a return type of `int`, so the function will expect a return value at the end of the function, which we return using the `return` keyword. The returned value is the a variable multiplied by the b variable.

In the `main` function, we create a new variable called `c`; call the `multiply` function and pass in 12 and 32. After being multiplied, the return value will be assigned to the value of `c`. After this, we print out the value of `c` in the `main` function.

The output of this is as follows:

```
Select C:\Users\siddesktop\source\repos\MyFirstProject\Debug\MyFirstProject.exe
Sum of 28 and 12 is 40
Value returned by multiply function is: 384
```

We can have a function with the same name, but we can pass in different variables or different numbers of them. This is called **function overloading**.

Create a new function called `multiply`, but this time pass in floats and set the return value to a float as well:

```
float multiply(float a, float b) {

    return a * b;

}
```

This is called function overloading, where the function name is the same, but it takes different types of arguments.

In the `main` function, after we've printed the value of `c`, add the following code:

```
float d = multiply(8.352f, -12.365f);
std::cout << "Value returned by multiply function is: " << d << std::endl;
```

So, what is this `f` after the float value? Well, `f` just converts the doubles to floats. If we don't add the `f`, then the value will be treated as a double by the compiler.

When you run the program, you'll get the value of `d` printed out:

```
C:\Users\siddesktop\source\repos\MyFirstProject\Debug\MyFirstProject.exe
Sum of 28 and 12 is 40
Value returned by multiply function is: 384
Value returned by multiply function is: -103.272
```

Scope of variables

You may have noticed that we have two variables called `c` in the program right now. There is a `c` in the `main` function as well as a `c` in the `add` function. How is it that they are both named `c` but have different values?

In C++, there is the concept of a local variable. This means that the definition of a variable is confined to the local block of code it is defined in. Consequently, the `c` variable in the `add` function is treated differently to the `c` variable in the `main` function.

There are also global variables, which need to be declared outside of the function or block of code. Any piece of code written between curly brackets is considered to be a block of code. Consequently, for a variable to be considered a global variable, it needs to be in the body of the program or it needs to be declared outside a block of code of a function.

Arrays

So far, we have only looked at single variables, but what if we want a bunch of variables grouped together? Like the ages of all the students in a class, for example. You can keep creating separate variables, `a`, `b`, `c`, `d`, and so on, and to access each you would have to call each of them, which is cumbersome, as you won't know the kind of data they hold.

To organize data better, we can use arrays. Arrays use continuous memory space to store values in a series, and you can access each element with an index number.

The syntax for arrays is as follows:

```
type name [size] = { value0, value1, ....., valuesize-1};
```

So, we can store the ages of five students as follows:

```
int age[5] = {12, 6, 18 , 7, 9 };
```

When creating an array with a set number of values, you don't have to specify a size but it is a good idea to do so. To access each value, we use the index from 0 - 4 as the first element with a value of 12 at the 0th index and the last element, 9, in the fourth index.

Let's see how to use this in code:

```cpp
#include <iostream>
#include <conio.h>

// Program prints out values to screen
int main()
{
    int age[5] = { 12, 6, 18 , 7, 9 };

    std::cout << "Element at the 0th index " << age[0]<< std::endl;
    std::cout << "Element at the 4th index " << age[4] << std::endl;

    _getch();
    return 0;
}
```

The output is as follows:

```
Select C:\Users\siddesktop\source\repos\MyFirstProject\Debug\MyFirstProject.exe
Element at the 0th index 12
Element at the 4th index 9
```

To access each element in the array, you can use a or loop:

```cpp
#include <iostream>
#include <conio.h>

// Program prints out values to screen
int main()
{
    int age[5] = { 12, 6, 18 , 7, 9 };

    for (int i = 0; i < 5; i++) {

        std::cout << "Element at the "<< i << "th index is: " <<
        age[i] << std::endl;
    }
```

```
    _getch();
    return 0;
}
```

The output of this is as follows:

Instead of calling `age[0]` and so on, we use the `i` index from the `for` loop itself and pass it into the `age` array to print out the index and the value stored at the index.

The `age` array is a single-dimension array. In graphics programming, we have seen that we use a two-dimensional array, which is mostly a 4x4 matrix. Let's look at an example of a two-dimensional 4x4 array. A two-dimensional array is defined as follows:

```
int matrix[4][4] = {
{2, 8, 10, -5},
{15, 21, 22, 32},
{3, 0, 19, 5},
{5, 7, -23, 18}
};
```

To access each element, you use a nested `for` loop.

Let's look at this in the following code:

```
#include <iostream>
#include <conio.h>

// Program prints out values to screen
int main()
{

    int matrix[4][4] = {
                        {2, 8, 10, -5},
                        {15, 21, 22, 32},
                        {3, 0, 19, 5},
                        {5, 7, -23, 18}

    };

    for (int x = 0; x < 4; x++) {
```

```
        for (int y = 0; y < 4; y++) {
            std::cout<< matrix[x][y] <<" ";
        }
        std::cout<<""<<std::endl;
    }


    _getch();
    return 0;
}
```

The output is as follows:

```
Select C:\Users\siddesktop\source\repos\MyFirstProject\Debug\MyFirstProject.exe
2 8 10 -5
15 21 22 32
3 0 19 5
5 7 -23 18
```

As a test, create two matrices and attempt to carry out matrix multiplication.

You can even pass arrays as parameters to functions, shown in the following example.

Here, the matrixPrinter function doesn't return anything but prints out the values stored in each element of the 4x4 matrix:

```
#include <iostream>
#include <conio.h>

void matrixPrinter(int a[4][4]) {

    for (int x = 0; x < 4; x++) {
        for (int y = 0; y < 4; y++) {
            std::cout << a[x][y] << " ";
        }
        std::cout << "" << std::endl;
    }
}


// Program prints out values to screen
int main()
{

    int matrix[4][4] = {
                        {2, 8, 10, -5},
                        {15, 21, 22, 32},
                        {3, 0, 19, 5},
```

```
                            {5, 7, -23, 18}
    };

    matrixPrinter(matrix);


    _getch();
    return 0;
}
```

We can even use an array of `char` to create a string of words. Unlike `int` and `float` arrays, the characters in an array don't have to be in curly brackets and they don't need to be separated by a comma.

To create a character array, you define it as follows:

```
    char name[] = "Hello, World !";
```

You can print out the values just by calling out the name of the array, as follows:

```
#include <iostream>
#include <conio.h>


// Program prints out values to screen
int main()
{

    char name[] = "Hello, World !";

    std::cout << name << std::endl;


    _getch();
    return 0;
}
```

The output of this is as follows:

```
C:\Users\siddesktop\source\repos\MyFirstProject\Debug\MyFirstProject.exe
Hello, World !
```

Pointers

Whenever we declare new variables so that we can store values in them, we actually send a memory allocation request to the operating system. The operating system will try to reserve a block of continuous memory for our application if there is enough free memory left.

When we want to access the value stored in that memory space, we call the variable name.

We don't have to worry about the memory location where we have stored the value. However, what if we want to get the address of the location where the variable is stored?

The address that locates the variable within the memory is called a reference to the variable. To access this, we use an address of the & operator. To get the address location, we place the operator before the variable.

Pointers are variables, and like any other variables they are used to store a value; however, this specific variable type allows the storage of the address—the reference—of another variable.

In C/C++, every variable can also be declared as a pointer that holds a reference to a value of a certain data type by preceding its variable name with an asterisk (*). This means, for example, that an int pointer holds a reference to a memory address where a value of an int may be stored.

A pointer can be used with any built-in or custom data type. If we access the value of a pointer variable, we will simply get the memory address it references. So, in order to access the actual value a pointer variable references, we have to use the so-called dereferencing operator (*).

If we have a variable called age and assign a value to it, to get the reference address location we use &age to store this address in a variable. To store the reference address, we can't just use a regular variable; we have to use a pointer variable and use the dereference operator before it to access the address, as follows:

```
int age = 10;
int *location = &age;
```

Here, the pointer location will store the address of where the age variable value is stored.

If we print the value of location, we will get the reference address where age is stored:

```
#include <iostream>
#include <conio.h>
// Program prints out values to screen
```

```
int main()
{
    int age = 10;
    int *location = &age;
    std::cout << location << std::endl;
    _getch();
    return 0;
}
```

This is the output:

This value might be different for you, as the location will be different from machine to machine.

To get the location of where the location variable itself is stored, we can print out &location as well.

This is the memory location of the variable on my system memory:

Let's look at another example:

```
#include <iostream>
#include <conio.h>

// Program prints out values to screen
int main()
{
    int age = 18;
    int *pointer;

    pointer = &age;

    *pointer = 12;

    std::cout << age << std::endl;
```

```
        _getch();
        return 0;
}
```

Here, we create two `int` variables; one is a regular `int` and the other is a pointer type.

We first set the `age` variable equal to `18`, then we set the address of `age`, and assign it to the `pointer` variable called `pointer`.

The `int` pointer is now pointing to the same address where the `age` variable stores its `int` value.

Next, use the dereference operator on the `pointer` variable to give us access to the `int` values stored at the referenced address and change the current value to `12`.

Now, when we print out the value of the `age` variable, we will see that the previous statement has indeed changed the value of the `age` variable. A null pointer is a pointer that is not pointing to anything, and is set as follows:

```
        int *p = nullptr;
```

Pointers are very much associated with arrays. As arrays are nothing but continuous sequences of memory, we can use pointers with them.

Consider our arrays example from the arrays section:

```
    int age[5] = { 12, 6, 18 , 7, 9 };
```

Instead of using the index, we can use pointers to point to the values in the array.

Consider the following code:

```
    #include <iostream>
    #include <conio.h>

    // Program prints out values to screen
    int main()
    {
        int *p = nullptr;
        int age[5] = { 12, 6, 18 , 7, 9 };
        p = age;
        std::cout << *p << std::endl;

        p++;

        std::cout << *p << std::endl;
```

```
    std::cout << *(p + 3) << std::endl;
std::cout << *p << std::endl;

    _getch();
    return 0;
}
```

In the `main` function, we create a pointer called `pointer`, as well as an array with five elements. We assign the array to the pointer. This causes the pointer to get the location of the address of the first element of the array. So, when we print the value pointed to by the pointer, we get the value of the first element of the array.

With `pointer`, we can also increment and decrement as a regular `int`. However, unlike a regular `int` increment, which increments the value of the variable when you increment a pointer, it will point to the next memory location. So, when we increment p it is now pointing to the next memory location of the array. Incrementing and decrementing a pointer means moving the referenced address by a certain number of bytes. The number of bytes depends on the data type that is used for the `pointer` variable.

Here, the pointer is the `int` type, so when we move the pointer by one, it moves 4 bytes and points to the next integer. When we print the value that p is pointing to now, it prints the second element's value.

We can also get the value of other elements in the array by getting the pointer's current location and by adding to it the nth number you want to get from the current location using `*(p + n)`, where n is the nth element from p. So, when we do `*(p + 3)`, we will get the third element from where p is pointing to currently. Since p was incremented to the second element, the third element from the second element is the fifth element, and so the value of the fifth element is printed out.

However, this doesn't change the location to which p is pointing, which is still the second position.

Here is the output:

Structs

Structures or structs are used to group data together. A `struct` can have different data elements in it, called members, integers, floats, chars, and so on. You can create many objects of a similar `struct` and store values in the `struct` for data management.

The syntax of `struct` is as follows:

```
struct name{

type1 name1;
type2 name2;
.
.
} ;
```

An object of `struct` can be created as follows:

```
struct_name     object_name;
```

An object is an instance of `struct` where we can assign properties to the data types we created while creating the `struct`. An example of this is as follows.

In a situation in which you want to maintain a database of student ages and the height of a section, your `struct` definition will look like this:

```
struct student {

    int age;
    float height;

};
```

Now you can create an array of objects and store the values for each student:

```
int main()
{

    student section[3];

    section[0].age = 17;
    section[0].height = 39.45f;

    section[1].age = 12;
    section[1].height = 29.45f;

    section[2].age = 8;
```

```
    section[2].height = 13.45f;


    for (int i = 0; i < 3; i++) {
        std::cout << "student " << i << " age: " << section[i].age <<
            " height: " << section[i].height << std::endl;
    }


    _getch();
    return 0;
}
```

Here is the output of this:

Enums

Enums are used for enumerating items in a list. When comparing items, it is easier to compare names rather than just numbers. For example, the days in a week are Monday to Sunday. In a program, we will assign Monday to 0, Tuesday to 1, and Sunday to 7, for example. To check whether today is Friday, you will have to count to and arrive at 5. However, wouldn't it be easier to just check if `Today == Friday`?

For this, we have enumerations, declared as follows:

```
enum name{
value1,
value2,
    .
    .
    .
};
```

So, in our example, it would be something like this:

```cpp
#include <iostream>
#include <conio.h>

// Program prints out values to screen

enum Weekdays {
    Monday = 0,
    Tuesday,
    Wednesday,
    Thursday,
    Friday,
    Saturday,
    Sunday,
};

int main()
{

    Weekdays today;

    today = Friday;

    if (today == Friday) {
        std::cout << "The weekend is here !!!!" << std::endl;
    }

    _getch();
    return 0;
}
```

The output of this is as follows:

```
Select C:\Users\siddesktop\source\repos\MyFirstProject\Debug\MyFirstProject.exe
The weekend is here !!!!
-
```

Also note that, Monday = 0. If we don't use initializers, the first item's value is set to 0. Each following item that does not use an initializer will use the value of the preceding item plus 1 for its value.

Classes

In C++, structs and classes are identical. You can do exactly the same thing with both of them. The only difference is the default access specifier: `public` for structs and `private` for classes.

The declaration of a class looks like the following code:

```
class name{

access specifier:

name();
~name();

member1;
member2;

} ;
```

A class starts with the `class` keyword, followed by the name of the class.

In a class, we first specify the access specifiers. There are three access specifiers: `public`, `private`, and `protected`:

- `public`: All members are accessible from anywhere.
- `private`: Members are accessible from within the class itself only.
- `protected`: Members are accessed by other classes that inherit from the class.

By default, all members are private.

Furthermore, `name();` and `~name();` are called the constructor and destructor of a class. They have the same name as the name of the class itself.

The constructor is a special function that gets called when you create a new object of the class. The destructor is called when the object is destroyed.

We can customize a constructor to set values before using the member variables. This is called constructor overloading.

Notice that although the constructor and destructor are functions no return is provided. This is because they are not there for returning values.

Let's look at an example of a class where we create a class called `shape`. This has two member variables for the `a` and `b` sides and a member function, which calculates and prints the area:

```
class shape {
    int a, b;
public:

    shape(int _length, int _width) {
        a = _length;
        b = _width;

        std::cout << "length is: " << a << " width is: " << b <<
                std::endl;
    }

    void area() {
        std::cout << "Area is: " << a * b << std::endl;
    }
};
```

We use the class by creating objects of the class.

Here, we create two objects, called `square` and `rectangle`. We set the values by calling the custom constructor, which sets the value of `a` and `b`. Then, we call the `area` function of the object by using the dot operator by pressing the `.` button on the keyboard after typing the name of the object:

```
int main()
{
    shape square(8, 8);
    square.area();

    shape rectangle(12, 20);
    rectangle.area();

    _getch();
    return 0;
}
```

The output is as follows:

Inheritance

One of the key features of C++ is inheritance, with which we can create classes that are derived from other classes so that derived or the child class automatically includes some of its parent's member variables and functions.

For example, we looked at the shape class. From this, we can have a separate class called circle and another class called triangle that has the same properties as other shapes, such as area.

The syntax for an inherited class is as follows:

```
class inheritedClassName: accessSpecifier parentClassName{



};
```

Note that accessSpecifier could be public, private, or protected depending on the minimum access level you want to provide to the parent member variables and functions.

Let's look at an example of inheritance. Consider the same shape class, which will be the parent class:

```
class shape {

protected:
    float a, b;
public:
    void setValues(float _length, float _width)
    {
```

```
            a = _length;
            b = _width;

            std::cout << "length is: " << a << " width is: " << b <<
            std::endl;
    }
    void area() {
            std::cout << "Area is: " << a * b << std::endl;
    }

};
```

Since we want the `triangle` class to access a and b of the parent class, we have to set the access specifier to protected, as shown previously; otherwise, it will be set to private by default. In addition to this, we also change the data type to floats for more precision. After doing this, we create a `setValues` function instead of the constructor to set the values for a and b. We then create a child class of `shape` and call it `triangle`:

```
class triangle : public shape {

public:
    void area() {

            std::cout << "Area of a Triangle is: " << 0.5f * a * b <<
                        std::endl;
    }

};
```

Due to inheritance from the `shape` class, we don't have to add the a and b member variables, and we don't need to add the `setValues` member function either, as this is inherited from the `shape` class. We just add a new function called `area`, which calculates the area of a triangle.

In the main function, we create an object of the `triangle` class, set the values, and print the area, as follows:

```
int main()
{

    shape rectangle;
    rectangle.setValues(8.0f, 12.0f);
    rectangle.area();

    triangle tri;
    tri.setValues(3.0f, 23.0f);
```

```
    tri.area();

    _getch();
    return 0;
}
```

Here is the output of this:

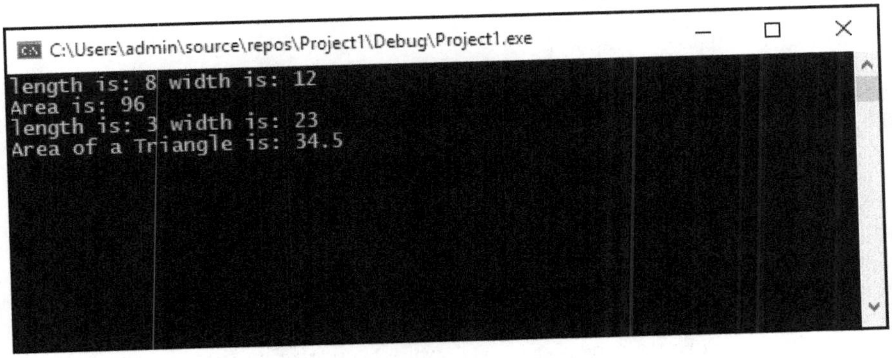

To calculate the area of circle, we modify the shape class and add a new overloaded setValues function, as follows:

```
#include <iostream>
#include <conio.h>

class shape {

protected:

    float a, b;

public:

    void setValues(float _length, float _width)
    {
        a = _length;
        b = _width;

        std::cout << "length is: " << a << " height is: " << b <<
                    std::endl;
    }

    void setValues(float _a)
    {
    a = _a;
    }
```

```
    void area() {

        std::cout << "Area is: " << a * b << std::endl;
    }

};
```

We will then add a new inherited class, called `circle`:

```
class circle : public shape {

public:
    void area() {

        std::cout << "Area of a Circle is: " << 3.14f * a * a <<
                     std::endl;
    }

};
```

In the main function, we create a new `circle` object, set the radius, and print the area:

```
int main()
{

    shape rectangle;
    rectangle.setValues(8.0f, 12.0f);
    rectangle.area();

    triangle tri;
    tri.setValues(3.0f, 23.0f);
    tri.area();

    circle c;
    c.setValues(5.0f);
    c.area();


    _getch();
    return 0;
}
```

Here is the output of this:

```
C:\Users\admin\source\repos\Project1\Debug\Project1.exe
length is: 8 height is: 12
Area is: 96
length is: 3 height is: 23
Area of a Triangle is: 34.5
Area of a Circle is: 78.5
```

Summary

In this chapter, we covered the basics of programming—from what variables are and how to store values in them, to looking at operators and statements, to how to decide when each is required. After that, we looked at iterators and functions, which can be used to make our job simpler and automate the code as much as possible. Arrays and pointers help us to group and store data of a similar type, and with `struct` and `enum` we can create custom data types. Finally, we looked at classes and inheritance, which is the crux of using C++ and makes it convenient to define our data types with custom properties.

In the next chapter, we will look at the foundation of graphics programming and explore how three-dimensional and two-dimensional objects are displayed on the screen.

Mathematics and Graphics Concepts

2

Before we begin rendering objects, it is essential that you are familiar with the math that will be used for the projects in this book. Mathematics plays a crucial role in game development, and graphics programming generally uses vectors and matrices extensively. In this chapter, you will understand where these math concepts can come in handy. First, we'll go over some key mathematical concepts and then apply them so that we can work with space transformations and render pipelines. There are dedicated books that cover all the math-related topics that you'll need for game development. However, since we will be covering graphics programming with C++, other mathematics topics are out of the scope of this book.

In the upcoming chapters, we will be using the OpenGL and Vulkan graphics APIs to render our objects and use the GLM math library to do the maths. In this chapter, we will explore the process of creating a 3D object in a virtual world using matrix and vector transforms. Then, we will look at how we can transform a 3D point into a 2D location using space transforms, as well as how the graphics pipeline helps us achieve this.

In this chapter, we will cover the following topics:

- 3D coordinate systems
- Vectors
- Matrices
- GLM OpenGL mathematics
- OpenGL data types
- Space transformations
- Render pipeline

3D coordinate systems

Before we can specify a location, we have to specify a coordinate system. A 3D coordinate system has three axes: the x axis, the y axis, and the z axis. These three axes start from the origin of where the three axes intersect.

The positive x axis starts from the origin and starts moving endlessly in a certain direction, while the negative x axis moves in the opposite direction. The positive y axis starts from the origin and moves in an upward direction at 90 degrees to the x axis, and the negative y axis moves in the opposite direction. This describes a 2D XY plane, which forms the basis of a 2D coordinate system.

The positive z axis starts from the same origin as the x and y axes and is perpendicular to the X and Y axes. The positive z axis can go in either direction of the XY plane in order to form a 3D coordinate system.

Assuming that the positive x axis is going to the right and the positive y axis is going up, then the z axis can either go into or out of the screen. This is because the z axis is perpendicular to the x and y axes.

When the positive z axis moves into the screen, this is known as a **left-handed coordinate system**. When the positive z axis comes out of the screen, this is known as a **ight-handed coordinate system**.

Extend your right arm so that it's in front of you, with your palm facing toward you, and make a fist. Extend your thumb to the right, and then extend your index finger upward. Now, extend your middle finger so that it faces you. This can be used to explain the right-handed coordinate system.

The thumb represents the direction of the positive x axis, the index finger represents the direction of the positive y axis, and the middle finger is the direction of the positive z axis. OpenGL, Vulkan, or any other graphics framework that uses these axes also use this coordinate system.

For the left-handed coordinate system, extend your left arm out so that it's in front of you, with the palm of your hand facing away from you, and make a fist. Next, extend your thumb and index finger in the right and upward directions, respectively. Now, extend your middle finger so that it's away from you. In this case, the thumb also represents the direction of the x axis and the index finger is pointing in the direction of the positive y axis. The z axis (the middle finger) is now facing away from you. Direct3D of DirectX uses this coordinate system.

In this book, since we are going to be covering OpenGL and Vulkan, we will be using the **right-handed coordinate system**:

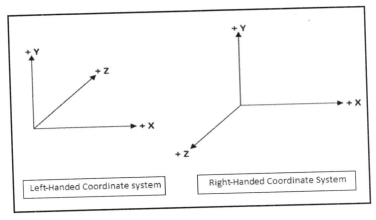

Points

Now that we have defined the coordinate system, we can specify what a point is. A 3D point is a location in 3D space that's specified by distance in terms of the **X**, **Y**, and **Z** axes and the origin of the coordinate system. It is specified as (X, Y, Z) where X, Y, and Z are the distance from the origin. But what is this origin we speak of? The origin is also the point where the three axes meet. The origin is at (0, 0, 0), and the location of the origin is specified in the coordinate system, as shown in the following diagram:

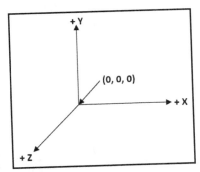

To specify points within a coordinate system, imagine that, in each direction, the axis is made of a smaller unit. This unit could be 1 millimeter, 1 centimeter, or 1 kilometer, depending on how much data you have.

If we just look at the X and Y axes, this would look something like this:

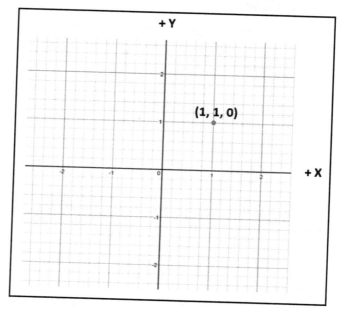

If we look at the x axis, the values 1 and 2 specify the distance along the axis of that point from the origin, which is at value 0. So, point 1 in the x axis is at (1, 0, 0) along the x axis. Similarly, point 1, which is along the y axis, is at (0, 1, 0).

In addition, the location of the red dot will be at (1, 1, 0); that is, 1 unit along the x axis and 1 unit along the y axis. Since Z is 0, we specify that its value is 0.

Similarly, the points in 3D space are represented as follows:

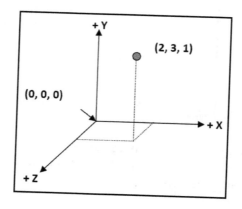

Vectors

A vector is a quantity that has a magnitude and a direction. Examples of quantities that have a magnitude and direction are displacement, velocity, acceleration, and force. With displacement, you can specify the direction as well as the net distance that the object has moved by.

The difference between speed and velocity is that speed only specifies the speed that an object is moving at, but doesn't establish the direction the object is moving in. However, velocity specifies the magnitude, which includes speed and direction. Similar to velocity, we have acceleration. A form of acceleration is gravity, and we know that this always acts downward and is always approximately 9.81 m/s^2 – well, at least on Earth. It is 1/6th of this on the moon.

An example of force is weight. Weight also acts downward and is calculated as mass multiplied by acceleration.

Vectors are graphically represented by a pointed line segment, with the length of the line denoting the magnitude of the vector and the pointed arrow denoting the direction of the vector. We can move around a vector since doing this doesn't change the magnitude or direction of it.

Two vectors are said to be equal if they both have the same magnitude and direction, even if they are in different locations. Vectors are denoted by arrow marks above the letter.

In the following diagram, vectors $\vec{A}$ and $\vec{B}$ start in different locations. Since the direction and magnitude of the are arrows the same, they are equal:

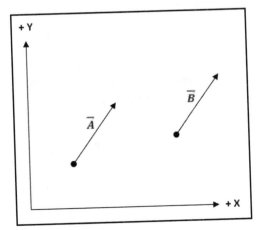

In a 3D coordinate system, a vector is specified by the coordinates with respect to the coordinate system. In the following diagram, the vector, $\vec{V}$ is equal to (2, 3, 1) and is denoted as $\vec{V} = \begin{bmatrix} 2 \\ 3 \\ 1 \end{bmatrix}$:

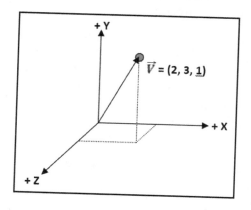

Vector operations

Just like scalar information, vectors can also be added, subtracted, and multiplied. Suppose you have two vectors, $\vec{A}$ and $\vec{B}$, where $\vec{A} = (a_x, a_y, a_z)$ and $\vec{B} = (b_x, b_y, b_z)$. Let's look at how we can add and subtract these vectors to/from each other.

When adding vectors, we add the components individually to create a new vector:

$$\vec{C} = \vec{A} + \vec{B}$$

$$\vec{C} = ((ax + bx), (ay + by), (az + bz))$$

Now, let's visualize the addition of two vectors in a graph. The Z value is kept as 0.0 for convenience. Here, $\vec{A} = (1.0, 0.4, 0.0)$ and $\vec{B} = (0.6, 2.0, 0.0)$, which means that the resultant vector, $\vec{C} = \vec{A} + \vec{B}, = (1.0 + 0.6, 0.4 + 2.0, 0.0 + 0.0) = (1.6, 2.4, 0.0)$:

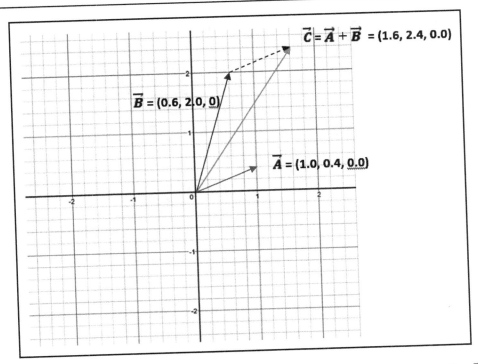

Vectors are also commutative, meaning that $\vec{A} + \vec{B}$ will give the same result as $\vec{B} + \vec{A}$.

However, if we add $\vec{B}$ to $\vec{A}$, then the dotted line will go from the vector $\vec{B}$ to vector $\vec{C}$ as shown in the preceding figure. Furthermore, in vector subtraction, we subtract the individual components of the vectors to create a new vector:

$$\vec{C} = \vec{A} - \vec{B}$$

$$\vec{C} = ((ax - bx), (ay - by), (az - bz))$$

Now, let's visualize the subtraction of two vectors in a graph.

Here, $\vec{A} = (1.0, 0.4, 0.0)$ and $\vec{B} = (0.6, 2.0, 0.0)$. Therefore, the resultant vector, $\vec{C} = \vec{A} - \vec{B}$, = $(1.0 - 0.6, 0.4 - 2.0, 0.0 - 0.0) = (0.4, -1.6, 0.0)$:

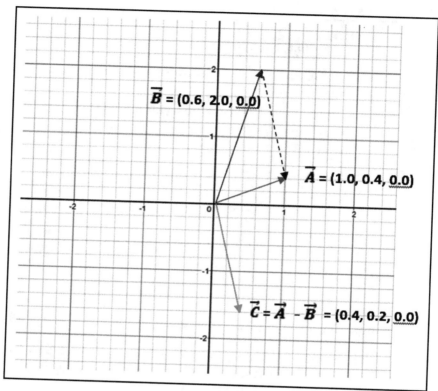

If vectors A and B are equal, the result will be a zero vector with all three components as zero.

If $\vec{A} = \vec{B}$, this means that $a_x = b_x$, $a_y = b_y$, $a_z = b_z$. If this is the case, then, $\vec{C} = \vec{A} - \vec{B} = (0, 0, 0)$.

We can multiply a scalar by a vector. The result is a vector with each component of the vector being multiplied by the scalar.

For example, if A is multiplied by a single value of s, we will have the following result:

$$\vec{C} = s \times \vec{A}$$

$$\vec{C} = s \times (a_x, a_y, a_z)$$

$$\vec{C} = (s \times a_x, s \times a_y, s \times a_z)$$

If $\vec{C} = (3, -5, 7)$ and $s = 0.5$ then;

$$\vec{C} = s\vec{A}$$

$$= (3 \times 0.5, -5 \times 0.5, 7 \times 0.5)$$

$$= (1.5, -2.5. 3.5)$$

Vector magnitude

The magnitude of the vector is equal to the length of the vector itself. But how do we calculate it mathematically?

The magnitude of a vector is given by the Pythagorean theorem, which specifies that, in a right-handed triangle, the square of the length of a diagonal is equal to the sum of the squares of the adjacent sides. Let's take a look at the following right-handed triangle, $c^2 = x^2 + y^2$:

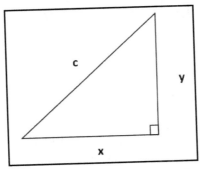

This can be extended to three dimensions with $c^2 = x^2 + y^2 + z^2$.

Magnitudes of vectors are indicated by double vertical bars, so the magnitude of a vector, $\vec{A}$ is denoted by $\|A\|$. The magnitude is always greater than or equal to zero.

So, if vector A = (X, Y, Z), then the magnitude is given by the following equation:

$$\|A\| = \sqrt{x^2 + y^2 + z^2}$$

If $\vec{A}$ = (3, -5, 7), then we get the following:

$$\|A\| = \sqrt{x^2 + y^2 + z^2}$$

$$= \sqrt{3^2 + (-5)^2 + 7^2}$$

$$= 9.110$$

Therefore, $\vec{A}$ is 9.11 units long.

Unit vectors

In some cases, we don't care about the magnitude of the vector; we just want to know the direction of the vector. To find this out, we want the length of the vector in the X, Y, and Z directions to be equal to 1. Such vectors are called unit vectors or normalized vectors.

In unit vectors, the X, Y, and Z components of the vector are divided by the magnitude to create a vector of unit length. They are denoted by a hat on top of the vector name instead of an arrow. So, a unit vector of A will be denoted as $\hat{a}$, like so:

$$\hat{a} = \vec{A}/\|A\|$$

$$\hat{a} = (x/\|A\|, y/\|A\|, z/\|A\|)$$

When a vector is converted into a unit vector, it is said to be normalized. This means that the value is always between 0.0 and 1.0. The original value has been rescaled to be in this range. Let's normalize the vector $\vec{A}$= (3, -5, 7).

First, we have to calculate the magnitude of $\vec{A}$, which we have already done (it's 9.11).

So, the unit vector is as follows:

$$\hat{a} = \vec{A} / \|A\|$$

$$= (3, -5, 7) / 9.11$$

$$= (3 / 9.11, -5 / 9.11, 7 / 9.11)$$

$$= (0.33, -0.51, 0.77)$$

The dot product

The dot product is a type of vector multiplication in which the resultant vector is a scalar. It is also referred to as a scalar product for the same reason. The scalar product of two vectors is the sum of the products of the corresponding components.

If you have two vectors, A = (a_x, a_y, a_z) and B = (b_x, b_y, b_z), this is given by the following equation:

$$\vec{A} \cdot \vec{B} = a_x \times b_x + a_y \times b_y + a_z \times b_z \; \text{--- (1)}$$

The dot product of two vectors is also equal to the cosine of the angle between the vectors that have been multiplied by the magnitudes of both vectors. Note that the dot product is represented as a dot between the vector:

$$\vec{A} \cdot \vec{B} = \|A\| \times \|B\| \times \cos(\theta)$$

θ is always between 0 and π. By putting an equation of 1 and 2 together, we can figure out the angle between two vectors:

$$\|A\| * \|B\| * cos\theta = ax * bx + ay * by + az * bz$$

$$cos\theta = (ax * bx + ay * by + az * bz) / (\|A\| * \|B\|)$$

Consequently we get:

$$\theta = cos - 1((ax * bx + ay * by + az * bz)/(\|A\| * \|B\|))$$

This form has some unique geometric properties:

- If $\vec{A}.\vec{B} = 0$, then $\vec{A}$ is perpendicular to $\vec{B}$, that is, cos 90 = 0.
- If $\vec{A}.\vec{B} = \|A\| * \|B\|$, then the two vectors are parallel to each other, that is, cos 0 = 1.
- If $\vec{A}.\vec{B} > 0$, then the angle between the vectors is less than 90 degrees.
- If $\vec{A}.\vec{B} < 0$, then the angle between the vectors is greater than 90 degrees.

Now, let's look at an example of a dot product.

If $\vec{A} = (3, -5, 7)$ and $\vec{B} = (2, 4, 1)$, then $\|A\| = 9.110$ and $\|B\| = \sqrt{2^2 + 4^2 + 1^2} = \sqrt{21}$.

Next, we calculate like so:

$$\vec{A}.\vec{B} = a_x * b_x + a_y * b_y + a_z * b_z,$$

$$\vec{A}.\vec{B} = 3 * 2 + (-5) * 4 + 7 * 1$$

$$= 6 - 20 + 7$$

$$= -7$$

$$cos\,\theta = -7/(9.110 * 4.582) = -7/41.74$$

$$\theta = cos-1(-7/41.74)$$

$$= cos-1(0.26770) = 99.65° \text{ (approx)}$$

The cross product

The c oss product is another form of vector multiplication in which the resultant product of the multiplication is another vector. Taking the cross product between $\vec{A}$ and $\vec{B}$ will result in a third vector that is perpendicular to vectors $\vec{A}$ and $\vec{B}$.

If you have two vectors, $\vec{A} = (a_x, a_y, a_z)$ and $\vec{B} = (b_x, b_y, b_z)$, then $\vec{A} \times \vec{B}$ is given as follows:

$$\vec{C} = \vec{A} \times \vec{B}$$
$$= (a_y b_z - a_z b_y, a_z b_x - a_x b_z, a_x b_y - a_y b_x)$$

The following are matrix and graphical implementations of the cross product between vectors:

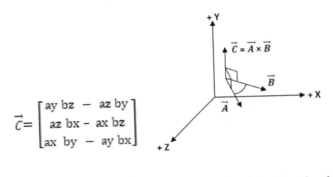

The direction of the resultant normal vector will obey the right-hand rule, where curling the fingers on your right hand (from $\vec{A}$ to $\vec{B}$) will cause the thumb to point in the direction of the resultant normal vector ($\vec{C}$).

Also, note that the order in which you multiply the vectors is important because if you multiply the other way around, then the resultant vector will point in the opposite direction.

The cross product is very useful when we want to find the normal of the face of a polygon, such as a triangle.

The following equation helps us find the cross product of vectors $\vec{A} = (3, -5, 7)$ and $\vec{B} = (2, 4, 1)$:

$$C = A \times B = (ay\ bz - az\ by, az\ bx - ax\ bz,\, , ax\ by - ay\ bx)$$

$$= (-5 * 1 - 7*4\, , 7 * 2 - 3 * 1, 3 * 4 - (-5) * 2\,)$$

$$= (-5-28, 14 - 3, 12 + 10)$$

$$= (-33, 11, 22)$$

Matrices

In computer graphics, matrices are used to calculate object transforms such as translation, that is, movement, scaling in the X, Y, and Z axes, and rotation around the X, Y, and Z axes. We will also be changing the position of objects from one coordinate system to an other, which is known as space transforms. We will see how matrices work and how they help to simplify the mathematics we have to use.

Matrices have rows and columns. A matrix with m number of rows and n number of columns is said to be a matrix of size $m \times n$. Each element of a matrix is represented as indices ij, where i specifies the row number and j represents the column number.

So, a matrix, M, of size 3×2 is represented as follows:

$$M = \begin{bmatrix} m11 & m12 \\ m21 & m22 \\ m31 & m32 \end{bmatrix}$$

Here, matrix M has three rows and two columns and each element is represented as m11, m12, and so on until m32, which is the size of the matrix.

In 3D graphics programming, we mostly deal with 4×4 matrices. Let's look at another matrix that's 4×4 in size:

$$M = \begin{bmatrix} m11 & m12 & m13 & m14 \\ m21 & m22 & m23 & m24 \\ m31 & m32 & m33 & m34 \\ m41 & m42 & m43 & m44 \end{bmatrix}$$

Matrix A can be presented as follows:

$$A = \begin{bmatrix} 3 & 1 & 0.5 & 0 \\ \sqrt{2} & -2 & 0 & 0 \\ 0 & 1 & 0 & 0 \\ 2 & 2.5 & 5 & 1 \end{bmatrix}$$

Here, the elements are $A_{11} = 3$, $A_{32} = 1$, and $A_{44} = 1$ and the dimension of the matrix is 4×4.

We can also have a single-dimension matrix with a vector shown as follows. Here, B is called the row vector and C is called a column vector:

$$B = \begin{bmatrix} b1 & b2 & b3 & b4 \end{bmatrix} \qquad C = \begin{bmatrix} c1 \\ c2 \\ c3 \\ c4 \end{bmatrix}$$

- Two matrices are equal if the number of rows and columns are the same and if the corresponding elements are of the same value.
- Two matrices can be added together if they have the same number of rows and columns. We add each element of the corresponding location to both matrices to get a third matrix that has the same dimensions as the added matrices.

Matrix addition and subtraction

Consider the following two matrices, A and B. Both of these are 3 x 3 in size:

$$A = \begin{bmatrix} A & B & C \\ D & E & F \\ G & H & I \end{bmatrix} \qquad B = \begin{bmatrix} a & b & c \\ d & e & f \\ g & h & i \end{bmatrix}$$

Here, if C = A + B, then this can be represented like so:

$$C = \begin{bmatrix} A+a & B+b & C+c \\ D+d & E+e & F+f \\ G+g & H+h & I+i \end{bmatrix}$$

Matrix subtraction works in the same way when each element of the matrix is subtracted from the corresponding element of the other matrix.

Matrix multiplication

Let's look at how a scalar value can be multiplied to a matrix. We can do this by multiplying each element of the matrix by the same scalar value. This will give us a new matrix that has the same dimensions as the original matrix.

Again, consider a Matrix, A, that's been multiplied by some scalars. Here, s×A, as follows:

$$C = s \times \begin{bmatrix} A & B & C \\ D & E & F \\ G & H & I \end{bmatrix} = \begin{bmatrix} s \times A & s \times B & s \times C \\ s \times D & s \times E & s \times F \\ s \times G & s \times H & s \times I \end{bmatrix}$$

Two A and B matrices can be multiplied together, provided that the number of columns in A is equal to the number of rows in B. So, if matrix A has the dimension a × b and B has the dimension X × Y, then for A to be multiplied by B, b should be equal to X:

The resultant size of the matrix will be a × Y. Two matrices can be multiplied together like so:

$$A = \begin{bmatrix} a11 & a12 \\ a21 & a22 \\ a31 & a32 \end{bmatrix} \qquad B = \begin{bmatrix} b11 & b12 & b13 \\ b21 & b22 & b23 \end{bmatrix}$$

Here, the size of A is 3 × 2 and the size of B is 2 × 3, which means that the resultant matrix, C, will be 3 × 3 in size:

$$C = A \times B =$$
$$\begin{bmatrix} a11 \times b11 + a12 \times b21 & a11 \times b12 + a12 \times b22 & a11 \times b13 + a12 \times b23 \\ a21 \times b11 + a22 \times b21 & a21 \times b12 + a22 \times b22 & a21 \times b13 + a22 \times b23 \\ a31 \times b11 + a32 \times b21 & a31 \times b12 + a32 \times b22 & a31 \times b13 + a32 \times b23 \end{bmatrix}$$

However, keep in mind that matrix multiplication is not commutative, meaning that A×B ≠ B×A. In fact, in some cases, it isn't even possible to multiply the other way around, just like it isn't in this case. Here, we can't even multiply B×A since the number of columns of B is not equal to the number of rows of A. In other words, the internal dimensions of the matrices should match so that the dimensions are in the form of [a×t] and [t×b].

You can also multiply a vector matrix with a regular matrix, as follows:

$$A = \begin{bmatrix} A & B & C \\ D & E & F \\ G & H & I \end{bmatrix} \qquad V = \begin{bmatrix} x \\ y \\ z \end{bmatrix}$$

The result will be a one-dimensional vector of size 3×1, as follows:

$$C = A \times V = \begin{bmatrix} A \times x + B \times y + C \times z \\ D \times x + E \times y + F \times z \\ G \times x + H \times y + I \times z \end{bmatrix}$$

Note that when multiplying the matrix with the vector-matrix, the vector is to the right of the matrix. This is done so that the matrix of size 3×3 is able to multiply the vector-matrix of size 3×1.

When we have a matrix with just one column, this is called a column-major matrix. So, matrix C is a column-major matrix, just like matrix V.

If the same vector, V, was expressed with just a row, it would be called a row-major matrix. This can be represented like so:

$$V = \begin{bmatrix} x & y & z \end{bmatrix}$$

So, how would we multiply a matrix, A, of size 3×3 with a row-major matrix, V, of size 1×3 if the internal dimensions don't match?

The simple solution here is, instead of multiplying matrix A × V, we multiply V × A. This way, the internal dimensions of the vector-matrix and the regular matrix will match 1×3 and 3×3, and the resultant matrix will also be a row-major matrix.

 Throughout this book, we will be using the column-major matrix.

If we were going to use 4×4 matrices, for example, how would we multiply a 4×4 matrix using the coordinates of x, y, and z?

When multiplying a 4 × 4 matrix with points X, Y, and Z, we add one more row to the column-major matrix and set the value of it to 1. The new point will be (X, Y, Z, 1), which is called a homogeneous point. This makes it easy to multiply a 4 × 4 matrix with a 4 × 1 vector:

$$A = \begin{bmatrix} A & B & C & D \\ E & F & G & H \\ I & J & K & L \\ M & N & O & P \end{bmatrix} \qquad P = \begin{bmatrix} x \\ y \\ z \\ 1 \end{bmatrix}$$

$$C = A \times P = \begin{bmatrix} Ax + By + Cz + D * 1 \\ Ex + Fy + Gz + H * 1 \\ Ix + Jy + Kz + L * 1 \\ Mx + Ny + Oz + P * 1 \end{bmatrix}$$

Matrix multiplication can be extrapolated to the multiplication of one 4 × 4 matrix with another 4 × 4 matrix. Let's look at how we can do this:

$$\text{Let } A = \begin{bmatrix} A & B & C & D \\ E & F & G & H \\ I & J & K & L \\ M & N & O & P \end{bmatrix} \qquad B = \begin{bmatrix} a & b & c & d \\ e & f & g & h \\ i & j & k & l \\ m & n & o & p \end{bmatrix}$$

$$A X B =$$

$$\begin{bmatrix} Aa + Be + Ci + Dm & Ab + Bf + Cj + Dn & Ac + Bg + Ck + Do & Ad + Bh + Cl + Dp \\ Ea + Fe + Gi + Hm & Eb + Ff + Gj + Hn & Ec + Fg + Gk + Ho & Ed + Fh + Gl + Hp \\ Ia + Je + Ki + Lm & Ib + Jf + Kj + Ln & Ic + Jg + Kk + Lo & Id + Jh + Kl + Lp \\ Ma + Ne + Oi + Pm & Mb + Nf + Oj + Pn & Mc + Ng + Ok + Po & Md + Nh + Ol + Pp \end{bmatrix}$$

Identity matrix

An identity matrix is a special kind of matrix in which the number of rows is equal to the number of columns. This is known as a square matrix. In an identity matrix, the elements in the diagonal of the matrix are all 1, while the rest of the elements are 0.

Here is an example of a 4 × 4 identity matrix:

$$I = \begin{bmatrix} 1 & 0 & 0 & 0 \\ 0 & 1 & 0 & 0 \\ 0 & 0 & 1 & 0 \\ 0 & 0 & 0 & 1 \end{bmatrix}$$

Identity matrices work similarly to how we get a result when we multiply any number with 1 and get the same number. Similarly, when we multiply any matrix with an identity matrix, we get the same matrix.

For example, A×I = A, where A is a 4 ×4 matrix and I is an identity matrix of the same size. Let's look at an example of this:

$$\text{Let A} = \begin{bmatrix} A & B & C & D \\ E & F & G & H \\ I & J & K & L \\ M & N & O & P \end{bmatrix} \quad I = \begin{bmatrix} 1 & 0 & 0 & 0 \\ 0 & 1 & 0 & 0 \\ 0 & 0 & 1 & 0 \\ 0 & 0 & 0 & 1 \end{bmatrix}$$

A × I =

$$\begin{bmatrix} A \times 1 + B \times 0 + C \times 0 + D \times 0 & A \times 0 + B \times 1 + C \times 0 + D \times 0 & A \times 0 + B \times 0 + C \times 1 + D \times 0 & A \times 0 + B \times 0 + C \times 0 + D \times 1 \\ E \times 1 + F \times 0 + G \times 0 + H \times 0 & E \times 0 + F \times 1 + G \times 0 + H \times 0 & E \times 0 + F \times 0 + G \times 1 + H \times 0 & E \times 0 + F \times 0 + G \times 0 + H \times 1 \\ I \times 1 + J \times 0 + K \times 0 + L \times 0 & I \times 0 + J \times 1 + K \times 0 + L \times 0 & I \times 0 + J \times 0 + K \times 1 + L \times 0 & I \times 0 + J \times 0 + K \times 0 + L \times 1 \\ M \times 1 + N \times 0 + O \times 0 + P \times 0 & M \times 0 + N \times 1 + O \times 0 + P \times 0 & M \times 0 + N \times 0 + O \times 1 + P \times 0 & M \times 0 + N \times 0 + O \times 0 + P \times 1 \end{bmatrix}$$

$$\text{A} \times I = \begin{bmatrix} A & B & C & D \\ E & F & G & H \\ I & J & K & L \\ M & N & O & P \end{bmatrix}$$

Matrix transpose

A matrix transpose occurs when the rows and columns are interchanged with each other. So, the transpose of an m X n matrix is n X m. The transpose of any matrix, M, is written as M^T. The transpose of a matrix is as follows:

$$A = \begin{bmatrix} A & B & C & D \\ E & F & G & H \\ I & J & K & L \\ M & N & O & P \end{bmatrix} \quad A^T = \begin{bmatrix} A & E & I & M \\ B & F & J & N \\ C & G & K & O \\ D & H & L & P \end{bmatrix}$$

Observe how the elements in the diagonal of the matrix remain in the same place but all the elements around the diagonal have been swapped.

In matrices, this diagonal of the matrix, which runs from the top left to the bottom right, is called the main diagonal.

Obviously, if you transpose a transposed matrix, you get the original matrix, so $(A^T)^T = A$.

Matrix inverse

The inverse of any matrix is where any matrix, when multiplied by its inverse, will result in an identity matrix. For matrix M, the inverse of the matrix is denoted as M^{-1}.

The inverse is very useful in graphics programming when we want to undo the multiplication of a matrix.

For example, Matrix M is equal to $A \times B \times C \times D$, where A, B, C and D are also matrices. Now, let's say we want to know what $A \times B \times C$ is instead of multiplying the three matrices, which is a two-step operation: first, you will multiply A with B and then multiply the resulting matrix with C. You can multiply M with D^{-1} as that will yield the same result:

$$M = A \times B \times C \times D$$
$$A \times B \times C = M \times D^{-1}$$

GLM OpenGL mathematics

To carry out the mathematical operations we've just looked at in OpenGL and Vulkan projects, we will be using a header-only C++ mathematics library called GLM. This was initially developed to be used with OpenGL, but it can be used with Vulkan as well:

The latest version of GLM can be downloaded from `https://glm.g-truc.net/0.9.9/index.html`.

Apart from being able to create points and perform vector addition and subtraction, GLM can also define matrices, carry out matrix transforms, generate random numbers, and generate noise. The following are a few examples of how these functions can be carried out:

- To define 2D and 3D points, we will need to include `#include <glm/glm.hpp>`, which uses the `glm` namespace. To define a 2D point in space, we use the following code:

  ```
  glm::vec2 p1 = glm::vec2(2.0f, 10.0f);
  ```

  ```
  Where the 2 arguments passed in are the x and y position.
  ```

- To define a 3D point, we use the following code:

  ```
  glm::vec3 p2 = glm::vec3(10.0f, 5.0f, 2.0f);
  ```

- A 4 x 4 matrix can also be created using `glm`, as shown in the following code. A 4 x 4 matrix is of the `mat4` type and can be created like this:

  ```
  glm::mat4 matrix = glm::mat4(1.0f);
  ```

  ```
  Here the 1.0f parameter passed in shows that the matrix is
  initialized as a identity matrix.
  ```

- For translation and rotation, you need to include the necessary GLM extensions, as shown in the following code:

  ```
  #include <glm/ext.hpp>
  glm::mat4 translation = glm::translate(glm::mat4(1.0f),
  glm::vec3(3.0f,4.0f, 8.0f));
  ```

- To translate the object so that it's (3.0, 4.0, 8.0) from its current position, do the following:

  ```
  glm:: mat4 scale = glm::scale(glm::mat4(1.0f),
  glm::vec3( 2.0f, 2.0f, 2.0f));
  ```

- We can also scale the value so that it's double its size in the *x*, *y*, and *z* directions:

  ```
  glm::mat4 rxMatrix = glm::rotate(glm::mat4(), glm::radians(45.0f),
  glm::vec3(1.0, 0.0, 0.0));
  glm::mat4 ryMatrix = glm::rotate(glm::mat4(), glm::radians(25.0f),
  glm::vec3(0.0, 1.0, 0.0));
  glm::mat4 rzMatrix = glm::rotate(glm::mat4(), glm::radians(10.0f),
  glm::vec3(0.0, 0.0, 1.0));
  ```

The preceding code rotates the object by `45,0f` degrees along the *x* axis, `25.0f` degrees along the *y* axis, and `10.0f` degrees along the *z* axis.

 Note that we use `glm::radians()` here. This `glm` function converts degrees into radians. More GLM functions will be introduced throughout this chapter.

OpenGL data types

OpenGL also has its own data types. These are portable across platforms.

OpenGL data types are prefixed with GL, followed by the data type. Consequently, a GL equivalent to an `int` variable is GLint, and so on. The following table shows a list of GL data types (the list can be viewed at `https://www.khronos.org/opengl/wiki/OpenGL_Type`):

C Type	Bitdepth	Description	Common Enum
GLboolean	1+	A boolean value, either GL_TRUE or GL_FALSE	
GLbyte	8	Signed, 2's complement binary integer	GL_BYTE
GLubyte	8	Unsigned binary integer	GL_UNSIGNED_BYTE
GLshort	16	Signed, 2's complement binary integer	GL_SHORT
GLushort	16	Unsigned binary integer	GL_UNSIGNED_SHORT
GLint	32	Signed, 2's complement binary integer	GL_INT
GLuint	32	Unsigned binary integer	GL_UNSIGNED_INT
GLfixed	32	Signed, 2's complement 16.16 integer	GL_FIXED
GLint64	64	Signed, 2's complement binary integer	
GLuint64	64	Unsigned binary integer	
GLsizei	32	A non-negative binary integer, for sizes.	
GLenum	32	An OpenGL enumerator value	
GLintptr	*ptrbits*[1]	Signed, 2's complement binary integer	
GLsizeiptr	*ptrbits*[1]	Non-negative binary integer size, for memory offsets and ranges	
GLsync	*ptrbits*[1]	Sync Object handle	
GLbitfield	32	A bitfield value	
GLhalf	16	An IEEE-754 floating-point value	GL_HALF_FLOAT
GLfloat	32	An IEEE-754 floating-point value	GL_FLOAT
GLclampf	32	An IEEE-754 floating-point value, clamped to the range [0,1]	
GLdouble	64	An IEEE-754 floating-point value	GL_DOUBLE
GLclampd	64	An IEEE-754 floating-point value, clamped to the range [0,1]	

Space transformations

The major job of 3D graphics is to simulate a 3D world and project that world into a 2D location, which is the viewport window. 3D or 2D objects that we want to render are nothing but collections of vertices. These vertices are then made into a collection of triangles to form the shape of the object sphere:

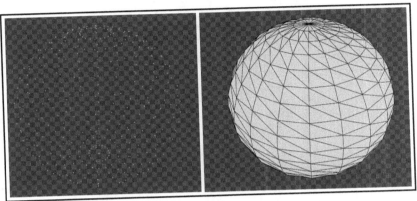

The screenshot on the left shows the vertices that were passed in, whereas the screenshot on the right shows that the vertices were used to create triangles. Each triangle forms a small piece of the surface for the final shape of the object.

Local/object space

When setting the vertices for any object, we start at the origin of a coordinate system. These vertices or points are placed and then connected to create the shape of the object, such as a triangle. This coordinate system that a model is created around is called the object space, model space, or local space:

World space

Now that we have specified the shape of the model, we want to place it in a scene, along with a couple of other shapes, such as a sphere and a cube. The cube and sphere shapes are also created using their own model space. When placing these objects into a 3D scene, we do so with respect to the coordinate system that the 3D objects will be placed in. This new coordinate system is called the world coordinate system, or world space.

Moving the object from the object space to the world space is done through matrix transforms. The local position of the object is multiplied by the world space matrix. Consequently, each vertex is multiplied by the world space matrix to transform its scale, rotation, and position from the local space to the world space.

The world space matrix is a product of scale, rotation, and translation matrices, as shown in the following formula:

$$World\ Matrix = W = T \times R \times S$$

S, R, and T are the scale, rotation, and translation of the local space relative to the world space, respectively. Let's take a look at each of them individually:

- The scale matrix for a 3D space is a 4 x 4 matrix whose diagonal represents the scale in the x, y, and z directions, as follows:

$$S = \begin{pmatrix} Sx & 0 & 0 & 0 \\ 0 & Sy & 0 & 0 \\ 0 & 0 & Sz & 0 \\ 0 & 0 & 0 & 1 \end{pmatrix}$$

- The rotation matrix can take three forms, depending on which axis you are rotating the object on. Rx, Ry, and Rz are the matrices we use for rotation along each axis, as shown in the following matrix:

$$R(\theta)x = \begin{pmatrix} 1 & 0 & 0 & 0 \\ 0 & \cos(\theta) & \sin(\theta) & 0 \\ 0 & -\sin(\theta) & \cos(\theta) & 0 \\ 0 & 0 & 0 & 1 \end{pmatrix}$$

$$R(\theta)y = \begin{pmatrix} \cos(\theta) & 0 & -\sin(\theta) & 0 \\ 0 & 1 & 0 & 0 \\ \sin(\theta) & 0 & \cos(\theta) & 0 \\ 0 & 0 & 0 & 1 \end{pmatrix}$$

$$R(\theta)z = \begin{pmatrix} \cos(\theta) & -\sin(\theta) & 0 & 0 \\ \sin(\theta) & \cos(\theta) & 0 & 0 \\ 0 & 0 & 1 & 0 \\ 0 & 0 & 0 & 1 \end{pmatrix}$$

- The translation matrix is an identity matrix where the last column represents the translation in the x, y, and z directions:

$$T = \begin{pmatrix} 1 & 0 & 0 & Tx \\ 0 & 1 & 0 & Ty \\ 0 & 0 & 1 & TZ \\ 0 & 0 & 0 & 1 \end{pmatrix}$$

Now, we can get the world position by multiplying the local position of the objects with the world matrix, as follows:

$$Position_{World} = Matrix_{World} \times Position_{local}$$

View space

For us to view the whole scene, we will need a camera. This camera will also decide which objects will be visible to us and which objects won't be rendered to the screen.

Consequently, we can place a virtual camera into the scene at a certain world location, as shown in the following diagram:

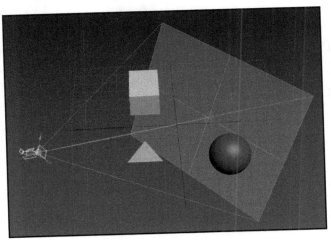

The objects in the scene are then transformed from the world space into a new coordinate system that's present at the location of the camera. This new coordinate system, which is at the location of the camera, is called the view space, camera space, or eye space. The x axis is red, the y axis is green, and the positive z axis is blue.

To transform the points from the world space to the camera space, we have to translate them using the negative of the virtual camera location and rotate them using the negative of the camera orientation.

However, there is an easier way to create the view matrix using GLM. We have to provide three variables to define the camera position, camera target position, and camera up vector, respectively:

```
glm::vec3cameraPos = glm::vec3(0.0f, 0.0f, 200.0f);
glm::vec3cameraFront = glm::vec3(0.0f, 0.0f, 0.0f);
glm::vec3cameraUp = glm::vec3(0.0f, 1.0f, 0.0f);
```

We can use these variables to create a view matrix by calling the `lookAt` function and passing the camera position, the look at position, and up vector, as follows:

```
glm::mat4 viewMatrix = glm::lookAt(cameraPos, cameraPos +
cameraFront, cameraUp);
```

Once we have the view matrix, the local positions can be multiplied by the world and the view matrix to get the position in the view space, as follows:

$$Position_{view} = View_{matrix} \times World_{matrix} \times Position_{local}$$

Projection space

The next task is to project the 3D objects that can be viewed by the camera onto the 2D plane. Projection needs to be done in such a way that the furthest object appears smaller and the objects that are closer appear bigger. Basically, when viewing an object, the points need to converge at a vanishing point.

In the following screenshot, the image on the right shows a cube being rendered. Note how the lines on the longer sides are actually parallel.

However, when the same box is viewed from the camera, the same side lines converge, and when these lines are extended, they will converge at a point behind the box:

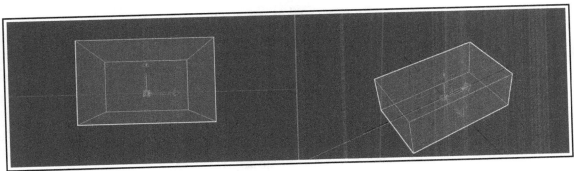

Now, we will introduce one more matrix, called the projection matrix, which allows objects to be rendered with perspective projection. The vertices of the objects will be transformed using what is called a projection matrix to perform the perspective projection transformation.

In the projection matrix, we define a projection volume called the frustum. All the objects inside the frustum will be projected onto the 2D display. The objects outside the projection plane will not be rendered:

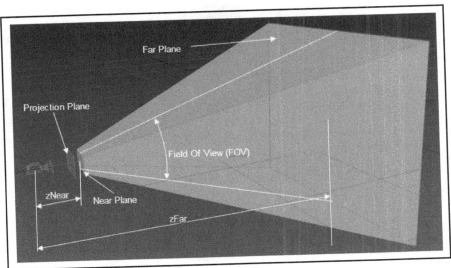

The projection matrix is created as follows:

$$\text{Martix}_{\text{Projection}} = \begin{pmatrix} A & 0 & 0 & 0 \\ 0 & q & 0 & 0 \\ 0 & 0 & B & C \\ 0 & 0 & -1 & 0 \end{pmatrix}$$

$$q = 1/tan(FieldOfView/2)$$

$$A = q/Aspect\ Ratio$$

$$B = (zNear + zFar)/(zNear - zFar)$$

$$C = 2\ {}^*(zNear\ {}^*\ zFar)/(zNear - zFar)$$

 The aspect ratio is the width of the projection plane divided by the height of the projection plane. *zNear* is the distance from the camera to the near plane. *zFar* is the distance from the camera to the far plane. The **field of view (FOV)** is the angle between the top and bottom planes of the view frustum.

In GLM, there is a function we can use to create the perspective projection matrix, as follows:

```
GLfloat FOV = 45.0f;
GLfloat width = 1280.0f;
GLfloat height = 720.0f;
GLfloat nearPlane = 0.1f;
Glfloat farPlane = 1000.0f;

glm::mat4 projectionMatrix = glm::perspective(FOV, width /height,
nearPlane, farPlane);
```

Note that `nearPlane` always needs to be greater than `0.0f` so that we can create the start of the frustum in front of the camera.

The `glm::perspective` function takes four parameters:

- The `FOV`
- The aspect ratio
- The distance to the near plane
- The distance to the far plane

So, after obtaining the projection matrix, we can finally perform a perspective projection transform on our view-transformed points to project the vertices onto the screen:

$$Position_{final} = Projection_{matrix} \times View_{matrix} \times World_{matrix} \times Position_{local}$$

Now that we understand this in theory, let's look at how we can actually implement this.

Screen space

After multiplying the local position by the model, view, and projection matrix, OpenGL will transform the scene into screen space.

If the screen size of your application has a resolution of 1,280 x 720, then it will project the scene onto the screen like so; this is what can be seen by the camera in the view-space heading:

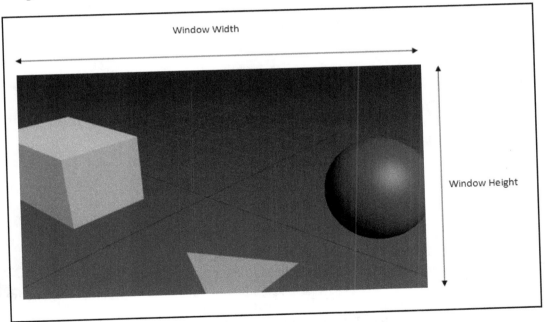

For this example, the width of the window will be 1,280 pixels and the height of the window will be 720 pixels.

Render pipeline

As I mentioned earlier, we have to convert 3D objects that are made up of vertices and textures and represent them on a 2D screen as pixels on the screen. This is done with what is called a render pipeline. The following diagram explains the steps involved:

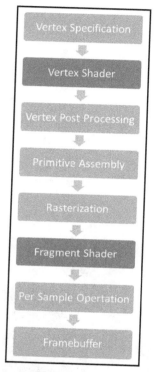

A pipeline is simply a series of steps that are carried out one after the other to achieve a certain objective. The stages that are highlighted in the orange boxes (or lightly shaded boxes, if you're reading a black and white copy of this book) in the preceding diagram are fixed, meaning that you cannot modify how the data in the stages is processed. The stages in the blue or darker boxes are programmable stages, meaning that you can write special programs to modify the output. The preceding diagram shows a basic pipeline, which includes the minimum stages we need to complete to render objects. There are other stages, such as Geometry, Tessellation, and Compute, which are all optional stages. However, these will not be discussed in this book since we are only introducing graphics programming.

The graphics pipeline itself is common for both OpenGL and Vulkan. However, their implementation is different, but we will see this in the upcoming chapters.

The render pipeline is used to render 2D or 3D objects onto a TV or monitor. Let's look at each of the stages in the graphics pipeline in detail.

Vertex specification

When we want to render an object to the screen, we set information regarding that object. The information that we will need to set is very basic, that is, the points or vertices that will make up the geometry. We will be creating the object by creating an array of vertices. This will be used to create a number of triangles that will make up the geometry we want to render. These vertices need to be sent to the graphics pipeline.

To send information to the pipeline in OpenGL, for example, we use **vertex array objects (VAO)** and **vertex buffer objects (VBO)**. VAOs are used to define what data each vertex has; VBOs have the actual vertex data.

Vertex data can have a series of attributes. A vertex could have property attributes, such as position, color, normal, and so on. Obviously, one of the main attributes that any vertex needs to have is the position information. Apart from the position, we will also look at other types of information that can be passed in, such as the color of each vertex. We will look at a few more attributes in future chapters in `Section 3`, *Modern OpenGL 3D Game Development*, when we cover rendering primitives using OpenGL.

Let's say that we have an array of three points. Let's look at how we would create the VAO and the VBO:

```
float vertices[] = {
    -0.5f, -0.5f, 0.0f,
     0.5f, -0.5f, 0.0f,
     0.0f,  0.5f, 0.0f
};
```

So, let's begin:

1. First, we generate a vertex array object of the Glint type. OpenGL returns a handle to the actual object for future reference, as follows:

   ```
   unsigned int VAO;
   glGenVertexArrays(1, &VAO);
   ```

2. Then, we generate a vertex buffer object, as follows:

```
unsigned int VBO;
glGenBuffers(1, &VBO);
```

3. Next, we specify the type of buffer object. Here, it is of the GL_ARRAY_BUFFER type, meaning that this is an array buffer:

```
glBindBuffer(GL_ARRAY_BUFFER, VBO);
```

4. Then, we bind the data to the buffer, as follows:

```
glBufferData(GL_ARRAY_BUFFER, sizeof(vertices), vertices,
GL_STATIC_DRAW);
```

The first parameter is a type of data buffer, which is of the GL_ARRAY_BUFFER type. The second parameter is the size of the data type that was passed in. sizeof() is a C++ keyword that gets the size of the data in bytes.

The next parameter is the data itself, while the last parameter is used to specify whether this data will change. GL_STATIC_DRAW means that the data will not be modified once the values have been stored.

5. Then, we specify the vertex attributes, as follows:

- The first parameter is the index of the attribute. In this case, we just have one attribute that has a position located at the 0th index.
- The second is the size of the attribute. Each vertex is represented by three floats for *x*, *y*, and *z*, so here, the value that's being specified is 3.
- The third parameter is the type of data that is being passed in, which is of the GL_FLOAT type.
- The fourth parameter is a Boolean asking whether the value should be normalized or used as is. We are specifying GL_FALSE since we don't want the data to be normalized.
- The fifth parameter is called the stride; this specifies the offset between the attributes. Here, the value for the next position is the size of three floats, that is, *x*, *y*, and *z*.
- The final parameter specifies the starting offset of the first component, which is 0 here. We are typecasting the data to a more generic data type (void*), called a void pointer:

```
glVertexAttribPointer(0, 3, GL_FLOAT, GL_FALSE, 3 *
sizeof(float), (void*)0);
```

6. Finally, we enable the attribute at the 0th index, as follows:

```
glEnableVertexAttribArray(0);
```

This is a basic example. This changes when we add additional attributes, such as color.

Vertex shader

The vertex shader stage performs operations on a per-vertex basis. Depending on the number of vertices you have passed into the vertex shader, the vertex shader will be called that many times. If you are passing three vertices to form a triangle, then the vertex shader will be called three times.

Depending on the attributes that are passed into the shader, the vertex shader modifies the value that is passed in and outputs the final value of that attribute. For example, when you pass in a position attribute, you can manipulate its value and send out the final position of that vertex at the end of the vertex shader.

The following code is for a basic vertex shader for the single attribute that we passed in previously:

```
#version 430 core
layout (location = 0) in vec3 position;

void main()
{
    gl_Position = vec4(position.x, position.y, position.z, 1.0);
}
```

 Shaders are programs written in a language similar to C. The shader will always begin with the version of the **GL Shader Language** (**GLSL**). There are other shader languages, including the **High-Level Shading Language** (**HLSL**), which is used by Direct 3D and CG. CG is also used in Unity.

Now, we will declare all the input attributes that we want to use. For this, we use the `layout` keyword and specify the location or the index of the attribute we want to use in brackets. Since we passed in one attribute for the vertex position and specified the index for it as 0 while specifying the attribute pointer, we set the location as 0. Then, we use the `in` keyword to say that we are receiving the information. We store each position's value in a variable type called `vec3`, along with a name position.

vec3, which is a variable type, is used for vectors that are GLSL-intrinsic data types that can store data that's been passed into the shader. Here, since we are passing in position information that has an *x*, *y*, and *z* component, it's convenient to use a vec3. We also have a vec4, which has an additional w component that can be used to store color information, for example.

Each shader needs to have a main function in which the major function that's relevant to the shader will be performed. Here, we are not doing anything too complicated: we're just getting the vec3, converting it into a vec4, and then setting the value to gl_Position. We have to convert vec3 into vec4 since gl_Position is a vec4. It is also GLSL's intrinsic variable, which is used to store and output values from the vertex shader.

Since this is a basic example of a vertex shader, we are not going to multiply each point with the ModelViewProjection matrix to transform the point onto the projection space. We will expand on this example later in this book.

Vertex post-processing

At this stage, clipping occurs. Objects that are not in the visible cone of the camera are not rendered to the screen. These primitives, which are not displayed, are said to be clipped.

Let's say that only part of a sphere is visible. The primitive is broken into smaller primitives and only the primitives that are visible will be displayed. The vertex positions of the primitives are transformed from the clip space into the window space.

For example, in the following diagram, only parts of the sphere, triangle, and cuboid are visible. The remaining parts of the shapes are not visible to the camera and so they have been clipped:

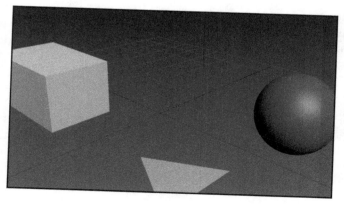

Primitive assembly

The primitive assembly stage gathers all the primitives that weren't clipped in the previous stage and creates a sequence of primitives.

Face culling is also performed at this stage. Face culling is the process in which primitives that are in front of the view but are facing backward will be culled since they won't be visible. For example, when you are looking at a cube, you only see the front face of the cube and not the back of the cube, so there is no point in rendering the back of the cube when it is not visible. This is called back-face culling.

Rasterization

The GPU needs to convert the geometry that's been described in terms of vectors into pixels. We call this rasterization. The primitives that pass the previous stages of clipping and culling will be processed further so that they can be rasterized. The rasterization process creates a series of fragments from these primitives. The process of converting a primitive into a rasterized image is done by the GPU. In the process of rasterization (vector to pixel), we always lose information, hence the name *fragments of primitives*. The fragment shader is used to calculate the final pixel's color value, which will be output to the screen.

Fragment shader

Fragments from the rasterization stage are then processed using the fragment shader. Just like the vertex shader stage, the fragment shader is also a program that can be written so that we can perform modifications on each fragment.

The fragment shader will be called for each fragment from the previous stage.

Here is an example of a basic fragment shader:

```
#version 430 core
out vec4 Color;

void main()
{
    Color = vec4(0.0f, 0.0f, 1.0f, 1.0f);
}
```

Just like the vertex shader, you need to specify the GLSL version to use.

We use the `out` keyword to send the output value from the fragment shader. Here, we want to send out a variable of the `vec4` type called `Color`. The main function is where all the magic happens. For each fragment that gets processed, we set the value of `Color` to `blue`. So, when the primitive gets rendered to the viewport, it will be completely blue.

This is how the sphere becomes blue.

Per-sample operation

In the same way that the vertex post-processing stage clipped a primitive, the per-sample operation also removes fragments that won't be shown. Whether a fragment needs to be displayed on the screen depends on certain tests that can be enabled by the user.

One of the more commonly used tests is the depth test. When enabled, this will check whether a fragment is behind another fragment. If this is the case, then the current fragment will be discarded. For example, here, only part of the cuboid is visible since it is behind the grey sphere:

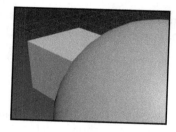

There are other tests we can perform as well, such as scissor and stencil tests, which will only show a portion of the screen or object based on certain conditions that we specify.

Color blending is also done at this stage. Here, based on certain blending equations, colors can be blended. For example, here, the sphere is transparent, so we can see the color of the cuboid blending into the color of the sphere:

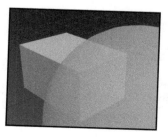

Framebuffer

Finally, when a per-sample operation is completed for all the fragments in a frame, the final image is rendered to the framebuffer, which is then presented on the screen.

A framebuffer is a collection of images that are drawn per frame. Each of these images is attached to the framebuffer. The framebuffer has attachments, such as the color image that's shown on the screen. There are also other attachments, such as the depth or the image/texture; this just stores the depth information of each pixel. The end user never sees this, but it is sometimes used for graphical purposes by games.

In OpenGL, the framebuffer is created automatically at the start. There are also user-created framebuffers that can be used to render the scene first, apply post-processing to it, and then hand it back to the system so that it can displayed on the screen.

Summary

In this chapter, we covered some of the basics of mathematics that we will be using throughout this book. In particular, we learned about coordinate systems, points, vectors, and matrices. Then, we learned how to apply these concepts to Open GL mathematics and space transforms. Afterward, we looked at GLM, which is a math library that we will be using to make our mathematic calculations easier. Finally, we covered space transforms and understood the flow of the graphics pipeline.

In the next chapter we will look at how to use a simple framework like SFML to make a 2D game

Section 2: SFML 2D Game Development

2

We will create a basic side-scrolling 2D action game in which we will cover basic game concepts, including creating a game loop, rendering a 2D game scene using SFML, 2D sprite creation, 2D sprite animations, UI text and buttons, physics, and collision detection.

The following chapters are in this section:

Chapter 3, *Setting Up Your Game*

Chapter 4, *Creating Your Game*

Chapter 5, *Finalizing Your Game*

Setting Up Your Game 3

In this chapter, we will start with the basics of how a game is made and what basic graphical components the game requires. Since this book is going to be covering graphics with C++, we will mostly look at what is graphically required from the graphics engine in a game. We will also cover the sound system so that we can make the game more interesting.

To create a basic graphics engine, we will be using the **Simple and Fast Multimedia Library** (**SFML**) since this includes most of the functionality that is needed to get a game up and running. The reason for choosing SFML is that it is very basic and easy to understand, unlike other engines and frameworks.

In this chapter, we will create a window for our game and add animations to it. We will also learn how to create and control our player's movements.

The following topics are covered in this chapter:

- An overview of SFML
- Downloading SFML and configuring Visual Studio
- Creating a window
- Drawing shapes
- Adding sprites
- Keyboard input
- Handing player movement

An overview of SFML

Games and video games (unlike other entertainment media) actually involve loading various resources, such as images, videos, sound, font types, and more. SFML provides functions for loading all of these features into games.

SFML is cross-platform compatible, which implies that it permits you to develop and run games on diverse platforms. It also supports various languages other than C++. Additionally, it is open source, so you can take a look at the source code and add a feature to it (if it is not included).

SFML is broken down into five modules, which can be defined as follows:

- **System**: This module directly interacts with a system such as Windows, which is essentially the **operating system** (**OS**) that it will use. Since SFML is cross-platform compatible and each OS is different in terms of how it handles data, this module takes care of interacting with the OS.
- **Window**: When rendering anything to the screen, the first thing we need is a viewport or a window. Once we have access to this, we can start sending our rendered scene to it. The window module takes care of how a window is created, how the input is handled, and more.
- **Graphics**: After we have access to a window, we can use the graphics module to begin rendering our scene to the window. In SFML, the graphics module is primarily rendered using OpenGL and deals with 2D scene rendering only. Therefore, it can't be used to make 3D games.
- **Audio**: The audio module is responsible for playing audio and audio streams, as well as recording audio.
- **Networking**: SFML also includes a networking library for sending and receiving data, which can be used for developing multiplayer games.

Downloading SFML and configuring Visual Studio

Now that we are familiar with the basics, let's get started:

1. Navigate to the SFML download page (`https://www.sfml-dev.org/download.php`):

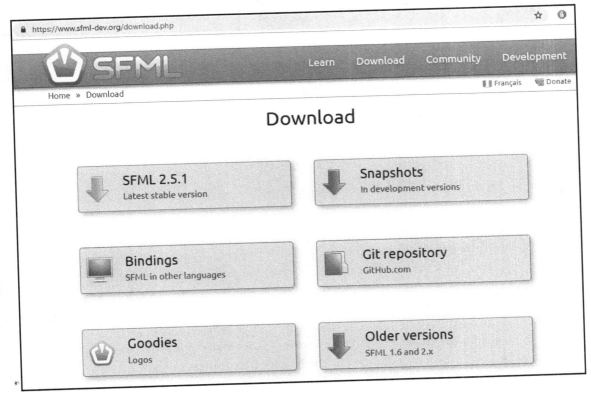

2. Select **SFML 2.5.1**. Alternatively, you can clone the repository and build the latest version using CMake.
3. Download either the 32-bit or 64-bit version (depending on your OS) for Visual Studio 2017.

Although we are going to be developing the game for Windows, you can download SFML for Linux or macOS from the same web page.

In the downloaded ZIP file, you will see the following directories:

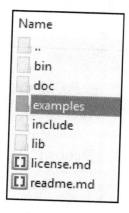

These directories can be defined as follows:

- `bin`: This contains all the **dynamic link libraries (DLLs)** that are required for running all the SFML modules. This has a `.dll` file, which contains the debug and release versions. The debug version has a `-d` suffix at the end of the file. Files that don't have this suffix are the release version `.dll` files.
- `doc`: This contains the documentation for SFML provided in HTML format.
- `examples`: This contains examples we can use to implement the modules and features of SFML. It tells us how to open a window, include OpenGL, carry out networking, and how to create a basic pong-like game.
- `include`: This contains all the header files for the modules. The graphics module has classes for creating sprites, loading textures, creating shapes, and more.
- `lib`: This contains all the library files that we will need in order to run SFML.

There are also two files: `readme.md` and `license.md`. The license file indicates that SFML can be used for commercial purposes. Therefore, it can be altered and redistributed, provided that you don't claim that you created it.

4. To set up a Visual Studio project, create a new project called `SFMLProject`. In this Visual Studio project root directory, where `SFMLProject.vcxproj` is located, extract the `SFML-2.5.1` folder and place it here.

5. Then, in the root directory, move all the `.dll` files from the `.bin` folder into the root directory. Your project root directory should look similar to the following screenshot:

```
SFML-2.5.1
    openal32.dll
    sfml-audio-2.dll
    sfml-audio-d-2.dll
    sfml-graphics-2.dll
    sfml-graphics-d-2.dll
    sfml-network-2.dll
    sfml-network-d-2.dll
    sfml-system-2.dll
    sfml-system-d-2.dll
    sfml-window-2.dll
    sfml-window-d-2.dll
    SFMLProject.vcxproj.user
    SFMLProject.vcxproj
    SFMLProject.vcxproj.filters
```

6. In the Visual Studio project, create a new `source.cpp` file.

7. Next, open **Project Properties** by right-clicking on the project in the **Solution Explorer**.

8. Make sure that the **Win32** configuration is selected. Under **Configuration Properties**, select **VC++ Directories**. Add **$(ProjectDir)\SFML-2.5.1\include** to the **Include Directories**. Then, add **$(ProjectDIr)\SFML-2.5.1\lib** in **Library Directories**, as shown in the following screenshot:

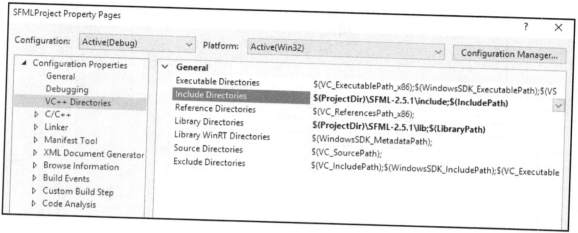

The $(ProjectDir) keyword always makes sure that files are searched with reference to the project directory, which is where the .vcxproj file is located. This makes the project portable and able to run on any Windows system.

9. Next, we have to set what libraries we want to use; select **Input** from the **Linker** dropdown menu and type in the following .lib files:

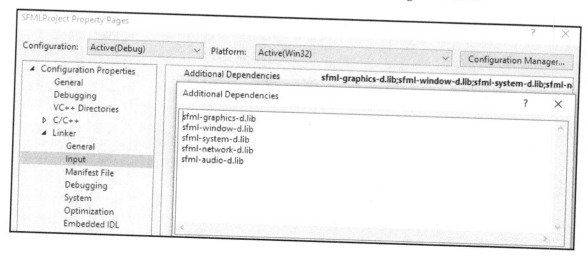

Although we won't be using `sfml-network-d.lib` in this book, it is better to include it so that, if you do want to make a multiplayer game later, then you will already be set up for it.

Now that we've completed the setup, we can finally start typing some code.

Creating a window

Before we draw anything, the first thing we need is a window so that we can display something on the screen. Let's create a window:

1. At the top of the `source.cpp` file, include the `Graphics.hpp` file to gain access to the SFML graphics library:

   ```
   #include "SFML-2.5.1\include\SFML\Graphics.hpp"
   ```

2. Next, add the main function, which will be the application's main entry point:

   ```
   int main(){
   return 0;
   }
   ```

3. To create the window, we have to specify the size of the window that we want to create. SFML has a `Vector2f` data type, which takes an `x` and a `y` value and uses them to define the size of the window that we will be using.

   Between `include` and `main`, add the following line of code. Create a variable called `viewSize` and set the `x` and `y` values to `1024` and `768`, respectively:

   ```
   sf::Vector2f viewSize(1024, 768);
   ```

   The assets for the game are created for the resolution, so I am using this view size; we also need to specify a `viewMode` class.

`viewMode` is an SFML class that sets the width and height of the window. It also gets the bits that are required to represent a color value in a pixel. `viewMode` also obtains the different resolutions that your monitor supports so that you can let the user set the resolution of the game to glorious 4K resolution if they desire.

4. To set the view mode, add the following code after setting the `viewSize` variable:

```
sf::videoMode vm(viewSize.x, viewSize.y);
```

5. Now, we can finally create a window. The window is created using the `RenderWindow` class. The `RenderWindow` constructor takes three parameters: a `viewMode` parameter, a window name parameter, and a `Style` parameter.

We have already created a `viewMode` parameter and we can pass in a window name here using a string. The third parameter, `Style`. `Style`, is an `enum` value; we can add a number of values, called a bitmask, to create the window style that we want:

- `sf::style::Titlebar`: This adds a title bar to the top of the window.
- `sf::style::Fullscreen`: This creates a full-screen mode window.
- `sf::style::Default`: This is the default style that combines the ability to resize a window, close it, and add a title bar.

6. Let's create a default-style window. First, create the window using the following command and add it after the creation of the `viewMode` parameter:

```
sf::RenderWindow window(vm, "Hello SFMLGame !!!",
sf::Style::Default);
```

7. In the `main()` class, we will create a `while` loop, which handles the main game loop for our game. This will check whether or not the window is open so that we can add some keyboard events by updating and rendering the objects in the scene. The `while` loop will run as long as the window is open. In the `main` function, add the following code:

```
int main() {
    //Initialize Game Objects
        while (window.isOpen()) {

                // Handle Keyboard Events
                // Update Game Objects in the scene
                // Render Game Objects

            }

    return 0;
}
```

Now, run the application. Here, you have your not-so-interesting game with a window that has a white background. Hey, at least you have a window now! To display something here, we have to clear the window and display whatever we draw in every frame. This is done using the `clear` and `display` functions.

8. We have to call `window.clear()` before we can render the scene and then call `window.display()` afterward to display the scene objects.

   In the `while` loop, add the `clear` and `display` functions. Game objects will be drawn between the `clear` function and the `display` function:

```cpp
int main() {
    //init game objects
        while (window.isOpen()) {
                // Handle Keyboard events
                // Update Game Objects in the scene
        window.clear(sf::Color::Red);
      // Render Game Objects
    window.display();
            }
        return 0;
}
```

The `clear` function takes in a clear color. Here, we are passing in the color red as a value into the function. This function fills in the whole window with this solid color value:

Drawing shapes

SFML provides us with the functionality to draw basic shapes such as a rectangle, circle, and triangle. The shape can be set to a certain size and has functions, such as `fillColor`, `Position`, and `Origin`, so that we can set the color, the position of the shape in the viewport, and the origin around which the shape can rotate respectively. Let's take a look at an example of a rectangular shape:

1. Before the `while` loop, add the following code to set up the rectangle:

```
sf::RectangleShape rect(sf::Vector2f(500.0f, 300.0f));
rect.setFillColor(sf::Color::Yellow);
rect.setPosition(viewSize.x / 2, viewSize.y / 2);
rect.setOrigin(sf::Vector2f(rect.getSize().x / 2,
rect.getSize().y / 2));
```

Here, we created a `Rectangle` parameter of the `RectangleShape` type and named it `rect`. The constructor of `RectangleShape` takes in the size of the rectangle. Its size is `500` by `300`. Then, we set the color of the rectangle to yellow. After this, we set the position of the rectangle to the center of the viewport and set the origin to the center of the rectangle.

2. To draw the rectangle, we have to call the `window.draw()` function and pass the rectangle into it. Make sure that you call this function between the `clear` and `display` functions in the `while` loop. Now, add the following code:

```
#include "SFML-2.5.1\include\SFML\Graphics.hpp"

sf::Vector2f viewSize(1024, 768);
sf::VideoMode vm(viewSize.x, viewSize.y);
sf::RenderWindow window(vm, "Hello Game SFML !!!",
sf::Style::Default);
int main() {
//init game objects
sf::RectangleShape rect(sf::Vector2f(500.0f, 300.0f));
rect.setFillColor(sf::Color::Yellow);
rect.setPosition(viewSize.x / 2, viewSize.y / 2);
rect.setOrigin(sf::Vector2f(rect.getSize().x / 2,
rect.getSize().y / 2));
        while (window.isOpen()) {
                // Handle Keyboard events
                // Update Game Objects in the scene
                window.clear(sf::Color::Red);
```

```
                    // Render Game Objects
                    window.draw(rect);
                    window.display();
            }
        return 0;
    }
```

3. Now, run the project; you will see a yellow rectangle in a red viewport, as follows:

4. If we set the position to `(0, 0)`, you will see where the origin is for the 2D rectangle in SFML—it is in the top left corner of the viewport:

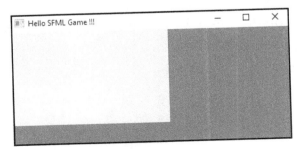

5. Move it back to the center of the viewport by undoing the previous action. Then, set the rectangle to the center of the viewport again, as follows:

```
rect.setPosition(viewSize.x / 2, viewSize.y / 2);
```

6. Now, we can add a few more shapes, such as a circle and a triangle. We can create a circle using the CircleShape class, whereas we can create a triangle using the ConvexShape class. Before the main loop, we will create a circle by using CircleShape and Triangle with ConvexShape, as follows:

```
sf::CircleShape circle(100);
circle.setFillColor(sf::Color::Green);
circle.setPosition(viewSize.x / 2, viewSize.y / 2);
circle.setOrigin(sf::Vector2f(circle.getRadius(),
circle.getRadius()));
sf::ConvexShape triangle;
triangle.setPointCount(3);
triangle.setPoint(0, sf::Vector2f(-100, 0));
triangle.setPoint(1, sf::Vector2f(0, -100));
triangle.setPoint(2, sf::Vector2f(100, 0));
triangle.setFillColor(sf::Color(128, 0, 128, 255));
triangle.setPosition(viewSize.x / 2, viewSize.y / 2);
```

The CircleShape class takes only one parameter (which is the radius of the circle), in comparison to the rectangle, which takes two parameters. We set the color of the circle to green using the setFIllColor function, and then set its position and origin.

To create the triangle, we use the ConvexShape class. To create a shape, we specify the setPointCount, which takes one parameter. We will use it to specify how many points will make up the shape. Next, using the setPoint function, we set the location of the points. This takes two parameters: the first is the index of the point and the second is the location of the point.

To create the triangle, we use three points: the first, with an index of 0 and a location of (-100, 0); the second, with an index of 1 and a location of (0, -100); and the third, with an index of 2 and a location of (100, 0).

Now, we need to set the color of the triangle. We do this by setting the values of the red, green, blue, and alpha values. Colors in SFML are 8-bit integer values. This means that each color range is between 0 and 255, where 0 is black and 255 is the maximum color range. So, when we set the color of the triangle to `triangle.setFillColor(sf::Color(128, 0, 128, 255));`, red is half of its maximum range, there is no green, blue is also half of its maximum range, and alpha is 255, making the triangle fully opaque. Then, we set the position of the triangle so that it's at the center of the screen.

7. Next, we draw the circle and triangle. Call the `draw` function for the circle and triangle after drawing the rectangle, as follows:

```
while (window.isOpen()) {
            // Handle Keyboard events
            // Update Game Objects in the scene
            window.clear(sf::Color::Red);
            // Render Game Objects
            window.draw(rect);
            window.draw(circle);
            window.draw(triangle);
            window.display();

    }
```

8. The output of the preceding code is as follows:

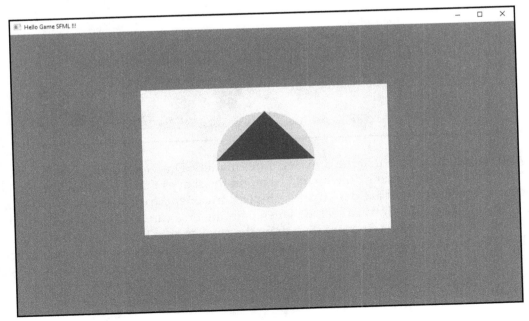

Note that, when creating the triangle, the second point was created with a negative *y* value of 100:

```
triangle.setPoint(0, sf::Vector2f(-100, 0));
triangle.setPoint(1, sf::Vector2f(0, -100));
triangle.setPoint(2, sf::Vector2f(100, 0));
```

However, the triangle is pointing upward. This means that the *+y* axis is pointing downward. You will find that this is mostly the case in 2D frameworks. Furthermore, the origin for the scene is in the top-left corner, so the coordinate system is as follows:

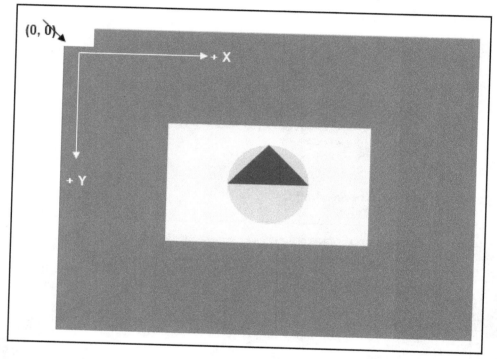

It is also important to note that the drawing order matters. Drawing happens from back to front. So, the first shape that's drawn will be behind the shapes that are drawn later in the same location. Objects that are drawn later simply draw over the earlier objects, in the same way that an artist would draw in real life when painting on a canvas. So, make sure that you draw the bigger objects first and then draw the smaller ones later. If you draw the smaller objects before the bigger ones, then the smaller objects will be behind the bigger objects and you won't be able to see them. Make sure this doesn't happen as you won't get any errors and everything in the code will be correct, so you won't know if something's gone wrong.

Adding sprites

A sprite is a rectangle with a picture applied to it. You may be wondering, *why not just use a picture?* Of course, we do load a picture up, then we won't be able to move or rotate it. Therefore, we apply a picture or texture to a rectangle that is able to move and rotate, making it look as if the picture is doing so. Let's learn how to do this:

1. Since we will be loading images into our game project, which is in the root directory of the project, let's create a folder called `Assets`.

2. In this folder, create another folder called `graphics`, and then copy and paste the `sky.png` file into the `graphics` folder:

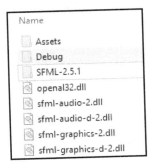

To create sprites, we use the `Sprite` class from SFML. The `Sprite` class takes in a texture. Then, the picture is loaded using the `Texture` class. While drawing, you need to call `window.draw.(sprite)` to draw the sprite. Let's take a look at how to do this.

3. Declare a `Texture` class called `skyTexture` and a `Sprite` class called `skySprite` globally. This should be done after the creation of the `RenderWindow` class:

```
sf::Texture skyTexture;
sf::Sprite skySprite;
```

4. Create a new function called `init` in the `source.cpp` file that appears right before the `main` function. Since we don't want the `main` function to be cluttered, we will add the code to initialize `skyTexture` and `skySprite` to it. In the `init` function, add the following code:

```
void init() {

// Load sky Texture
```

```
    skyTexture.loadFromFile("Assets/graphics/sky.png");
// Set and  Attacha Texture to Sprite
    skySprite.setTexture(skyTexture);

}
```

First, we load the `skyTexture` function by calling the `loadFromFile` function. We pass in the path and filename of the file that we want to load. Here, we want to load the `sky.png` file from the `Assets` folder.

Next, we use the `setTexture` function of the sprite and pass the `skyTexture` function into it.

5. To do this, create a new function called `draw()` above the `main` and `init` functions. We call `draw(skySprite)` in it in order to draw the sprite, as follows:

```
void draw() {
    window.draw(skySprite);

}
```

6. Now, we have to call `init()` at the beginning of the `main` function and `draw()` in the `while` loop that we added to the `main` function. You can remove all the code that was used for creating and drawing the shapes from the `main` function. Your `main` function should look as follows:

```
#include "SFML-2.5.1\include\SFML\Graphics.hpp"

sf::Vector2f viewSize(1024, 768);
sf::VideoMode vm(viewSize.x, viewSize.y);
sf::RenderWindow window(vm, "Hello Game SFML !!!",
sf::Style::Default);

sf::Texture skyTexture;
sf::Sprite skySprite;

void init() {

    skyTexture.loadFromFile("Assets/graphics/sky.png");
    skySprite.setTexture(skyTexture);

}

void draw() {
    window.draw(skySprite);
```

```
}

int main() {
    init();

    while (window.isOpen()) {
        window.clear(sf::Color::Red);
        draw();

        window.display();
    }

    return 0;
}
```

The output is as follows:

Praise the sun! Lo and behold, we have the sky texture loaded and have drawn it as a sprite in the window.

7. I have included a background texture picture as well, called bg.png, which is available in the Assets folder of this chapter's project. Try and load the texture and draw the texture in the same way.

8. I named the variables of the background texture and sprite bgTexture and bgSprite, respectively, and drew the bgSprite variable into the scene. Don't forget to add the bg.png file to the Assets/graphics directory.

Your scene should now look as follows:

9. Next, add another sprite called `heroSprite` and load in the picture with `heroTexture`. Set the origin of the sprite to its center and place it in the middle of the scene. The `hero.png` file image is provided here, so make sure you place it in the `Assets/graphics` folder. Now, declare `heroSprite` and `heroTexture`, as follows:

```
sf::Texture heroTexture;
sf::Sprite heroSprite;
```

```
In the init function initialize the following values:
    heroTexture.loadFromFile("Assets/graphics/hero.png");
    heroSprite.setTexture(heroTexture);
    heroSprite.setPosition(sf::Vector2f(viewSize.x/2,
        viewSize.y/2));
    heroSprite.setOrigin(heroTexture.getSize().x / 2,
        heroTexture.getSize().y / 2);
```

10. To set the origin of the sprite, we take the textures and the height and divide them by 2.

    Using the `draw` function, draw the `heroSprite` sprite, as follows:

```
void draw() {
    window.draw(skySprite);
    window.draw(bgSprite);
    window.draw(heroSprite);
}
```

11. Our hero will now appear in the scene, as follows:

Keyboard input

It is great that we are able to add shapes, sprites, and textures; however, computer games, by nature, are interactive. We will need to allow players to use keyboard inputs so that they can access the game's content. But how do we know which button the player is pressing? Well, that is handled through the polling of events. Polling just checks the status of the keys regularly; events are used to check whether an event was triggered, such as the closing of the viewport.

SFML provides the sf::Event class so that we can poll events. We can use the pollEvent function of the window to check for events that may be occurring, such as a player pressing a button.

Create a new function called updateInput(). Here, we will create a new object of the sf::Event class called event. We will create a while loop called window.pollEvent and then pass in the event variable to check for events.

So far, we have been using *Shift + F5* or the stop button in Visual Studio to stop the application. One of the basic things we can do is check whether the *Esc* key has been pressed. If it has been pressed, we want to close the window. To do this, add the following code:

```
void updateInput() {

    sf::Event event;

    while (window.pollEvent(event)) {

    if (event.key.code == sf::Keyboard::Escape ||
            event.type ==sf::Event::Closed)
                    window.close();

    }

}
```

In the while loop, we need to check whether the event key code is that of the *Esc* key code, or whether the event is Event::closed. Then, we call the window.close() function to close the window. When we close the window, it shuts down the application.

Call the updateInput() function in the main while loop before the window.clear() function. Now, when you press *Esc* while the application is running, it will close. SFML doesn't limit inputs just to keyboards; it also provides functionality for mouse, joystick, and touch input.

Handing player movement

Now that we have access to the player's keyboard, we can learn how to move game objects. Let's move the player character to the right when the right arrow key is pressed on the keyboard. We will stop moving the hero when the right arrow key is released:

1. Create a global `Vector2f` called `playerPosition`, right after `heroSprite`.
2. Create a Boolean data type called `playerMoving` and set it to `false`.
3. In the `updateInput` function, we will check whether the right key has been pressed or released. If the button is pressed, we set `playerMoving` to `true`. If the button is released, then we set `playerMoving` to `false`.

The `updateInput` function should be as follows:

```
void updateInput() {

    sf::Event event;

    while (window.pollEvent(event)) {

        if (event.type == sf::Event::KeyPressed) {


            if (event.key.code == sf::Keyboard::Right) {

                playerMoving = true;
            }
        }
        if (event.type == sf::Event::KeyReleased) {

            if (event.key.code == sf::Keyboard::Right) {
                playerMoving = false;
            }
        }
        if (event.key.code == sf::Keyboard::Escape || event.type
        == sf::Event::Closed)
            window.close();
    }
}
```

4. To update the objects in the scene, we will create a function called update, which will take a float called dt. This stands for delta time and refers to the time that has passed between the previous update and the current update call. In the update function, we will check whether the player is moving. If the player is moving, then we will move the position of the player in the +x direction and multiply this by dt.

The reason we multiply by delta time is because if we don't, then the update will not be time-dependent, but processor-dependent instead. If you don't multiply the position by dt, then the update will happen faster on a faster PC and will be slower on a slower PC. So, make sure that any movement is always multiplied by dt.

The update function should look as follows. Make sure that this function appears before the main function:

```
void update(float dt) {

    if (playerMoving) {
        heroSprite.move(50.0f * dt, 0);
    }
}
```

5. At the beginning of the main function, create an object of the sf::Clock type called Clock. The Clock class takes care of getting the system clock and allows us to get the delta time in seconds, milliseconds, or microseconds.

6. In the while loop, after calling updateInput(), create a variable called dt of the sf::Time type and set the dt variable by calling clock.restart().

7. Now, call the update function and pass in dt.asSeconds(), which will give the delta time as 60 frames per second, which is approximately .0167 seconds.

The main function should appear as follows:

```
int main() {
    sf::Clock clock;
    init();
    while (window.isOpen()) {
        // Update input
        updateInput();

        // Update Game
        sf::Time dt = clock.restart();
        update(dt.asSeconds());
```

```
window.clear(sf::Color::Red);
        //Draw Game
        draw();

        window.display();
    }
    return 0;
}
```

8. Now, when you run the project and press the right arrow key on the keyboard, the player will start moving right, and will stop when you release the right arrow key:

Summary

In this chapter, we looked at how to set up SFML so that we can start creating a game. We covered the five basic modules that make up SFML, and also looked at creating shapes using SFML and adding the background and player sprite to the scene. We also added keyboard input and used this to make the player character move within the scene.

In the next chapter, we will create the basic skeleton of the game. We will also move the player character to a separate class and add some basic physics to the character to allow them to jump in the game.

4
Creating Your Game

In this chapter, we will make our project more flexible by adding game objects as classes instead of adding them to the source.cpp file. In this case, we will use classes to make the main character and the enemy. We will create a new rocket class that the player will be able to shoot at the enemy. We will then spawn enemies at regular intervals along with new rockets when we press a button. We will finally check for a collision between the rocket and the enemy and, accordingly, remove the enemy from the scene.

This chapter will cover the following topics:

- Starting afresh
- Creating the Hero class
- Creating the Enemy class
- Adding enemies
- Creating the Rocket class
- Adding rockets
- Collision detection

Starting afresh

Since we are going to create a new class for the main character, we will remove the code pertaining to the player character in the main file. Let's learn how to do this.

Remove all player-related code from the main.cpp file. After doing this, the file should appear as follows:

```
#include "SFML-2.5.1\include\SFML\Graphics.hpp"


sf::Vector2f viewSize(1024, 768);
sf::VideoMode vm(viewSize.x, viewSize.y);
sf::RenderWindow window(vm, "Hello SFML Game !!!", sf::Style::Default);
```

```cpp
    sf::Vector2f playerPosition;
    bool playerMoving = false;

    sf::Texture skyTexture;
    sf::Sprite skySprite;

    sf::Texture bgTexture;
    sf::Sprite bgSprite;


    void init() {


        skyTexture.loadFromFile("Assets/graphics/sky.png");
        skySprite.setTexture(skyTexture);

        bgTexture.loadFromFile("Assets/graphics/bg.png");
        bgSprite.setTexture(bgTexture);

    }


    void updateInput() {

        sf::Event event;

        // while there are pending events...
        while (window.pollEvent(event)) {

            if (event.key.code == sf::Keyboard::Escape || event.type ==
                sf::Event::Closed)
                window.close();


        }

    }


    void update(float dt) {

    }

    void draw() {

        window.draw(skySprite);
```

```cpp
    window.draw(bgSprite);

}


int main() {

    sf::Clock clock;
    window.setFramerateLimit(60);

    init();

    while (window.isOpen()) {

        updateInput();

        sf::Time dt = clock.restart();
        update(dt.asSeconds());


        window.clear(sf::Color::Red);

        draw();

        window.display();

    }

    return 0;
}
```

Creating the Hero class

We will now move on to create a new class by going through the following steps:

1. Select the project in the solution explorer and then right-click and select **Add** |
   Class. In this class name, specify the name as Hero. You will see the .h and .cpp
   file sections automatically populated as Hero.h and Hero.cpp respectively.
   Click on **Ok**.

2. In the `Hero.h` file, add the SFML graphics header and create the `Hero` class:

```
#include "SFML-2.5.0\include\SFML\Graphics.hpp"

class Hero{

};
```

3. In the `Hero` class, we will create the methods and variables that will be required by the class. We will also create some public properties that will be accessible outside the class, as follows:

```
public:
    Hero();
    ~Hero();

    void init(std::string textureName, sf::Vector2f position, float
    mass);
    void update(float dt);
    void jump(float velocity);
    sf::Sprite getSprite();
```

Here, we have the constructor and destructor, which will be respectively called when an object is created and destroyed. We add an `init` function to pass a texture name, spawn the player, and specify a mass. We are specifying a mass here because we will be creating some very basic physics so that when we hit the jump button, the player will jump up and land back down on their feet.

Additionally, the `update`, `jump`, and `getSprite` functions will update the player position, make the player jump, and get the sprite of the player that is used for depicting the player character respectively.

4. Apart from these `public` variables, we will also need some `private` variables that can only be accessed within the class. Add these in the `Hero` class, as follows:

```
private:

    sf::Texture m_texture;
    sf::Sprite m_sprite;
    sf::Vector2f m_position;

int jumpCount = 0;
float m_mass;
    float m_velocity;
    const float m_gravity = 9.80f;
        bool m_grounded;
```

In the `private` section, we create variables for `texture`, `sprite`, and `position` so that we can set these values locally. We have the `int` variable called `jumpCount` so that we can check the number of times the player character has jumped. This is needed because the player can sometimes double jump, which is something we don't want.

We will also need the `float` variables to store the player's mass, the velocity when they jump, and the gravitational force when they fall back to the ground, which is a constant. The `const` keyword tells the program that it is a constant and under no circumstance should the value be made changeable.

Lastly, we add a `bool` value to check whether the player is on the ground. Only when the player is on the ground can they start jumping.

5. Next, in the `Hero.cpp` file, we will implement the functions that we added in the `.h` file. At the top of the `.cpp` file, include the `Hero.h` file and then add the constructor and destructor:

```
#include "Hero.h"
Hero::Hero(){

}
```

 The `::` symbol represents the scope resolution operator. Functions that have the same name can be defined in two different classes. In order to access the methods of a particular class, the scope resolution operator is used.

6. Here, the `Hero` function is scoped to the `Hero` class:

```
Hero::~Hero(){

}
```

7. Next, we will set up the `init` function, as follows:

```
void Hero::init(std::string textureName, sf::Vector2f position,
float mass){

    m_position = position;
    m_mass = mass;

    m_grounded = false;
    // Load a Texture
    m_texture.loadFromFile(textureName.c_str());
```

```
// Create Sprite and Attach a Texture
m_sprite.setTexture(m_texture);
m_sprite.setPosition(m_position);
m_sprite.setOrigin(m_texture.getSize().x / 2,
m_texture.getSize().y / 2);

}
```

We set the position and mass to the local variable and set the grounded state to `false`. Then, we set the texture by calling `loadFromFile` and passing in the string of the texture name to it. The `c_str()` phrase returns a pointer to an array that contains a null-terminated sequence of characters (that is, a C string) representing the current value of the `string` object (http://www.cplusplus.com/reference/string/string/c_str/). We then set the sprite texture, position, and the origin of the sprite itself.

8. Now, we add the `update` function where we implement the logic for updating the player position. The player's character cannot move left or right; instead, it can only move up, which is the *y* direction. When an initial velocity is applied, the player will jump up and then start falling down because of gravity. Add the `update` function to update the position of the hero, as follows:

```
void Hero::update(float dt){

    m_force -= m_mass * m_gravity * dt;

    m_position.y -= m_force * dt;

    m_sprite.setPosition(m_position);


    if (m_position.y >= 768 * 0.75f) {

        m_position.y = 768 * 0.75f;
        m_force = 0;
        m_grounded = true;
        jumpCount = 0;
    }

}
```

When the velocity is applied to the character, the player will initially go up because of the force, but will then start coming down because of gravity. The resulting velocity acts in the downward direction, and is calculated by the following formula:

$$Velocity = Acceleration \times Time$$

We multiply the acceleration by the mass so that the player falls faster. To calculate the distance moved vertically, we use the following formula:

$$Distance = Velocity \times Time$$

Then, we calculate the distance moved between the previous and the current frame. We then set the position of the sprite based on the position that we calculated.

We also have a condition to check whether the player is at one-fourth of the distance from the bottom of the screen. We multiply this by 768, which is the height of the window, and then multiply it by .75f, at which point the player is considered to be on the ground. If that condition is satisfied, we set the position of the player, set the resulting velocity to 0, set the grounded Boolean to true, and, finally, reset the jump counter to 0.

9. When we want to make the player jump, we call the jump function, which takes an initial velocity. We will now add the jump function, as follows:

```
void Hero::jump(float velocity){

    if (jumpCount < 2) {
        jumpCount++;

        m_velocity = VELOCITY;
        m_grounded = false;
    }

}
```

Here, we first check whether jumpCount is less than 2 as we only want the player to jump twice. If jumpCount is less than 2, then increase the jumpCount value by 1, set the initial velocity, and set the grounded Boolean to false.

10. Finally, we add the `getSprite` function, which simply gets the current sprite, as follows:

```
sf::Sprite Hero::getSprite(){

    return m_sprite;
}
```

Congrats! We now have our `Hero` class ready. Let's use it in the `source.cpp` file by going through the following steps:

1. Include `Hero.h` at the top of the `main.cpp` file:

```
#include "SFML-2.5.1\include\SFML\Graphics.hpp"
#include "Hero.h"
```

2. Next, add an instance of the `Hero` class, as follows:

```
sf::Texture skyTexture;
sf::Sprite skySprite;

sf::Texture bgTexture;
sf::Sprite bgSprite;
Hero hero;
```

3. In the `init` function, initialize the `Hero` class:

```
// Load bg Texture

bgTexture.loadFromFile("Assets/graphics/bg.png");

// Create Sprite and Attach a Texture
bgSprite.setTexture(bgTexture);
hero.init("Assets/graphics/hero.png", sf::Vector2f(viewSize.x *
0.25f, viewSize.y * 0.5f), 200);
```

Here, we set the texture picture; to do so, set the position to be at `.25` (or 25%) from the left of the screen and center it along the `y` axis. We also set the mass as `200`, as our character is quite chubby.

4. Next, we want the player to jump when we press the up arrow key. Therefore, in the `updateInput` function, while polling for window events, we add the following code:

```
while (window.pollEvent(event)) {
    if (event.type == sf::Event::KeyPressed) {
        if (event.key.code == sf::Keyboard::Up) {
            hero.jump(750.0f);
        }
    }
    if (event.key.code == sf::Keyboard::Escape || event.type ==
    sf::Event::Closed)
        window.close();

}
```

Here, we check whether a key was pressed by the player. If a key is pressed and the button is the up arrow on the keyboard, then we call the `hero.jump` function and pass in an initial velocity value of `750`.

5. Next, in the `update` function, we call the `hero.update` function, as follows:

```
void update(float dt) {
    hero.update(dt);
}
```

6. Finally, in the `draw` function, we draw the hero sprite:

```
void draw() {

    window.draw(skySprite);
    window.draw(bgSprite);
    window.draw(hero.getSprite());

}
```

7. You can now run the game. When the player is on the ground, press the up arrow button on the keyboard to see the player jump. When the player is in the air, press the jump button again and you will see the player jump again in midair:

Creating the Enemy class

The player character looks very lonely. She is ready to cause some mayhem, but there is nothing to shoot right now. Let's add some enemies to solve this problem:

1. The enemies will be created using an enemy class; let's create a new class and call it Enemy.

2. Just like the Hero class, the Enemy class will have a .h file and a .cpp file. In the Enemy.h file, add the following code:

```cpp
#pragma once
#include "SFML-2.5.1\include\SFML\Graphics.hpp"

class Enemy
{
public:
    Enemy();
    ~Enemy();

    void init(std::string textureName, sf::Vector2f position,
        float_speed);
    void update(float dt);
    sf::Sprite getSprite();

private:

    sf::Texture m_texture;
    sf::Sprite m_sprite;
    sf::Vector2f m_position;
    float m_speed;

};
```

Here, the Enemy class, just like the Hero class, also has a constructor and destructor. Additionally, it has an init function that takes in the texture and position; however, instead of mass, it takes in a float variable that will be used to set the initial velocity of the enemy. The enemy won't be affected by gravity and will only spawn from the right of the screen and move toward the left of the screen. There are also update and getSprite functions; since the enemy won't be jumping, there won't be a jump function. Lastly, in the private section, we create local variables for texture, sprite, position, and speed.

3. In the `Enemy.cpp` file, we add the constructor, destructor, `init`, `update`, and `getSprite` functions:

```cpp
#include "Enemy.h"

Enemy::Enemy(){}

Enemy::~Enemy(){}

void Enemy::init(std::string textureName, sf::Vector2f position,
    float _speed) {

    m_speed = _speed;
    m_position = position;

    // Load a Texture
    m_texture.loadFromFile(textureName.c_str());

    // Create Sprite and Attach a Texture
    m_sprite.setTexture(m_texture);
    m_sprite.setPosition(m_position);
    m_sprite.setOrigin(m_texture.getSize().x / 2,
    m_texture.getSize().y / 2);

}
```

Don't forget to include `Enemy.h` at the top of the main function. We then add the constructor and destructor. In the `init` function, we set the local speed and position values. Next, we load `Texture` from the file and set the texture, position, and origin of the enemy sprite.

4. In the `update` and `getSprite` functions, we update the position and get the enemy sprite:

```cpp
void Enemy::update(float dt) {

    m_sprite.move(m_speed * dt, 0);

}


sf::Sprite Enemy::getSprite() {

    return m_sprite;
}
```

5. We have our `Enemy` class ready. Let's now see how we can use it in the game.

Adding enemies

In the `main.cpp` class, include the `Enemy` header file. Since we want more than one enemy instance, we need to add a vector called `enemies` and then add all the newly-created enemies to it.

In the context of the following code, the `vector` phrase has absolutely nothing to do with math, but rather with a list of objects. In fact, it is like an array in which we can store multiple objects. Vectors are used instead of an array because vectors are dynamic in nature, so it makes it easier to add and remove objects from the list (unlike an array, which, by comparison, is a static list). Let's get started:

1. We need to include `<vector>` in the `main.cpp` file, as follows:

```
#include "SFML-2.5.1\include\SFML\Graphics.hpp"
#include <vector>

#include "Hero.h"
#include "Enemy.h"
```

2. Next, add a new variable called `enemies` of the `vector` type, which will store the `Enemy` data type in it:

```
sf::Texture bgTexture;
sf::Sprite bgSprite;

Hero hero;

std::vector<Enemy*> enemies;
```

3. In order to create a vector of a certain object type, you use the `vector` keyword, and inside the arrow brackets, specify the data type that the vector will hold, and then specify a name for the vector you have created. In this way, we can create a new function called `spawnEnemy()` and add a prototype for it at the top of the main function.

When any function is written below the main function, the main function will not be aware that such a function exists. Therefore, a prototype will be created and placed above the main function. This means that the function can now be implemented below the main function—essentially, the prototype tells the main function that there is a function that will be implemented below it, and so to keep a lookout for it.

```
sf::Vector2f viewSize(1024, 768);
sf::VideoMode vm(viewSize.x, viewSize.y);
sf::RenderWindow window(vm, "Hello SFML Game !!!",
sf::Style::Default);
```

void spawnEnemy();

Now, we want the enemy to spawn from the right of the screen, but we also want the enemy to spawn at either the same height as the player, slightly higher than the player, or much higher than the player, so that the player will have to use a single jump or a double jump to attack the enemy.

4. To do this, we add some randomness to the game to make it less predictable. For this, we add the following line of code underneath the init function:

```
hero.init("Assets/graphics/hero.png", sf::Vector2f(viewSize.x *
0.25f, viewSize.y * 0.5f), 200);

srand((int)time(0));
```

The srand phrase is a pseudorandom number that is initialized by passing a seed value. In this case, we are passing in the current time as a seed value.

For each seed value, a series of numbers will be generated. If the seed value is always the same, then the same series of numbers will be generated. That is why we pass in the time value—so that the sequence of numbers that is generated will be different each time. We can get the next random number in the series by calling the rand function.

5. Next, we add the spawnEnemy function, as follows:

```
void spawnEnemy() {

    int randLoc = rand() % 3;

    sf::Vector2f enemyPos;

    float speed;
```

```
switch (randLoc) {

case 0: enemyPos = sf::Vector2f(viewSize.x, viewSize.y * 0.75f);
speed = -400; break;

case 1: enemyPos = sf::Vector2f(viewSize.x, viewSize.y * 0.60f);
speed = -550; break;

case 2: enemyPos = sf::Vector2f(viewSize.x, viewSize.y * 0.40f);
speed = -650; break;

default: printf("incorrect y value \n"); return;

}

Enemy* enemy = new Enemy();
enemy->init("Assets/graphics/enemy.png", enemyPos, speed);

enemies.push_back(enemy);
}
```

Here, we first get a random number—this will create a new random number from 0 to 2 because of the modulo operator while getting the random location. So the value of randLoc will either be 0, 1, or 2 each time the function is called.

A new enemyPos variable is created that will be assigned depending upon the randLoc value. We will also set the speed of the enemy depending on the randLoc value; for this, we create a new float called speed, which we will assign later. We then create a switch statement that takes in the randLoc value—this enables the random location to spawn the enemy.

Depending upon the scenario, we can set the enemyPosition variable and the speed of the enemy:

- When randLoc is 0, the enemy spawns from the bottom and moves with a speed of -400.
- When randLoc is 1, the enemy spawns from the middle of the screen and moves at a speed of -500.
- When the value of randLoc is 2, then the enemy spawns from the top of the screen and moves at the faster speed of -650.
- If randLoc is none of these values, then a message is printed out saying that the value of *y* is incorrect, and instead of breaking, we return to make sure that the enemy doesn't spawn in a random location.

To print out the message to the console, we can use the `printf` function, which takes a string value. At the end of the string, we specify \n; this is a keyword to tell the compiler that it is the end of the line, and whatever is written after needs to be put in a new line, similar to when calling `std::cout`.

6. Once we know the position and speed, we can then create the enemy object itself and initialize it. Note that the enemy is created as a pointer; otherwise, the reference to the texture is lost and the texture won't display when the enemy is spawned. Additionally, when we create the enemy as a raw pointer with a new keyword, the system allocates memory, which we will have to delete later.

7. After the enemy is created, we add it to the `enemies` vector by calling the `push` function of the vectors.

8. We want the enemy to spawn automatically at regular intervals. For this, we create two new variables to keep track of the current time and spawn a new enemy every `1.125` seconds.

9. Next, create two new variables of the `float` type, called `currentTime` and `prevTime`:

```
Hero hero;

std::vector<Enemy*> enemies;

float currentTime;
float prevTime = 0.0f;
```

10. Then, in the `update` function, after updating the `hero` function, add the following lines of code in order to create a new enemy:

```
hero.update(dt);
currentTime += dt;
// Spawn Enemies
if (currentTime >= prevTime + 1.125f)))) {
spawnEnemy();
prevTime = currentTime;
}
```

First, we increment the `currentTime` variable. This variable will begin increasing as soon as the game starts so that we can track how long it has been since we started the game. Next, we check whether the current time is greater than or equal to the previous time plus `1.125` seconds, as that is when we want the new enemy to spawn. If it is `true`, then we call the `spawnEnemy` function, which will create a new enemy. We also set the previous time as equal to the current time so that we know when the last enemy was spawned. Good! So, now that we have enemies spawning in the game, we can `update` the enemies and also `draw` them.

11. In the `update` function, we also create a `for` loop to update the enemies and delete the enemies once they go beyond the left of the screen. To do this, we add the following code to the `update` function:

```
// Update Enemies

for (int i = 0; i < enemies.size(); i++) {

    Enemy *enemy = enemies[i];

    enemy->update(dt);

    if (enemy->getSprite().getPosition().x < 0) {

        enemies.erase(enemies.begin() + i);
        delete(enemy);

    }
}
```

This is where the use of vectors is really helpful. With vectors, we are able to add, delete, and insert elements in the vector. In the example here, we get the reference of the enemy at the location index of `i` in the vector. If that enemy goes offscreen and needs to be deleted, then we can just use the `erase` function and pass the location index from the beginning of the vector to remove the enemy at that index. When we reset the game, we also delete the local reference of the enemy we created. This will also free the memory space that was allocated when we created the new enemy.

12. In the `draw` function, we go through each of the enemies in a `for...each` loop and draw them:

```
window.draw(skySprite);
window.draw(bgSprite);

window.draw(hero.getSprite());
```

```
for (Enemy *enemy : enemies) {
  window.draw(enemy->getSprite());
}
```

We use the `for...each` loop to go through all the enemies, since the `getSprite` function needs to be called on all of them. Interestingly, we didn't use `for...each` when we had to update the enemies because with the `for` loop, we can simply use the index of the enemy if we have to delete it.

13. Finally, add the `Enemy.png` file to the `Assets/graphics` folder. Now, when you run the game, you will see enemies spawning at different heights and moving toward the left of the screen:

Creating the Rocket class

The game has enemies in it now, but the player still can't shoot at them. Let's create some rockets so that these can be launched from the player's bazooka by going through the following steps:

1. In the project, create a new class called `Rocket`. As you can see from the following code block, the `Rocket.h` class is very similar to the `Enemy.h` class:

```cpp
#pragma once

#include "SFML-2.5.1\include\SFML\Graphics.hpp"

class Rocket
{
public:
    Rocket();
    ~Rocket();

    void init(std::string textureName, sf::Vector2f position,
        float_speed);
    void update(float dt);
    sf::Sprite getSprite();

private:

    sf::Texture m_texture;
    sf::Sprite m_sprite;
    sf::Vector2f m_position;
    float m_speed;

};
```

The `public` section contains the `init`, `update`, and `getSprite` functions. The `init` function takes in the name of the texture to load, the position to set, and the speed at which the object is initialized. The `private` section has local variables for the `texture`, `sprite`, `position`, and `speed`.

2. In the `Rocket.cpp` file, we add the constructor and destructor, as follows:

```cpp
#include "Rocket.h"


Rocket::Rocket(){
}

Rocket::~Rocket(){
}
```

In the `init` function, we set the speed and `position` variables. Then, we set the `texture` variable and initialize the sprite with the `texture` variable.

3. Next, we set the `position` variable and origin of the sprite, as follows:

```cpp
void Rocket::init(std::string textureName, sf::Vector2f position,
float _speed){

    m_speed = _speed;
    m_position = position;

    // Load a Texture
    m_texture.loadFromFile(textureName.c_str());

    // Create Sprite and Attach a Texture
    m_sprite.setTexture(m_texture);
    m_sprite.setPosition(m_position);
    m_sprite.setOrigin(m_texture.getSize().x / 2,
      m_texture.getSize().y / 2);

}
```

4. In the `update` function, the object is moved according to the `speed` variable:

```cpp
void Rocket::update(float dt){
    \
    m_sprite.move(m_speed * dt, 0);

}
```

5. The `getSprite` function returns the current sprite, as follows:

```cpp
sf::Sprite Rocket::getSprite() {

    return m_sprite;
}
```

Adding rockets

Now that we have created the rockets, let's learn how to add them:

1. In the `main.cpp` file, we include the `Rocket.h` class as follows:

```
#include "Hero.h"
#include "Enemy.h"
#include "Rocket.h"
```

2. We then create a new vector of `Rocket` called `rockets`, which takes in `Rocket`:

```
std::vector<Enemy*> enemies;
std::vector<Rocket*> rockets;
```

3. In the `update` function, after we have updated all the enemies, we update all the rockets. We also delete the rockets that go beyond the right of the screen:

```cpp
// Update Enemies

for (int i = 0; i < enemies.size(); i++) {

    Enemy* enemy = enemies[i];

    enemy->update(dt);

    if (enemy->getSprite().getPosition().x < 0) {

        enemies.erase(enemies.begin() + i);
        delete(enemy);

    }

}
// Update rockets

for (int i = 0; i < rockets.size(); i++) {

Rocket* rocket = rockets[i];

rocket->update(dt);

if (rocket->getSprite().getPosition().x > viewSize.x) {
    rockets.erase(rockets.begin() + i);
    delete(rocket);
    }
}
```

4. Finally, we draw all the rockets with the `draw` function by going through each rocket in the scene:

```
for (Enemy *enemy : enemies) {

    window.draw(enemy->getSprite());
}

for (Rocket *rocket : rockets) {
    window.draw(rocket->getSprite());
}
```

5. Now, we can actually shoot the rockets. In the `main.cpp`, class, create a new function called `shoot()` and add a prototype for it at the top of the main function.

```
void spawnEnemy();
void shoot();
```

6. In the `shoot` function, we will add the functionality to shoot the rockets. We will spawn new rockets and push them back to the `rockets` vector. You can add the shoot function as follows:

```
void shoot() {

    Rocket* rocket = new Rocket();

    rocket->init("Assets/graphics/rocket.png",
                hero.getSprite().getPosition(),
        400.0f);

    rockets.push_back(rocket);

}
```

When this function is called, it creates a new `Rocket` and initializes it with the `Rocket.png` file, sets the position of it as equal to the position of the hero sprite, and then sets the velocity to `400.0f`. The rocket is then added to the `rockets` vector.

7. Now, in the `updateInput` function, add the following code so that when the down arrow key is pressed, the `shoot` function is called:

```
if (event.type == sf::Event::KeyPressed) {

    if (event.key.code == sf::Keyboard::Up) {
```

```
        hero.jump(750.0f);
    }

    if (event.key.code == sf::Keyboard::Down) {

        shoot();
    }
}
```

8. Don't forget to place the `rocket.png` file in the `assets` folder. Now, when you run the game and press the down arrow key, a rocket is fired:

Collision detection

For the final section of this chapter, let's add some collision detection so that the rocket actually kills an enemy when they both come into contact with each other:

1. Create a new function called checkCollision, and then create a prototype for it at the top of the main function:

    ```
    void spawnEnemy();
    void shoot();

    bool checkCollision(sf::Sprite sprite1, sf::Sprite sprite2);
    ```

2. This function takes two sprites so that we can check the intersection of one with the other. Add the following code for the function in the same place that we added the shoot function:

    ```
    void shoot() {

        Rocket* rocket = new Rocket();

        rocket->init("Assets/graphics/rocket.png",
          hero.getSprite().getPosition(), 400.0f);

        rockets.push_back(rocket);

    }


    bool checkCollision(sf::Sprite sprite1, sf::Sprite sprite2) {

        sf::FloatRect shape1 = sprite1.getGlobalBounds();
        sf::FloatRect shape2 = sprite2.getGlobalBounds();

        if (shape1.intersects(shape2)) {

            return true;

        }
        else {

            return false;

        }

    }
    ```

Inside this `checkCollision` function, we create two local variables of the `FloatRect` type. We then assign the `GlobalBounds` of the sprites to each `FloatRect` variable named `shape1` and `shape2`. The `GlobalBounds` gets the rectangular region of the sprite that the object is spanning from where it is currently.

The `FloatRect` type is simply a rectangle; we can use the `intersects` function to check whether this rectangle intersects with another rectangle. If the first rectangle intersects with another rectangle, then we return `true` to say that there is an intersection or collision between the sprites. If there is no intersection, then we return `false`.

3. In the `update` function, after updating the `enemy` and `rocket` classes, we check the collision between each rocket and each enemy in a nested `for` loop. You can add the collision check as follows:

```
// Update rockets

for (int i = 0; i < rockets.size(); i++) {

    Rocket* rocket = rockets[i];

    rocket->update(dt);
    if (rocket->getSprite().getPosition().x > viewSize.x) {

        rockets.erase(rockets.begin() + i);
        delete(rocket);

    }

}

// Check collision between Rocket and Enemies

for (int i = 0; i < rockets.size(); i++) {
    for (int j = 0; j < enemies.size(); j++) {
        Rocket* rocket = rockets[i];
        Enemy* enemy = enemies[j];

        if (checkCollision(rocket->getSprite(),
            enemy->getSprite())) {

            rockets.erase(rockets.begin() + i);
            enemies.erase(enemies.begin() + j);

            delete(rocket);
```

```
        delete(enemy);

        printf(" rocket intersects enemy \n");
    }

 }

}
```

Here, we create a double `for` loop, call the `checkCollision` function, and then pass each rocket and enemy into it to check the intersection between them.

4. If there is an intersection, we remove the rocket and enemy from the vector and delete them from the scene. With this, we are done with collision detection.

Summary

In this chapter, we created a separate `Hero` class so that all the code pertaining to the `Hero` class was in one single file. In this `Hero` class, we managed jumping and the shooting of the rockets in the class. Next, we created the `Enemy` class, because for every hero, there needs to be a villain in the story! We learned how to add enemies to a vector so that it is easier to loop between the enemies in order to update their position. We also created a `Rocket` class and managed the rockets using a vector. Finally, we learned how to check for collisions between the enemies and the rockets. This creates the foundation of the gameplay loop.

In the next chapter, we will finish the game, adding sound and text to it in order to give audio feedback to the player and show the current score.

5
Finalizing Your Game

In the previous chapter, we looked at how to create the game; in this chapter, we will finish the **Gameloop** so that you can play the game. The objective of the game is to make sure that none of the enemies are able to make it to the left of the screen. If they do, it is game over.

We will add a scoring system so that the player knows how much they have scored in a round. For each enemy that is shot down, the player will get one point. We will also add text to the game in order to display the title of the game, the player's score, and a small tutorial that shows you how to play the game.

At the end of this chapter, we will embellish the game. We will add audio that will be used as background music, as well as sound effects for when the player shoots the rocket and when the player's rockets hit the enemy. We will also add some animation to the player so that the character looks more lively.

In this chapter, we will cover the following topics:

- Finishing the Gameloop and adding scoring
- Adding text
- Adding audio
- Adding player animations

So, let's begin!

Finishing the Gameloop and adding scoring

The following steps will show you how to finish the Gameloop and add scoring to the game code:

1. Add two new variables to the `source.cpp` file: one of the `int` type, called `score`, and one of the `bool` type, called `gameover`. Initialize the score to `0` and gameover to `true`:

```
std::vector<Enemy*> enemies;
std::vector<Rocket*> rockets;

float currentTime;
float prevTime = 0.0f;

int score = 0;
bool gameover = true;
```

2. Create a new function called `reset()`. We will use this to reset the variables. Create a prototype for the reset function at the top of the `source.cpp` file:

```
bool checkCollision(sf::Sprite sprite1, sf::Sprite sprite2);
void reset();
```

At the bottom of the `source.cpp` file, after where we created the `checkCollision` function, add the reset function itself so that when the game resets, all the values are also reset. To do this, use the following code:

```
void reset() {

    score = 0;
    currentTime = 0.0f;
    prevTime = 0.0;

    for (Enemy *enemy : enemies) {
        delete(enemy);
    }
    for (Rocket *rocket : rockets) {
        delete(rocket);
    }

    enemies.clear();
    rockets.clear();
}
```

If the game is over, pressing the down arrow key once will restart the game. Once the game starts again, the `reset()` function will be called. In the `reset()` function, we need to set `score`, `currentTime`, and `prevTime` to 0.

When the game resets, remove any instantiated enemy and rocket objects by deleting and thus freeing the memory. This also clears the vectors that were holding a reference to the now-deleted objects. Now that we've set up the variables and the reset function, let's use them in the game to reset the values when we restart the game.

In the `UpdateInput` function, in the `while` loop, where we check whether the down arrow key on the keyboard was pressed, we will add an `if` condition to check whether the game is over. If it is over, we'll set the `gameover` bool to `false` so that the game is ready to start, and we'll reset the variables by calling the `reset` function, as follows:

```
if (event.key.code == sf::Keyboard::Down) {

    if (gameover) {
        gameover = false;
        reset();
    }
    else {
        shoot();
        }
}
```

Here, `shoot()` is moved into an `else` statement so that the player can only shoot if the game is running.

Next, we will set the `gameover` condition to `true` when an enemy goes beyond the left-hand side of the screen.

When we update the enemies, the enemy will be deleted when it disappears from the screen, and we will also set the `gameover` condition to `true`.

Add the following code for updating the enemies to the `update()` function:

```
// Update Enemies
    for (int i = 0; i < enemies.size(); i++) {

        Enemy* enemy = enemies[i];

        enemy->update(dt);
```

```
if (enemy->getSprite().getPosition().x < 0) {

        enemies.erase(enemies.begin() + i);
        delete(enemy);
        gameover = true;
    }
}
```

3. Here, we want to update the game if `gameover` is `false`. In the `main` function, before we update the game, we will add a check to find out whether the game is over. If the game is over, we will not update the game. To do this, use the following code:

```
while (window.isOpen()) {
    ////update input
    updateInput();
    //// +++ Update Game Here +++
    sf::Time dt = clock.restart();
    if(!gameover)
        update(dt.asSeconds());
    //// +++ Draw Game Here ++
    window.clear(sf::Color::Red);
    draw();

    // Show everything we just drew
    window.display();

}
```

We will also increase the score when the rocket collides with an enemy. This means that, in the `update()` function, when we delete the rocket and enemy after the intersection, we will also update the score:

```
// Check collision between Rocket and Enemies

for (int i = 0; i < rockets.size(); i++) {
    for (int j = 0; j < enemies.size(); j++) {

        Rocket* rocket = rockets[i];
        Enemy* enemy = enemies[j];

        if (checkCollision(rocket->getSprite(), enemy-
            >getSprite())) {

            score++;

            rockets.erase(rockets.begin() + i);
```

```
                    enemies.erase(enemies.begin() + j);

                    delete(rocket);
                    delete(enemy);

                    printf(" rocket intersects enemy \n");

                }

            }

        }
```

When you run the game, start the game by pressing the down arrow key. When one of the enemies goes past the left-side of the screen, the game will end. When you press the down arrow key again, the game will restart.

The gameloop is now complete, but we still can't see the score. To do this, let's add some text to the game.

Adding text

These steps will guide you through how to add text to the game:

1. Create an `sf::Font` called `headingFont` so that we can load the font and then use it to display the name of the game. At the top of the screen, where we created all the variables, create the `headingFont` variable, as follows:

```
int score = 0;
bool gameover = true;

// Text
sf::Font headingFont;
```

2. In the `init()` function, right after we loaded `bgSprite`, load the font using the `loadFromFile` function:

```
// Create Sprite and Attach a Texture
bgSprite.setTexture(bgTexture);

// Load font

headingFont.loadFromFile("Assets/fonts/SnackerComic.ttf");
```

Since we will need a font to be loaded in from the system, we have to place the font in the `fonts` directory, which can be found under the `Assets` directory. Make sure you place the font file there. The font we will be using for the heading is the `SnackerComic.ttf` file. I have also included the `arial.ttf` file, which we will use to display the score, so make sure you add that as well.

3. Create the `headingText` variable using the `sf::Text` type so that we can display the heading of the game. Do this at the start of the code:

```
sf::Text headingText;
```

4. In the `init()` function, after loading `headingFont`, we will add the code to create the heading for the game:

```
// Set Heading Text
headingText.setFont(headingFont);
headingText.setString("Tiny Bazooka");
headingText.setCharacterSize(84);
headingText.setFillColor(sf::Color::Red);
```

We need to set the font for the heading text using the `setFont` function. In `setFont`, pass the `headingFont` variable that we just created.

We need to tell `headingText` what needs to be displayed. For that, we will use the `setString` function and pass in the `TinyBazooka` string since that is the name of the game we just made. Pretty cool name, huh?

Let's set the size of the font itself. To do this, we will use the `setCharacterSize` function and pass in `84` as the size in pixels so that it is clearly visible. Now, we can set the color to red using the `setFillColor` function.

5. We want the heading to be centered on the viewport, so we will get the bounds of the text and set its origin to the `center` of the viewport in the x and y directions. Set the position of the text so that it's at the center of the x-direction and `0.10` of the height from the top along the y-direction:

```
sf::FloatRect headingbounds = headingText.getLocalBounds();
headingText.setOrigin(headingbounds.width/2,
    headingbounds.height / 2);
headingText.setPosition(sf::Vector2f(viewSize.x * 0.5f,
    viewSize.y * 0.10f));
```

6. To display the text, call `window.draw` and pass `headingText` into it. We also want the text to be drawn when the game is over. To do this, add an `if` statement, which checks whether the game is over:

```
if (gameover) {
        window.draw(headingText);
}
```

7. Run the game. You will see the name of the game displayed at the top:

8. We still can't see the score, so let's add a `Font` variable and a `Text` variable and call them `scoreFont` and `scoreText`, respectively. In the `scoreFont` variable, load the `arial.ttf` font and set the text for the score using the `scoreText` variable:

```
sf::Font headingFont;
sf::Text headingText;

sf::Font scoreFont;
sf::Text scoreText;
```

9. Load the `ScoreFont` string and then set the `ScoreText` string:

```
scoreFont.loadFromFile("Assets/fonts/arial.ttf");

// Set Score Text

scoreText.setFont(scoreFont);
scoreText.setString("Score: 0");
scoreText.setCharacterSize(45);
scoreText.setFillColor(sf::Color::Red);

sf::FloatRect scorebounds = scoreText.getLocalBounds();
scoreText.setOrigin(scorebounds.width / 2,
    scorebounds.height / 2);
scoreText.setPosition(sf::Vector2f(viewSize.x * 0.5f,
    viewSize.y * 0.10f));
```

Here, we set the `scoreText` string to a score of `0`, which we will change once the score increases. Set the size of the font to `45`.

Set the score so that it's in the same position as `headingText` since it will only be displayed when the game is over. When the game is running, `scoreText` will be displayed.

10. In the `update` function, where we update the score, update `scoreText`:

```
score++;
std::string finalScore = "Score: " + std::to_string(score);
scoreText.setString(finalScore);
sf::FloatRect scorebounds = scoreText.getLocalBounds();
scoreText.setOrigin(scorebounds.width / 2,
    scorebounds.height / 2);
scoreText.setPosition(sf::Vector2f(viewSize.x * 0.5f, viewSize.y
    * 0.10f));
```

For convenience, we created a new string called `finalScore`. Here, we set the `"Score: "` string and concatenated it with the score, which is an int that's been converted into a string by the `toString` property of the string class. Then, we used the `setString` function of `sf::Text` to set the string. We had to get the new bounds of the text since the text would have changed. Set the origin, center, and position of the updated text.

11. In the `draw` function, create a new `else` statement. If the game is not over, draw `scoreText`:

```
if (gameover) {
        window.draw(headingText);
} else {
        window.draw(scoreText);
}
```

12. Reset the `scoreText` in the `reset()` function:

```
prevTime = 0.0;
scoreText.setString("Score: 0");
```

When you run the game now, the score will continue to update. The values will reset when you restart the game.

The scoring system looks as follows:

13. Add a tutorial so that the player knows what to do when the game starts. Create a new `sf::Text` called `tutorialText`:

    ```
    sf::Text tutorialText;
    ```

14. Initialize the text after `scoreText` in the `init()` function:

    ```
    // Tutorial Text

    tutorialText.setFont(scoreFont);
    tutorialText.setString("Press Down Arrow to Fire and Start Game,
    Up Arrow to Jump");
    tutorialText.setCharacterSize(35);
    tutorialText.setFillColor(sf::Color::Red);

    sf::FloatRect tutorialbounds = tutorialText.getLocalBounds();
    tutorialText.setOrigin(tutorialbounds.width / 2,
    ```

```
tutorialbounds.height / 2);
    tutorialText.setPosition(sf::Vector2f(viewSize.x * 0.5f,
viewSize.y * 0.20f));
```

15. We only want to show the tutorial at the start of the game, along with the heading text. Add the following code to the draw function:

```
if (gameover) {
        window.draw(headingText);
    window.draw(tutorialText);
    }
    else {
        window.draw(scoreText);
    }
```

Now, when you start the game, the player will see that the game will start if they press the down arrow key. They will also know that, when the game is running, they can press the down arrow key to shoot a rocket and use the up arrow key to jump. The following screenshot shows this on screen text:

Adding audio

Let's add some audio to the game to make it a little more interesting. This will also provide audio feedback to the player to tell them whether the rocket was fired or an enemy was hit.

SFML supports .wav or .ogg files, but it doesn't support .mp3 files. For this project, all the files will be in the .ogg file format as it is good for compression and is also cross-platform compatible. To start, place the audio files in the Audio directory in the Assets folder of the system. With the audio files in place, we can start playing the audio files.

Audio files can be of two types:

- The background music, which is of a longer duration and a much higher quality than other files in the game. These files are played using the sf::Music class.
- Other sound files, such as sound effects – which are smaller in size and sometimes of lower quality – are played using the sf::Sound class. To play the files, you also need an sf::SoundBuffer class, which is used to store the file and play it later.

To add audio to the game, follow these steps:

1. Let's play the background music file, bgMusic.ogg. Audio files use the Audio.hpp header, which needs to be included at the top of the main.cpp file. This can be done as follows:

   ```
   #include "SFML-2.5.1\include\SFML\Audio.hpp"
   ```

2. At the top of the main.cpp file, create a new instance of sf::Music and call it bgMusic:

   ```
   sf::Music bgMusic;
   ```

3. In the init() function, add the following lines to open the bgMusic.ogg file and play the bgMusic file:

   ```
   // Audio

   bgMusic.openFromFile("Assets/audio/bgMusic.ogg");
   bgMusic.play();
   ```

4. Run the game. You will hear the background music playing as soon as the game starts.

5. To add the sound files that are for the rockets being fired and the enemies being hit, we need two sound buffers to store both of the effects and two sound files to play the sound files. Create two variables of the `sf::SoundBuffer` type called `fireBuffer` and `hitBuffer`:

```
sf::SoundBuffer fireBuffer;
sf::SoundBuffer hitBuffer;
```

6. Now, create two `sf::Sound` variables called `fireSound` and `hitSound`. Both can be initialized by being passed into their respective buffers, as follows:

```
sf::Sound fireSound(fireBuffer);
sf::Sound hitSound(hitBuffer);
```

7. In the `init` function, initialize the buffers first, as follows:

```
bgMusic.openFromFile("Assets/audio/bgMusic.ogg");
    bgMusic.play();

    hitBuffer.loadFromFile("Assets/audio/hit.ogg");
    fireBuffer.loadFromFile("Assets/audio/fire.ogg");
```

8. When the rocket intersects with the enemy, we will play the `hitSound` effect:

```
hitSound.play();
        score++;

        std::string finalScore = "Score: " +
                        std::to_string(score);

        scoreText.setString(finalScore);

        sf::FloatRect scorebounds = scoreText.getLocalBounds();
        scoreText.setOrigin(scorebounds.width / 2,
        scorebounds.height / 2);
        scoreText.setPosition(sf::Vector2f(viewSize.x * 0.5f,
        viewSize.y * 0.10f));
```

9. In the `shoot` function, we will play the `fireSound` file, as follows:

```
void shoot() {
    Rocket* rocket = new Rocket();

    rocket->init("Assets/graphics/rocket.png",
```

```
hero.getSprite().getPosition(), 400.0f);

    rockets.push_back(rocket);
    fireSound.play();
}
```

Now, when you play the game, you will hear a sound effect when you shoot the rocket and when the rocket hits the enemy.

Adding player animations

The game has now reached its final stages of development. Let's add some animation to the game to make it really come alive. To animate 2D sprites, we need a sprite sheet. We can use other techniques to add 2D animations, such as skeletal animation, but sprite sheet-based 2D animations are faster to make. Hence, we will use sprite sheets to add animations to the main character.

A sprite sheet is an image file; however, instead of just one single image, it contains a collection of images in a sequence so that we can loop them to create the animation. Each image in the sequence is called a frame.

Here is the sprite sheet we are going to be using to animate the player:

Looking from left to right, we can see that each frame is slightly different from the last. The main things that are being animated here are the jet pack of the player character and the player character's eyes (so that the character looks like it's blinking). Each picture will be shown as an animation frame when the game runs, just like in a flip-book animation, where one image is quickly replaced with another image to create the effect of animation.

SFML makes it really easy to animate 2D characters since we can choose which frame to display in the `update` function. Let's start animating the character:

1. Add the sprite sheet file to the `Assets/graphics` folder. We need to make some changes to the `Hero.h` and `Hero.cpp` files. Let's look at the changes for the `Hero.h` file first:

```
class Hero{

public:
    Hero();
    ~Hero();

    void init(std::string textureName, int frameCount,
        float animDuration, sf::Vector2f position, float mass);
    void update(float dt);
    void jump(float velocity);
    sf::Sprite getSprite();

private:

    int jumpCount = 0;
    sf::Texture m_texture;
    sf::Sprite m_sprite;
    sf::Vector2f m_position;
    float m_mass;
    float m_velocity;
    const float m_gravity = 9.81f;
    bool m_grounded;

    int m_frameCount;
    float m_animDuration;
    float m_elapsedTime;;
    sf::Vector2i m_spriteSize;

};
```

We need to add two more parameters to the `init` function. The first is an int called `frameCount`, which is the number of frames in the animation. In our case, there are four frames in the hero sprite sheet. The other parameter is a float, called `animDuration`, which basically sets how long you want the animation to be played. This will determine the speed of the animation.

We will also create some variables. The first two variables we'll create, m_frameCount and m_animDuration, will be used for storing frameCount and animDuration locally. We will also create a float called m_elapsedTime, which will keep track of how long the game has been running, and a vector2 int called m_spriteSize, which will store the size of each frame.

2. Let's move on to the Hero.cpp file and see what changes are needed there. Here is the modified init function:

```
void Hero::init(std::string textureName, int frameCount,
    float animDuration, sf::Vector2f position, float mass){

    m_position = position;
    m_mass = mass;
    m_grounded = false;

    m_frameCount = frameCount;
    m_animDuration = animDuration;
    // Load a Texture
    m_texture.loadFromFile(textureName.c_str());

    m_spriteSize = sf::Vector2i(92, 126);

    // Create Sprite and Attach a Texture
    m_sprite.setTexture(m_texture);
    m_sprite.setTextureRect(sf::IntRect(0, 0, m_spriteSize.x,
        m_spriteSize.y));
    m_sprite.setPosition(m_position);
    m_sprite.setOrigin(m_spriteSize.x / 2, m_spriteSize.y / 2);

}
```

In the init function, we set m_frameCount and m_animationDuration locally. We need to hardcode the value of the width (as 92) and height (as 126) of each frame. If you are loading in your own images, these values will be different.

After calling setTexture, we will call the setTextureRect function of the Sprite class to set which part of the sprite sheet we want to display. Start at the origin of the sprite and get the first frame of the sprite sheet by passing the width and height of spriteSHere, we passed the new heroAnim.png file instead of theize.

Set the position and origin, which is equal to the center of the width and height of spriteSize.

3. Let's make some changes to the `update` function, which is where the major magic happens:

```
void Hero::update(float dt){
    // Animate Sprite
    M_elapsedTime += dt;
    int animFrame = static_cast<int> ((m_elapsedTime /
                    m_animDuration) * m_frameCount) % m_frameCount;

    m_sprite.setTextureRect(sf::IntRect(animFrame * m_spriteSize.x,
        0, m_spriteSize.x, m_spriteSize.y));

    // Update Position
    m_velocity -= m_mass * m_gravity * dt;

    m_position.y -= m_velocity * dt;

    m_sprite.setPosition(m_position);


    if (m_position.y >= 768 * 0.75) {

            m_position.y = 768 * 0.75;
            m_velocity = 0;
            m_grounded = true;
            jumpCount = 0;

    }


}
```

In the `update` function, increase the elapsed time by the delta time. Then, calculate the current animation frame number.

Update the part of the sprite sheet to be shown by calling `setTextureRect` and move the origin of the frame to the `x-axis`, which depends on `animFrame`, by multiplying it by the width of the frame. The height of the new frame doesn't change, so we set it to 0. The width and height of the frame remain the same, so we pass in the size of the frame itself.

The rest of the functions in `Hero.cpp` remain as they are, and no changes need to be made to them.

4. Go back to `main.cpp` so that we can change how we call `hero.init`. In the `init` function, make the required change:

```
hero.init("Assets/graphics/heroAnim.png", 4, 1.0f,
sf::Vector2f(viewSize.x * 0.25f, viewSize.y * 0.5f), 200);
```

Here, we passed the new `heroAnim.png` file instead of the single-frame `.png` file we loaded previously. Set the number of frames to 4 and set `animDuration` to `1.0f`.

5. Run the game. You will see that the player character is now animated and blinks every four frames:

Summary

In this chapter, we completed the gameloop and added the `gameover` condition. We added scoring so that the player knows how many points they have scored. We also added text so that the name of the game is displayed, the player's score is displayed, and a tutorial is displayed that tells the user how to play the game. Then, we learned how to place these elements in the center of the viewport. Finally, we added sound effects and animations to make our game come to life.

In the next chapter, we will look at how to render 3D and 2D objects in a scene. Instead of using a framework, we will start creating a basic engine and begin our journey of understanding the basics of rendering.

Section 3: Modern OpenGL 3D Game Development

3

Using the game-development concepts learned in Section 2, in this section we will create a 3D physics puzzle game using modern OpenGL and the bullet physics engine. We will learn about the graphics pipeline and the creation of 3D objects using vertex and index buffers. Then we will add them to the scene using vertex and fragment shaders, add textures, and use text rendering, including the bullet physics library, lighting models, post-processing effects, and 3D particle-system generation. The following chapters are covered in this section:

Chapter 6, *Getting Started with OpenGL*

Chapter 7, *Building on the Game Objects*

Chapter 8, *Enhancing Your Game with Collision, Loop, and Lighting*

Getting Started with OpenGL 6

In the previous three chapters, we rendered 2D objects called sprites in our tiny Bazooka game using the **Simple and Fast Media Library** (**SFML**). At the core of SFML is OpenGL; this is used to render anything on screen, including 2D objects.

SFML does a great job of putting everything in a nice little package, and this allows us to get a 3D game going very quickly. However, in order to understand how a graphics library actually works, we need to learn how OpenGL works by delving deeper into how to use it so that we can render anything on the screen.

In this chapter, we will discover how to use a graphics library, such as OpenGL, in order to render 3D objects in any scene. We will cover the following topics:

- What is OpenGL?
- Creating our first OpenGL project
- Creating a window and ClearScreen
- Creating a `Mesh` class
- Creating a Camera class
- The Shaderloader class
- The Light Renderer class
- Drawing the object

What is OpenGL?

So, what is this OpenGL that we speak of? Well, OpenGL is a collection of graphics APIs; essentially, this is a collection of code that allows you to gain access to the features of your graphics hardware. The current version of OpenGL is 4.6, but any graphics hardware that is capable of running OpenGL 4.5 can run 4.6 as well.

OpenGL is entirely hardware and operating system independent, so it doesn't matter if you have a NVIDIA or AMD GPU; it will work the same on both hardware. The way in which OpenGL's features work is defined by a specification that is used by graphics hardware manufacturers while they're developing the drivers for their hardware. This is why we sometimes have to update the graphics hardware drivers if something doesn't look right or if the game is not performing well.

Furthermore, OpenGL runs the same, regardless of whether you are running a Windows or a Linux machine. It is, however, deprecated on macOS Mojave, but if you are running a macOS version earlier than Mojave, then it is still compatible.

OpenGL is only responsible for rendering objects in the scene. Unlike SFML, which allows you to create a window and then gain access to the keyboard and mouse input, we will need to add a separate library that will handle all of this for us.

So, let's start preparing our project by rendering a 3D OpenGL object in the scene.

Creating our first OpenGL project

Now that we have gained an understanding of what OpenGL is, let's examine how to create our first OpenGL project, as follows:

1. Create a new empty C++ project in Visual Studio and call it `OpenGLProject`.
2. Then, download GLEW; this is a C/C++ extension loader library. OpenGL supports extensions that various GPU vendors can use to write and extend the functionality of OpenGL. This library will determine what extensions are supported on the platform.
3. Go to `http://glew.sourceforge.net/` and download the Windows 32-bit and 64-bit **Binaries**:

> **Downloads**
>
> GLEW is distributed as source and precompiled binaries. The latest release is 2.1.0[07-31-17]:
>
> | | |
> |---|---|
> | **Source** | ZIP \| TGZ |
> | **Binaries** | Windows 32-bit and 64-bit |

4. Next, we need to download GLFW; this is a platform-independent API that is used for creating a window, reading inputs, and handling events. Go to `https://www.glfw.org/download.html` and download the 64-bit Windows binary. In this book, we will be primarily looking at implementing it on the Windows platform:

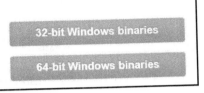

Windows pre-compiled binaries

These packages contain complete GLFW header file, documentation and release mode DLL and static library binaries for Visual C++ 2010 (32-bit only), Visual C++ 2012, Visual C++ 2013, Visual C++ 2015, MinGW (32-bit only) and MinGW-w64.

| 32-bit Windows binaries |
| 64-bit Windows binaries |

5. Next, we need to download `glm`, which is used to do all the math for our graphics calculations. Go to `https://glm.g-truc.net/0.9.9/index.html` and download GLM from the site.

6. Now that we have downloaded all the required libraries and headers, we can start adding them to our project.

7. In the root directory (where the Visual Studio project file is stored) of the project, create a new directory called `Dependencies`.

8. From this directory, extract `glew`, `glfw`, and `glm`; the `Dependencies` directory should now look as follows:

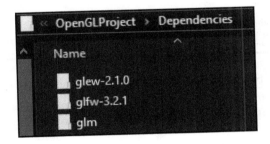

9. Open the Visual Studio project. We need to set the location of the headers and library files. To do this, open the project properties of `OpenGLProject` and set **Configuration** to **Release** and **Platform** to **x64**.

10. Under **C/C++ | General**, select **Additional Include Directories** and select the following directories for GLEW and GLFW:

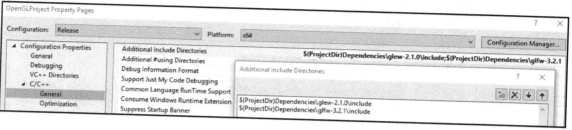

11. Next, under **Linker |General**, select **Additional Library Directories**, and then select the location of the `.lib` files in the `glew` and `glfw` directories, as follows:

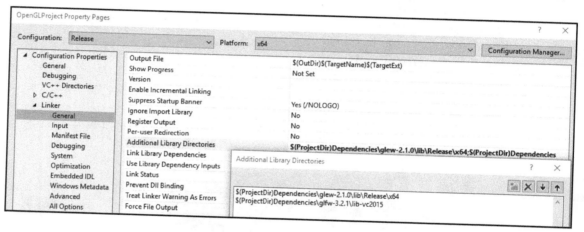

12. Next, we have to go to **Linker | Input** and specify which `.lib` files we are using.
13. Under **Linker | Input**, select **Additional Dependencies** and then add **opengl32.lib**, **glfw3.lib**, and **glew32.lib**, as follows:

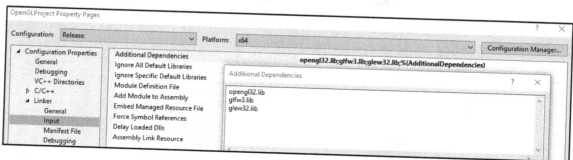

14. Although we didn't specifically download `opengl32.lib`, it is included when you update the driver of the graphics hardware. Therefore, make sure that you are running the most recent drivers for your GPU; if not, download them from the manufacturer's website.

15. Finally, we have to add the `glew32.dll` and `glfw3.dll` files to the root directory of the project. `glew32.dll` is inside `glew-2.1.0/ bin/Release/64`, whereas `glfw3.dll` is inside `glfw-3.2.1/lib-vc2015`.

16. The root directory of the project file should now look as follows:

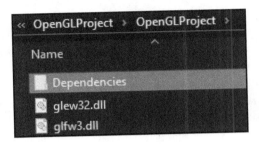

17. With this out of the way, we can finally start working on the project.

Creating a window and ClearScreen

Now, let's explore how we can work with the OpenGL project that we created:

1. The first thing we have to do is create a window so that we can start rendering the game objects to the screen.

2. Create a new `.cpp` file; Visual Studio will automatically call this `source.cpp`, so keep it as it is.

3. At the top of the file, include the `glew` and `glfw` headers. Make sure that you include `glew.h` first since it contains the correct OpenGL header files to be included:

```
#include <GL/glew.h>
#include <GLFW/glfw3.h>
```

Then create a main function and add the following to it.

```
int main(int argc, char **argv)
{

    glfwInit();
```

```
GLFWwindow* window = glfwCreateWindow(800, 600,
 " Hello OpenGL ", NULL, NULL);
return 0;
}
```

4. The first thing we need to do here is initialize `glfw` by calling `glfwInit()`.

5. Once initialized, we can create the window that our game scene will be rendered to. To create a window, we need to create a new instance of `GLFWWindow` called window and call `glfwCreateWindow`. This takes five parameters, including the width and height of the window, along with the name of the window. The final two parameters—`monitor` and `share`—are set to `NULL`. The `monitor` parameter takes a specific monitor on which the window will be created. If it is set to `null`, then the default monitor is chosen. The `share` parameter will let us share the window resource with our users. Here, we set it to `NULL` as we don't want to share the window resources.

6. Now, run the project; you will see that a window briefly appears before the application closes.

7. Well, that's not very fun. Let's add the rest of the code so that we can see something being rendered on the viewport.

8. The first thing we need to do is initialize OpenGL Context. OpenGL Context is a collection of all the current states of OpenGL. We will discuss the different states in the upcoming sections.

9. To do this, call `glfwMakeCurrentContext` and pass in the window that we just created:

```
glfwMakeContextCurrent(window);
```

10. We can now initialize GLEW by calling `glewInit()`.

11. Next, we will add the following code between `glewInit()` and `return 0` in the `main` function:

```
while (!glfwWindowShouldClose(window)){
            // render our scene

    glfwSwapBuffers(window);
    glfwPollEvents();
}

    glfwTerminate();
```

12. Here, we are creating a `while` loop, calling `glfwWindowShouldClose`, and then passing it in the current window. While the window is open, the `glfwSwapBuffers(window);` and `glfwPollEvents();` commands will be executed.

13. In the `while` loop, we will render our scene. Then, we will swap display buffers. The display buffer is where the current frame is rendered and stored. While the current frame is being shown, the next frame is actually being rendered in the background, which we don't get to see. When the next frame is ready, the current frame is swapped with the new frame. This swapping of frames is done by `glfwSwapBuffer` and is managed by OpenGL.

14. After we swap the display buffer, we need to check for any events that were triggered, such as the window being closed in `glfwPollEvents()`. Once the window is closed, `glfw` is terminated.

15. If you run the project now, you will see a black window; while it doesn't vanish, it is still not very impressive. We can use OpenGL to clear the viewport with a color of our choice, so let's do that next.

16. Create a new function called `void renderScene()`. Whatever we render to the scene from now on will also be added to this function. Add a new prototype for `void renderScene()` to the top of the `source.cpp` file.

17. In the `renderScene` function, add the following lines of code:

```
void renderScene(){

    glClear(GL_COLOR_BUFFER_BIT | GL_DEPTH_BUFFER_BIT);
    glClearColor(1.0, 0.0, 0.0, 1.0);//clear yellow

    // Draw game objects here

}
```

In the first function, we call `glClear()`. All OpenGL functions start with the `gl` prefix; the `glClear` function clears the buffer. In this case, we are asking OpenGL to clear the color buffer and the depth buffer. The color buffer is where all the color information is stored for the scene. The depth buffer stores whichever pixel is in front; this means that if a pixel is behind another pixel, then that pixel will not be stored. This is especially important for 3D scenes, where some objects can be behind other objects and get occluded by the objects that are in front of it. We only require the pixel information regarding the objects that are in front as we will only get to see those objects and not the objects that are behind them.

Next, we call the `glClearColor` function and pass in an RGBA value; in this case, red. The `glCearColor` function clears the color buffer with the specific color in every frame. The buffers need to be cleared in every frame; otherwise, the previous frame will be overwritten with the image in the current frame. Imagine this to be like clearing the blackboard before drawing anything on it in every frame.

The depth buffer is also cleared after every frame using a default white color. This means that we don't have to clear it manually as this will be done by default.

18. Now, call `renderScene` before swapping the buffer and run the project again. You should see a nice yellow viewport, as follows:

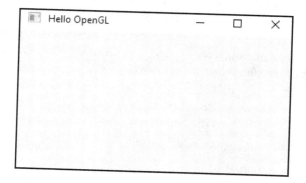

Before drawing the objects, we have to create some additional classes that will help us define the shape that we want to draw. We also need to create a camera class in order to set up a virtual camera through which we can view the scene. Furthermore, we need to write a basic vertex, a `shader` fragment, and a `Shaderloader` class, which will create a `shader` program that we can use to render our shape.

First, let's create the `Mesh` class, which is where we will define the different shapes that we want to draw.

Creating a Mesh class

The following steps explain how to create a Mesh class:

1. Create new .h and .cpp files called Mesh.h and Mesh.cpp, respectively. These will be used to create a new Mesh class. In the Mesh.h file, add the following code:

```
#include <vector>
#include "Dependencies/glm/glm/glm.hpp"

enum MeshType {

    kTriangle = 0,
    kQuad = 1,
    kCube = 2,
    kSphere = 3

};

struct Vertex {

    glm::vec3 pos;
    glm::vec3 normal;
    glm::vec3 color;
    glm::vec2 texCoords;

};


class Mesh {

public:
    static void setTriData(std::vector<Vertex>& vertices,
        std::vector<uint32_t>&indices);
    static void setQuadData(std::vector<Vertex>& vertices,
        std::vector<uint32_t>&indices);
    static void setCubeData(std::vector<Vertex>& vertices,
        std::vector<uint32_t>&indices);
    static void setSphereData(std::vector<Vertex>& vertices,
        std::vector<uint32_t>&indices);

};
```

2. At the top of the Mesh.h file, we include a vector so that we can store points in a vector and include glm.hpp. This will help us define points in the space using the vec3 variable.

3. Then, we create a new `enum` type called `MeshType` and create four types: `Mesh Triangle`, `Quad`, `Cube`, and `Sphere`. We've done this so that we can specify the kind of mesh we are using and so the data will be populated accordingly.

4. Next, we create a new `struct` type called `Vertex`, which has `vec3` properties called `pos`, `Color`, and `Normal`, and a `vec2` property called `textCoords`.

   Each vertex has certain properties, such as `Position`, `Color`, `Normal`, and `Texture Coordinate`. `Position` and `Color` store the position and color information for each vertex, respectively. `Normal` specifies which direction the normal attribute is pointing to while `Texture Coordinate` specifies how a texture needs to be laid out. We will cover the normal and texture coordinate attributes when we cover lighting and how to apply textures to our objects.

5. Then, the `Mesh` class is created. This has four functions, which are for setting the vertex and the index data per vertex.

6. In the `Mesh.cpp` file, we include the `Mesh.h` file and then set the data for the four shapes. Here is an example of how `setTriData` sets the values for the vertices and indices:

```cpp
#include "Mesh.h"

void Mesh::setTriData(std::vector<Vertex>& vertices,
std::vector<uint32_t>& indices) {

    std::vector<Vertex> _vertices = {
{ { 0.0f, -1.0f, 0.0f },            // Position
{ 0.0f, 0.0f, 1.0 },                // Normal
{ 1.0f, 0.0f, 0.0 },                // Color
{ 0.0, 1.0 }                        // Texture Coordinate
},                                  // 0

        { { 1.0f, 1.0f, 0.0f },{ 0.0f, 0.0f, 1.0 },{ 0.0f, 1.0f,
        0.0 },{ 0.0, 0.0 } }, // 1

        { { -1.0f, 1.0f, 0.0f },{ 0.0f, 0.0f, 1.0 },{ 0.0f, 0.0f,
        1.0 },{ 1.0, 0.0 } }, // 2
    };

    std::vector<uint32_t> _indices = {
        0, 1, 2,
    };

    vertices.clear(); indices.clear();
```

```
        vertices = _vertices;
        indices = _indices;
    }
```

7. For each of the three vertices of the triangle, we set the position, normal, color, and texture coordinate information in the `vertices` vector.

Next, we set the indices in the `indices` vector. For definitions of the other functions, you can refer to the project that comes with this book. Then, we set the `_vertices` and `_indices` vectors to the reference vertices and indices, respectively.

Creating a Camera class

The following steps will help you create a `Camera` class:

1. Create two files: `Camera.h` and `Camera.cpp`. In the `Camera.h` file, include the following code:

```
#include <GL/glew.h>

#include "Dependencies/glm/glm/glm.hpp"
#include "Dependencies/glm/glm/gtc/matrix_transform.hpp"
```

2. Then, create the `Camera` class itself, as follows:

```
class Camera
{
public:
    Camera(GLfloat FOV, GLfloat width, GLfloat height, GLfloat
      nearPlane, GLfloat farPlane, glm::vec3 camPos);
    ~Camera();

    glm::mat4 getViewMatrix();
    glm::mat4 getProjectionMatrix();
    glm::vec3 getCameraPosition();

private:

    glm::mat4 viewMatrix;
    glm::mat4 projectionMatrix;
    glm::vec3 cameraPos;

};
```

3. In the constructor and the public region of the `camera` class, we get the **field of view (FOV)**, the width and height of the viewport, the distance to `nearPlane`, the distance to `farPlane`, and the position that we want to set the camera at.

4. We also add three getters to get the view matrix, projection matrix, and the camera position.

5. In the private section, we create three variables: two 4 x 4 matrices for setting the view and projection matrices and a `vec3` property to specify the camera position.

6. In the `Camera.cpp` file, we include the `Camera.h` file at the top and create the `camera` constructor, as follows:

```
#include "Camera.h"

Camera::Camera(GLfloat FOV, GLfloat width, GLfloat height, GLfloat
nearPlane, GLfloat farPlane, glm::vec3 camPos){

    cameraPos = camPos;
    glm::vec3 cameraFront = glm::vec3(0.0f, 0.0f, 0.0f);
    glm::vec3 cameraUp = glm::vec3(0.0f, 1.0f, 0.0f);

    viewMatrix = glm::lookAt(cameraPos, cameraFront, cameraUp);
    projectionMatrix = glm::perspective(FOV, width /height,
                        nearPlane, farPlane);
}
```

7. In the constructor, we set the camera position to the local variable and set up two `vec3` properties called `cameraFront` and `cameraUp`. Our camera is going to be a stationary camera that will always be looking toward the center of the world coordinates; the up vector will always be pointing toward the positive y-axis.

8. To create `viewMatrix`, we call the `glm::lookAt` function and pass in the `cameraPos`, `cameraFront`, and `cameraUp` vectors.

9. We create the projection matrix by setting the `FOV` value of the FOV; this is an aspect ratio that is given by the `width` value over the `height`, `nearPlane`, and `farPlane` values.

10. With the view and projection matrices set, we can now create the getter functions, as follows:

```
glm::mat4 Camera::getViewMatrix() {

    return viewMatrix;
}
glm::mat4 Camera::getProjectionMatrix() {
```

```
        return projectionMatrix;
}

glm::vec3 Camera::getCameraPosition() {

        return cameraPos;
}
```

Next, we'll create the `shaderLoader` class, which will let us create the `shader` program.

The ShaderLoader class

The following steps will show you how to implement the `ShaderLoader` class in an OpenGL project:

1. In the `ShaderLoader` class, create a public function called `createProgram` that takes a vertex and fragment `shader` file.
2. We'll also create two private functions: `readShader`, which returns a string, and `createShader`, which returns an unsigned GL `int`:

```
#include <GL/glew.h>

class ShaderLoader {

    public:

            GLuint CreateProgram(const char* vertexShaderFilename,
                const char* fragmentShaderFilename);

    private:

            std::string readShader(const char *filename);
            GLuint createShader(GLenum shaderType, std::string source,
                const char* shaderName);
};
```

3. In the `ShaderLoader.cpp` file, we include our `ShaderLoader.h` header file, the `iostream` system header file, and the `fstream` vector, as follows:

```
#include "ShaderLoader.h"

#include<iostream>
#include<fstream>
#include<vector>
```

`iostream` is used when you want to print something to the console; `fstream` is used for reading a file. We'll need this as we will be passing in vertex and shader files for the `fstream` to read, as well as vectors for storing character strings.

4. First, we create the `readerShader` function; this will be used to read the `shader` file that we passed in:

```
std::string ShaderLoader::readShader(const char *filename)
{
    std::string shaderCode;
    std::ifstream file(filename, std::ios::in);

    if (!file.good()){
        std::cout << "Can't read file " << filename << std::endl;
        std::terminate();
    }

    file.seekg(0, std::ios::end);
    shaderCode.resize((unsigned int)file.tellg());
    file.seekg(0, std::ios::beg);
    file.read(&shaderCode[0], shaderCode.size());
    file.close();
    return shaderCode;
}
```

The contents of the `shader` file are then stored in a string and returned.

5. Next, we create the `createShader` function, which will actually compile the shader, as follows:

```
GLuint ShaderLoader::createShader(GLenum shaderType,
std::string source, const char* shaderName)
{

    int compile_result = 0;

    GLuint shader = glCreateShader(shaderType);
    const char *shader_code_ptr = source.c_str();
    const int shader_code_size = source.size();

    glShaderSource(shader, 1, &shader_code_ptr,
      &shader_code_size);
    glCompileShader(shader);
    glGetShaderiv(shader, GL_COMPILE_STATUS,
      &compile_result);

    //check for errors
```

```
        if (compile_result == GL_FALSE)
        {

            int info_log_length = 0;
            glGetShaderiv(shader, GL_INFO_LOG_LENGTH,
              &info_log_length);
            std::vector<char> shader_log(info_log_length);
            glGetShaderInfoLog(shader, info_log_length, NULL,
              &shader_log[0]);
            std::cout << "ERROR compiling shader: " <<
              shaderName << std::endl <<&shader_log[0] <<
              std::endl;
            return 0;

        }
        return shader;

    }
```

6. The `CreateShader` function takes the following three parameters:

   - The first parameter is the `enum` parameter, called `shaderType`, which specifies the type of `shader` being sent to be compiled. In this case, it could be a vertex shader or a fragment shader.
   - The second parameter is the string that contains the shader code.
   - The final parameter is a string with the `shader` type, which will be used to specify whether there is a problem compiling the `shader` type.

7. In the `CreateShader` function, we call `glCreateShader` in order to specify the type of shader that is being created; then, `glCompileShader` is called to compile the shader. Afterward, we get the compiled result of the shader.

8. If there is a problem with compiling the shader, then we send out a message stating that there is an error compiling the shader alongside `shaderLog`, which will detail the compilation error. If there are no errors during compilation, then the shader is returned.

9. The final function is the `createProgram` function, which takes the `vertex` and `fragment` shaders:

```
GLuint ShaderLoader::createProgram (const char*
vertexShaderFilename, const char* fragmentShaderFilename){

  std::string vertex_shader_code = readShader
                      (vertexShaderFilename);


  std::string fragment_shader_code = readShader
                      (fragmentShaderFilename);
```

```
GLuint vertex_shader = createShader (GL_VERTEX_SHADER,
                              vertex_shader_code,
                              "vertex shader" );

GLuint fragment_shader = createShader (GL_FRAGMENT_SHADER,
                                fragment_shader_code,
                                "fragment shader");

int link_result = 0;
//create the program handle, attach the shaders and link it
GLuint program = glCreateProgram();
glAttachShader(program, vertex_shader);
glAttachShader(program, fragment_shader);

glLinkProgram(program);
glGetProgramiv(program, GL_LINK_STATUS, &link_result);
//check for link errors
if (link_result == GL_FALSE) {

  int info_log_length = 0;
  glGetProgramiv(program, GL_INFO_LOG_LENGTH, &info_log_length);
  std::vector<char> program_log(info_log_length);

  glGetProgramInfoLog(program, info_log_length, NULL,
    &program_log[0]);
  std::cout << "Shader Loader : LINK ERROR" << std::endl
    <<&program_log[0] << std::endl;
  return 0;
}
return program;
}
```

10. This function takes the vertex and fragment shader files, reads them, and then compiles both files.

11. Then, we create a new `shaderProgram` function by calling `glCreateProgram()` and assigned to program.

12. Now, we have to attach both shaders to the program by calling `glAttachShader` and passing the program and the shader.

13. Finally, we link the program by calling `glLinkProgram`. After, we pass in the program and check for any linking errors.

14. If there are any linking errors, we send out an error message to the console, along with a program log that will detail the linking error. If not, then the program is returned.

The Light Renderer class

Now, it's time to draw our first object; to do so, perform the following steps:

1. We will draw a basic light source that will appear above the current scene so that we can visualize the location of the light source in the scene. We will use this location of the light source later to calculate the lighting on our object. Note that a flat-shaded object doesn't need to have lighting calculations made on it.

2. First, create a `LightRenderer.h` file and a `.cpp` file, and then create the `LightRenderer` class.

3. At the top of the `LightRenderer.h` file, include the following headers:

```
#include <GL/glew.h>

#include "Dependencies/glm/glm/glm.hpp"
#include "Dependencies/glm/glm/gtc/type_ptr.hpp"

#include "Mesh.h"
#include "ShaderLoader.h";
#include "Camera.h"
```

4. We will need `glew.h` to call the OpenGL commands, while we'll need the `glm` headers to define `vec3` and the matrices.

5. We will also need `Mesh.h`, which allows us to define the shape of the light in the light source. You can use the `ShaderLoader` class to load in the shaders in order to render the object and `Camera.h` to get the camera's location, view, and projection matrices onto the scene.

6. We will create the `LightRenderer` class next:

```
class LightRenderer
{


};
```

We will add the following `public` section to this class:

```
public:
    LightRenderer(MeshType meshType, Camera* camera);
    ~LightRenderer();

    void draw();

    void setPosition(glm::vec3 _position);
```

```
void setColor(glm::vec3 _color);
void setProgram(GLuint program);

glm::vec3 getPosition();
glm::vec3 getColor();
```

7. In the public section, we create the constructor that we pass `MeshType` to; this will be used to set the shape of the object that we want to render. Then, we have the destructor. Here, we have a function called `draw`, which will be used to draw the mesh. Then, we have a couple of setters for setting the position, color, and shader program for the object.

8. After defining the public section, we set the `private` section, as follows:

```
private:

    Camera* camera;

    std::vector<Vertex>vertices;
    std::vector<GLuint>indices;

glm::vec3 position, color;
GLuint vbo, ebo, vao, program;
```

9. In the private section, we have a `private` variable so that we can store the camera locally. We create vectors to store the vertex and index data; we also create local variables to store the position and color information. Then, we have `GLuint`, which will store `vbo`, `ebo`, `vao`, and the program variable.

The program variable will have the shader program that we want to use to draw the object. Then, we have `vbo`, which stands for vertex buffer object; `ebo`, which stands for Element Buffer Object; and `vao`, which stands for Vertex Array Object. Let's examine each of these buffer objects and find out what they do:

- **Vertex Buffer Object (VBO)**: This is the geometrical information; it includes attributes such as position, color, normal, and texture coordinates. These are stored on a per vertex basis on the GPU.
- **Element Buffer Object (EBO)**: This is used to store the index of each vertex and will be used while drawing the mesh.
- **Vertex Array Object (VAO)**: This is a helper container object that stores all the VBOs and attributes. This is used as you may have more than one VBO per object, and it would be tedious to bind the VBOs all over again when you render each frame.

Buffers are used to store information in the GPU memory for fast and efficient access to the data. Modern GPUs have a memory bandwidth of approximately 600 GB/s, which is enormous compared to the current high-end CPUs that only have approximately 12 GB/s.

Buffer objects are used to store, retrieve, and move data. It is very easy to generate a buffer object in OpenGL. You can easily generate one by calling `glGenBuffers()`.

That is all for `LightRender.h`; now, let's move on to `LightRenderer.cpp`, as follows:

1. At the top of `LightRenderer.cpp`, include `LightRenderer.h`. Then, add the constructor, as follows:

```
LightRenderer::LightRenderer(MeshType meshType, Camera* camera) {

}
```

2. In the `LightRenderer` constructor, we start adding the code. First, we initialize the local camera, as follows:

```
this->camera = camera;
```

3. Next, we set the shape of the object that we want to draw, depending on the `MeshType` type. For this, we will create a `switch` statement and call the appropriate `setData` function, depending on the type, as follows:

```
switch (modelType) {

    case kTriangle: Mesh::setTriData(vertices, indices);
        break;
    case kQuad: Mesh::setQuadData(vertices, indices); break;
    case kCube: Mesh::setCubeData(vertices, indices); break;
    case kSphere: Mesh::setSphereData(vertices, indices);
        break;

}
```

4. Next, we will generate and bind the `vao` buffer object, as follows:

```
glGenVertexArrays(1, &vao);
glBindVertexArray(vao);
```

The `glGenVertexArrays` function takes two parameters; the first parameter is the number of vertex array object names that we want to generate. In this case, we just want to create one, so it is specified as such. The second parameter takes in an array where the vertex array names are stored, so we pass in the `vao` buffer object.

5. The `glBindVertexArray` function is called `next`, and `vao` is passed into it in order to bind the `vao` buffer object. The `vao` buffer object will be bound for the duration of the application. A buffer is an object that's managing a certain piece of memory; buffers can be of different types and, therefore, they need to be bound to a specific buffer target so that they can give meaning to the buffer.

6. Once the `vao` buffer object has been bound, we can generate the vertex buffer object and store the vertex attributes.

7. To generate the vertex buffer object, we call `glGenBuffers()`; this also takes two parameters. The first parameter is the number of buffers that we want to generate, while the second is the array of VBOs. In this case, since we have one `vbo` buffer object, we will just pass in `1` for the first parameter and pass in the `vbo` as the second parameter:

   ```
   glGenBuffers(1, &vbo);
   ```

8. Next, we have to specify the buffer type. This is done by using the `glBindBuffer()` function; this takes two parameters again. The first is the buffer type and, in this case, it is of the `GL_ARRAY_BUFFER` type, while the second parameter is the name of the buffer object, which is `vbo`. Now, add the following line of code:

   ```
   glBindBuffer(GL_ARRAY_BUFFER, vbo);
   ```

9. In the next step, we actually pass in the data that we want to store in the buffer. This is done by calling `glBufferData`; the `glBufferData` function takes four parameters:

   - The first parameter is the buffer type, which, in this case, is `GL_ARRAY_BUFFER`.
   - The second parameter is the size in bytes of the buffer data to store.
   - The third parameter is the pointer to the data, which will be copied.
   - The fourth parameter is the expected usage of the data being stored.

   In our case, we will just modify the data once and use it many times, so it will be called `GL_STATIC_DRAW`.

10. Now, add the `glBufferData` function for storing the data, as follows:

    ```
    glBufferData(GL_ARRAY_BUFFER,
    sizeof(Vertex) * vertices.size(),
    &vertices[0],
    GL_STATIC_DRAW);
    ```

Now, we have to set the vertex attributes that we are going to use. While creating the `struct` vertex, we have attributes such as position, color, normal, and texture coordinates; however, we may not need all of these attributes all of the time. Therefore, we only need to specify the ones that we need. In our case, since we are not using any lighting calculation or applying any textures to the object, we don't need to specify this – we will just need the position and color attributes for now. However, these attributes need to be enabled first.

11. To enable these attributes, we'll call `glEnableVertexAttribArray` and pass in the index that we want to enable. The position will be in the 0th index, so we will set the value as follows:

    ```
    glEnableVertexAttribArray(0);
    ```

12. Next, we call `glVertexAttribPointer` so that we can set the attribute that we want to use. The first attribute will be positioned at the 0th index. This takes six parameters, as follows:

    - The first parameter is the index of the vertex attribute, which, in this case, is 0.
    - The second parameter is the size of the attribute. Essentially, this is the number of components that the vertex attribute has. In this case, it is the position of the x, y, and z components, so it is specified as 3.
    - The third parameter is for the variable types of the components; since they are specified in `GLfloat`, we specify `GL_FLOAT`.
    - The fourth parameter is a Boolean that specifies whether the values should be normalized or whether they should be converted into fixed-point values. Since we don't want the values to be normalized, we specify `GL_FALSE`.
    - The fifth parameter is called the stride, which is the offset of consecutive vertex attributes. Imagine the vertices being laid out in the memory as follows. The stride refers to the blocks of memory that you will have to go through to get to the next set of vertex attributes; this is the size of the `struct` vertex:

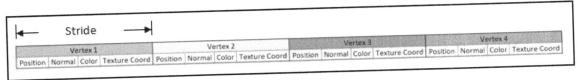

- The sixth parameter is the offset of the first component of the vertex attribute within the `struct` vertex. The attribute that we are looking at here is the position attribute, which is at the start of the `struct` vertex, so we will pass 0:

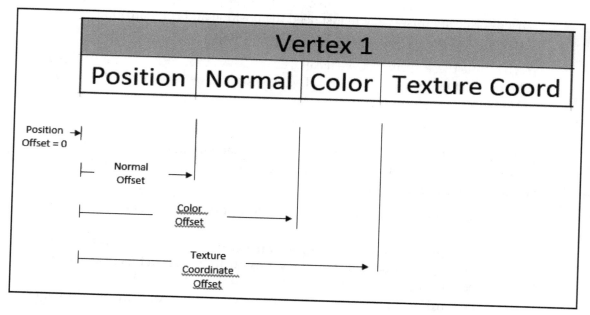

13. Set the `glVertexAttribute` pointer, as follows:

```
glVertexAttribPointer(0, 3, GL_FLOAT, GL_FALSE, sizeof(Vertex),
(GLvoid*)0);
```

14. Let's create one more attribute pointer so that we can color the object. Like we did previously, we need to enable the attribute and set the `attrib` pointer, as follows:

```
glEnableVertexAttribArray(1);
glVertexAttribPointer(1, 3, GL_FLOAT, GL_FALSE, sizeof(Vertex),
(void*)(offsetof(Vertex, Vertex::color)));
```

15. Since the next attribute index is 1, we enable the attribute array using 1. While setting the attribute pointer, the first parameter is 1, since this is the first index. `color` has three components – *r*, *g*, and *b* – so the next parameter is 3. Colors are defined as floats, and so we specify `GL_FLOAT` for this parameter.

16. Since we don't want the fourth parameter to be normalized, we set the parameter to `GL_FALSE`. The fifth parameter is the stride and it is still equal to the size of the `struct` vertex. Finally, for the offset, we use the `offsetof` function to set the offset of `vertex::color` in the `struct` vertex.

Next, we have to set the element buffer object. This is done in the same way as setting the vertex buffer object: we need to generate the element, set the binding, and then bind the data to the buffer, as follows:

1. First, we generate the buffer by calling `glGenBuffers`. This is done by passing in the number of buffers that we want to create, which is 1, and then passing in the name of the buffer object to generate it:

```
glGenBuffers(1, &ebo);
glBindBuffer(GL_ELEMENT_ARRAY_BUFFER, ebo);

glBufferData(GL_ELEMENT_ARRAY_BUFFER, sizeof(GLuint) *
indices.size(), &indices[0], GL_STATIC_DRAW);
```

2. Next, we bind the buffer type to the buffer object, which, in this case, is `GL_ELEMENT_ARRAY_BUFFER`. It will store the element or index data.

3. Then, we set the index data itself by calling `glBufferData`. We pass in the buffer type first, set the size of the element data, and then pass in the data and the usage with `GL_STATIC_DRAW`, like we did previously.

4. At the end of the constructor, we unbind the buffer and the vertex array as a precaution:

```
glBindBuffer(GL_ARRAY_BUFFER, 0);
glBindVertexArray(0);
```

5. Next, we will create the `draw` function; this will be used to draw the object itself. To do this, add the `draw` function, as follows:

```
void LightRenderer::draw() {

}
```

6. We will use this function to add the code for drawing the object. The first thing we will do is create a `glm::mat4` function called `model` and initialize it; then, we will use the `glm::translate` function to translate the object to the required position:

```
glm::mat4 model = glm::mat4(1.0f);

model = glm::translate(glm::mat4(1.0),position);
```

Next, we will set the model, view, and projection matrices to transform the object from its local space. This was covered in Chapter 2, *Mathematics and Graphics Concepts*, so now is a good time for you to go and refresh your memory of graphics concepts.

The model, view, and projection matrices are set in the vertex shader. Information is sent to the shader by calling `glUseProgram`, which takes in a shader program:

```
glUseProgram(this->program);
```

Then, we can send the required information through the uniform variables. We will create a uniform data type in the shader using a name. In the `draw` function, we need to get the location of this uniform variable by calling `glGetUniformLocation`, and then passing in the program and the variable string in the shader that we set, as follows:

```
GLint modelLoc = glGetUniformLocation(program, "model");
```

This will return a `GLuint` value with the location of the variable, which is the model matrix here.

Now, we can set the value of the model matrix using the `glUniform` function. Since we are setting a matrix uniform, we use the `glUniformMatrix3fv` function; this takes four parameters. The first parameter is the location that we obtained in the previous step, whereas the second parameter is the amount of data that we are passing in; in this case, we are just passing in one matrix, so we specify this as 1. The third parameter is a Boolean value, which specifies whether the data needs to be transposed. We don't want the matrix to be transposed, so we specify it as `GL_FALSE`. The final parameter is the pointer to the data, `gl::ptr_value`; we pass this into the model matrix.

Now, add the function to set the model matrix, as follows:

```
glUniformMatrix4fv(modelLoc, 1, GL_FALSE, glm::value_ptr(model));
```

Similar to the model matrix, we have to pass in the view and projection matrices to the shader as well. To do this, we get the view and projection matrices from the camera class. Then, we get the location of the uniform variable that we defined in the shader and set the value of the view and projection matrices using the glUniformMatrix4fv function:

```
glm::mat4 view = camera->getViewMatrix();
GLint vLoc = glGetUniformLocation(program, "view");
glUniformMatrix4fv(vLoc, 1, GL_FALSE, glm::value_ptr(view));

glm::mat4 proj = camera->getprojectionMatrix();
GLint pLoc = glGetUniformLocation(program, "projection");
glUniformMatrix4fv(pLoc, 1, GL_FALSE, glm::value_ptr(proj));
```

Once we have all the required data to draw the object, we can finally draw the object. At this point, we call glBindVertexArray, bind the vao buffer object, and then call the glDrawElements function to draw the object.

The glDrawElements function takes four parameters. The first parameter is the mode that we can use to draw the lines by calling GL_LINES. Alternatively, we can draw triangles by using GL_TRIANGLES. There are, in fact, many more types of modes that can be specified, but in our case, we will only specify GL_TRIANGLES.

The second parameter is the number of elements or the number of indices that need to be drawn. This is specified when we created the object. The third parameter is the type of index data that we will be passing, which is of the GL_UNSIGNED_INT type. The final parameter is the location where the indices are stored – this is set to 0.

Add the following lines of code:

```
glBindVertexArray(vao);
glDrawElements(GL_TRIANGLES, indices.size(), GL_UNSIGNED_INT, 0);
```

For safety purposes, we will unbind the vertex array and the program variable by setting their values to 0:

```
glBindVertexArray(0);
glUseProgram(0);
```

This marks the end of the `draw` function.

Add the destructor and the rest of the setters and getters to finish the class, as follows:

```
LightRenderer::~LightRenderer() {

}

void LightRenderer::setPosition(glm::vec3 _position) {

  position = _position;
}

void LightRenderer::setColor(glm::vec3 _color) {

  this->color = _color;
}

void LightRenderer::setProgram(GLuint _program) {

  this->program = _program;
}


//getters
glm::vec3 LightRenderer::getPosition() {

  return position;
}

glm::vec3 LightRenderer::getColor() {

  return color;
}
```

Drawing the object

Let's go back to the `source.cpp` file and render `LightRenderer`, as follows:

1. At the top of the file, include `ShaderLoader.h`, `Camera.h`, and `LightRenderer.h`, and then create an instance of the `Camera` and `LightRenderer` classes called `camera` and `light`, as follows:

```
#include "ShaderLoader.h"
#include "Camera.h"
```

```
#include "LightRenderer.h"
Camera* camera;
LightRenderer* light;
```

2. Create a new function called `initGame` and add the prototype for it to the top of the file. In the `gameInit` function, load the shader and initialize the camera and light.

3. Add the new function, as follows:

```
void initGame(){
...

}
```

4. The first thing we do is enable depth testing so that only the pixels in the front are drawn. This is done by calling the `glEnable()` function and passing in the `GL_DEPTH_TEST` variable; this will enable the following depth test:

```
glEnable(GL_DEPTH_TEST);
```

5. Next, we will create a new instance of `ShaderLoader` called `shader` in the `init` function. Then, we need to call the `createProgram` function and pass in the vertex and fragment shader files to shade in the light source. The program will return a `GLuint` value, which we store in a variable called `flatShaderProgram`, as follows:

```
ShaderLoader shader;

GLuint flatShaderProgram =
shader.createProgram("Assets/Shaders/FlatModel.vs",
"Assets/Shaders/FlatModel.fs");
```

6. The vertex and shader files are located in the `Assets` folder under `Shaders`; the `FlatModel.vs` file will look as follows:

```
#version 450 core

layout (location = 0) in vec3 Position;
layout (location = 1) in vec3 Color;

uniform mat4 projection;
uniform mat4 view;
uniform mat4 model;

out vec3 outColor;
```

```
void main(){
    gl_Position = projection * view * model * vec4(Position, 1.0);

    outColor = Color;
}
```

`#version` specifies the version of GLSL that we are using, which is `450`. This stands for OpenGL version 4.50. Next, `layout (location = 0)` and `layout (location = 1)` specify the location of the vertex attributes that are passed in; in this case, this is the position and color. The `0` and `1` indices correspond to the index numbers while setting `vertexAttribPointer`. In the variables that are specified, this data is placed in the shader and stored in shader-specific `vec3` data types called `Position` and `Color`.

The three uniforms that we sent from the `draw` call for storing the model, view, and projection matrices are stored in a variable type called `uniform` and a `mat4` store data type, both of which are matrices. After this, we create another variable of the `out` type, which specifies that this will be sent out of the vertex shader; this is of the `vec3` type and is called `outColor`. Next, all the actual work is done inside the `main` function. For this, we transform the local coordinate system by multiplying the position by the model, view, and projection matrices. The result is stored in a GLSL intrinsic variable called `gl_Position`—this is the final position of the object. Then, we store the `Color` attribute in the `out vec3` variable that we created called `outColor`—that's it for the vertex shader!

7. Next, let's take a look at the fragment shader's `FlatModel.fs` file:

```
#version 450 core

in vec3 outColor;

out vec4 color;


void main(){
    color = vec4(outColor, 1.0f);

}
```

In the fragment shader file, we also specify the version of GLSL that we are using.

Next, we specify an `in vec3` variable called `outColor`, which will be the color that was sent out of the vertex shader. This can be used in the fragment shader. We also create an `out vec4` variable called `color`, which will be sent out of the fragment shader and will be used to color the object. The color that's being sent out of the fragment shader is expected to be a `vec4` variable. Then, in the main function, we convert `outColor` from a `vec3` variable into a `vec4` variable, and then set it to the `color` variable.

In the shaders, we can convert a `vec3` variable into a `vec4` variable by simply performing the following operation. This may look a bit strange, but for the sake of convenience, this unique feature is available in shader programming to make our lives a little easier.

8. Going back to the `source.cpp` file, when we pass in the vertex and fragment shader files, they will create `flatShaderProgram`. Next, in the `initGame` function, we create and initialize the camera, as follows:

```
camera = new Camera(45.0f, 800, 600, 0.1f, 100.0f, glm::vec3(0.0f,
    4.0f, 6.0f));
```

Here, we create a new camera with an FOV of 45, a width and height of 800 x 600, a near and far plane of 0.1f and 100.0f, as well as a position of 0 along the X-axis, 4.0 along the Y-axis, and 6.0 along the Z-axis.

9. Next, we create `light`, as follows:

```
light = new LightRenderer(MeshType::kTriangle, camera);
light->setProgram(flatShaderProgram);
light->setPosition(glm::vec3(0.0f, 0.0f, 0.0f));
```

10. This is done with the shape of a triangle, which is then passed to the camera. Then, we set the shader to `flatShaderProgram` and set the position to the center of the world.

11. Now, we call the `draw` function of the light in the `renderScene()` function, as follows:

```
void renderScene(){

    glClear(GL_COLOR_BUFFER_BIT | GL_DEPTH_BUFFER_BIT);
    glClearColor(1.0, 1.0, 0.0, 1.0);//clear yellow
    light->draw();

}
```

12. I changed the clear screen color to yellow so that the triangle can be seen clearly. Next, call the `initGame` function in the `main` function, as follows:

```
int main(int argc, char **argv)
{

    glfwInit();

    GLFWwindow* window = glfwCreateWindow(800, 600,
                        " Hello OpenGL ", NULL, NULL);
    glfwMakeContextCurrent(window);

    glewInit();

    initGame();


    while (!glfwWindowShouldClose(window)){

            renderScene();

            glfwSwapBuffers(window);
            glfwPollEvents();
    }

    glfwTerminate();

    delete camera;
    delete light;

    return 0;
}
```

13. Delete the camera and light at the end so that the system resource is released.
14. Now, run the project to see the glorious triangle that we set as the shape of the light source:

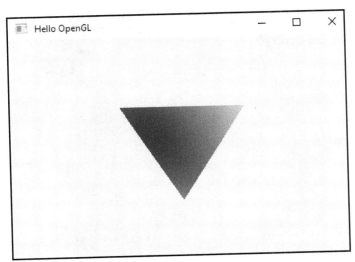

15. Change the `MeshType` type to cube to see a cube being drawn instead:

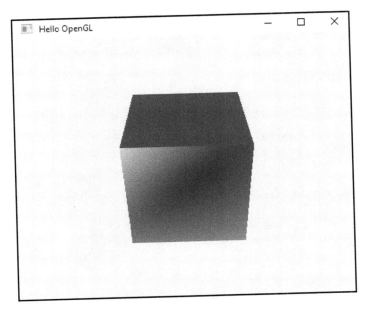

If you get an error instead of the colored object as output, then this could either mean that you have done something incorrectly or that your drivers haven't been updated and that your GPU doesn't support OpenGL 4.5.

16. To make sure GLFW supports the version of your driver, add the following code, which checks for any GLFW errors. Then, run the project and look at the console output for any errors:

```
static void glfwError(int id, const char* description)
{
  std::cout << description << std::endl;
}

int main(int argc, char **argv)
{

  glfwSetErrorCallback(&glfwError);

  glfwInit();

  GLFWwindow* window = glfwCreateWindow(800, 600, " Hello OpenGL ",
                       NULL, NULL);
  glfwMakeContextCurrent(window);

  glewInit();

  initGame();



  while (!glfwWindowShouldClose(window)){

    renderScene();

    glfwSwapBuffers(window);
    glfwPollEvents();
  }

  glfwTerminate();


  delete camera;
  delete light;

  return 0;
}
```

If you get the following output, then this could mean that the OpenGL version you're using is not supported:

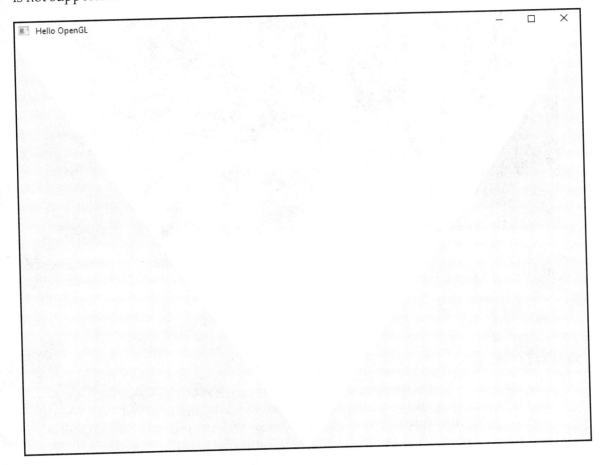

This will be accompanied by the following error, suggesting that the GLSL version you're using is not supported:

```
ERROR compiling shader: vertex shader
ERROR: 0:2: '' :  incorrect GLSL version: 450
WARNING: 0:3: 'GL_ARB_explicit_attrib_location' :  extension is not available
 current GLSL version
WARNING: 0:3: 'GL_ARB_explicit_attrib_location' :  extension is not available
 current GLSL version
WARNING: 0:4: 'GL_ARB_explicit_attrib_location' :  extension is not available
 current GLSL version
WARNING: 0:4: 'GL_ARB_explicit_attrib_location' :  extension is not available
 current GLSL version
WARNING: 0:4: 'GL_ARB_explicit_attrib_location' :  extension is not available
 current GLSL version
WARNING: 0:5: 'GL_ARB_explicit_attrib_location' :  extension is not available
 current GLSL version

ERROR compiling shader: fragment shader
ERROR: 0:2: '' :  incorrect GLSL version: 450

Shader Loader : LINK ERROR
Link called without any attached shader objects.
```

In this case, change the version of the shader code at the top of the shader to 330 instead of 450, and then try running the project again.

This should give you the desired output.

Summary

In this chapter, we created a new OpenGL project and added the necessary libraries to get the project working. Then, we created a new window to work with using GLFW. After using a couple more lines of code, we were able to clear the viewport with the color of our choice.

Next, we started preparing some classes that could help us draw objects such as the Mesh class, which defined the shape of the object, and the Camera class, which we use in order to view the object. Then, we created a ShaderLoader class, which helped us create the shader program that is used to draw the object.

With the necessary preparation done, we created a LightRenderer class. This is used to draw an object that represents a light position that's defined by a shape. We used this class to draw our first object.

In the next chapter, we will explore how to draw other objects by adding textures and physics to the rendering engine.

Building on the Game Objects

7

n the last chapter, we looked at how to draw basic shapes using OpenGL. Now that we have covered the basics, let's improve our objects by adding some textures to them so that the objects don't just look like a plain cube and sphere.

We can write our physics as we did last time, but when dealing with 3D objects, writing our own physics can become difficult and time consuming. To simplify the process, we will use the help of an external physics library to handle the physics and collision detection.

We will cover the following topics in this chapter:

- Creating the `MeshRenderer` class
- Creating the `TextureLoader` class
- Adding Bullet Physics
- Adding rigid bodies

Creating the MeshRenderer class

For drawing regular game objects, we will create a separate class from the `LightRenderer` class by adding texture, and we will also add motion to the object by adding physical properties. We will draw a textured object and then add physics to this object in the next section of this chapter. To do this, we will create a new `.h` and `.cpp` file called `MeshRenderer`.

In the `MeshRenderer.h` file, we will do the following:

1. First, we will add the includes as follows:

```
#include <vector>

#include "Camera.h"
#include "LightRenderer.h"

#include <GL/glew.h>

#include "Dependencies/glm/glm/glm.hpp"
#include "Dependencies/glm/glm/gtc/matrix_transform.hpp"
#include "Dependencies/glm/glm/gtc/type_ptr.hpp"
```

2. Next, we will create the class itself as follows:

```
Class MeshRenderer{

};
```

3. We will create the `public` section first as follows:

```
public:
    MeshRenderer(MeshType modelType, Camera* _camera);
    ~MeshRenderer();
     void draw();

    void setPosition(glm::vec3 _position);
    void setScale(glm::vec3 _scale);
    void setProgram(GLuint _program);
    void setTexture(GLuint _textureID);
```

In this section, we create the constructor, which takes a `ModelType` and the `_camera`. We add the destructor afterward. We have a separate function for drawing the object.

4. We then use some `setter` functions to set the position, scale, the shader program, and the `textureID` function , which we will be using to set the texture on the object.

5. Next, we will add the `private` section as follows:

```
private:

    std::vector<Vertex>vertices;
    std::vector<GLuint>indices;
    glm::mat4 modelMatrix;

    Camera* camera;

    glm::vec3 position, scale;
        GLuint vao, vbo, ebo, texture, program;
```

In the `private` section, we have vectors to store the vertices and the indices. Then, we have a `glm::mat4` variable called `modelMatrix` to store the model matrix value in.

6. We create a local variable for the camera and `vec3s` for storing the position and scale value.

7. Finally, we have `GLuint` to store `vao`, `vbo`, `ebo`, `textureID`, and the shader program.

We will now move on to setting up the `MeshRenderer.cpp` file by going through the following steps:

1. First, we will include the `MeshRenderer.h` file at the top of `MeshRenderer.cpp`.

2. Next, we will create the constructor for `MeshRenderer` as follows:

```
MeshRenderer::MeshRenderer(MeshType modelType, Camera* _camera) {


}
```

3. For this, we first initialize the `camera`, `position`, and `scale` local values as follows:

```
camera = _camera;

scale = glm::vec3(1.0f, 1.0f, 1.0f);
position = glm::vec3(0.0, 0.0, 0.0);
```

4. Then we create a `switch` statement, as we did in `LightRenderer`, to get the mesh data, as follows:

```
switch (modelType){

    case kTriangle: Mesh::setTriData(vertices, indices);
        break;
    case kQuad: Mesh::setQuadData(vertices, indices);
        break;
    case kCube: Mesh::setCubeData(vertices, indices);
        break;
    case kSphere: Mesh::setSphereData(vertices, indices);
        break;
}
```

5. Then, we generate and bind vao, vbo, and ebo. In addition to this, we set the data for vbo and ebo as follows:

```
glGenVertexArrays(1, &vao);
glBindVertexArray(vao);

glGenBuffers(1, &vbo);
glBindBuffer(GL_ARRAY_BUFFER, vbo);
glBufferData(GL_ARRAY_BUFFER, sizeof(Vertex) * vertices.size(),
    &vertices[0], GL_STATIC_DRAW);

glGenBuffers(1, &ebo);
glBindBuffer(GL_ELEMENT_ARRAY_BUFFER, ebo);
glBufferData(GL_ELEMENT_ARRAY_BUFFER, sizeof(GLuint) *
    indices.size(), &indices[0], GL_STATIC_DRAW);
```

6. The next step is to set the attributes. In this case, we will be setting the `position` attribute, but instead of color, we will set the texture coordinate attribute, as it will be required to set the texture on top of the object.

7. The attribute at the 0th index will still be a vertex position, but the attribute of the first index will be a texture coordinate this time, as shown in the following code:

```
glEnableVertexAttribArray(0);

glVertexAttribPointer(0, 3, GL_FLOAT, GL_FALSE, sizeof(Vertex),
    (GLvoid*)0);

glEnableVertexAttribArray(1);

glVertexAttribPointer(1, 2, GL_FLOAT, GL_FALSE, sizeof(Vertex),
    (void*)(offsetof(Vertex, Vertex::texCoords)));
```

Here, the attribute for the vertex position remains the same, but for the texture coordinate, the first index is enabled as before. The change occurs in the number of components. The texture coordinate is defined in the *x*- and *y*-axes, as this is a 2D texture, so for the second parameter, we specify 2 instead of 3. The stride still remains the same, but the offset is changed to texCoords.

8. To close the constructor, we unbind the buffers and vertexArray as follows:

```
glBindBuffer(GL_ARRAY_BUFFER, 0);
glBindVertexArray(0);
```

9. We now add the draw function as follows:

```
void MeshRenderer::draw() {

}
```

10. In this draw function, we will first set the model matrix as follows:

```
glm::mat4 TranslationMatrix = glm::translate(glm::mat4(1.0f),
    position);

glm::mat4 scaleMatrix = glm::scale(glm::mat4(1.0f), scale);

modelMatrix = glm::mat4(1.0f);

modelMatrix = TranslationMatrix *scaleMatrix;
```

11. We will create two matrices for storing translationMatrix and scaleMatrix and then we set the values.
12. We will then initialize the modelMatrix variable and the multiply scale and translation matrix and assign them to the modelMatrix variable.
13. Next, instead of creating a separate view and projection matrix, we can create a single matrix called vp and assign the multiplied view and projection matrices to it as follows:

```
glm::mat4 vp = camera->getprojectionMatrix() * camera->
    getViewMatrix();
```

Obviously, the order in which the view and projection matrices are multiplied matters and cannot be reversed.

14. We can now send the values to the GPU.

15. Before we send the values to the shader, the first thing we have to do is call `glUseProgram` and set the shader program so that the data is sent to the correct program. Once this is complete, we can set the values for vp and `modelMatrix` as follows:

```
glUseProgram(this->program);
GLint vpLoc = glGetUniformLocation(program, "vp");
glUniformMatrix4fv(vpLoc, 1, GL_FALSE, glm::value_ptr(vp));

GLint modelLoc = glGetUniformLocation(program, "model");
glUniformMatrix4fv(modelLoc, 1, GL_FALSE,
glm::value_ptr(modelMatrix));
```

16. Next, we will bind the `texture` object. We use the `glBindTexture` function to bind the texture. The function takes two parameters, with the first being the texture target. We have a 2D texture, so we pass in `GL_TEXTURE_2D` as the first parameter and the second parameter as a texture ID. To do this, we add the following line to bind the texture:

```
glBindTexture(GL_TEXTURE_2D, texture);
```

You might be wondering why we aren't using `glUniformMatrix4fv` or something similar while setting the texture location, as we did for the matrices. Well, since we have just the one texture, the program sets the uniform location as the 0th index by default so we don't have to worry about it. This all that we require to bind the texture.

17. Next, we can bind the vao and draw the object as follows:

```
glBindVertexArray(vao);
glDrawElements(GL_TRIANGLES, indices.size(), GL_UNSIGNED_INT, 0);
```

18. Unbind the `VertexArray` at the end as follows:

```
glBindVertexArray(0);
```

19. Next, we will add the definition for the destructor and `setters` as follows:

```
MeshRenderer::~MeshRenderer() {

}

// setters

void MeshRenderer::setTexture(GLuint textureID) {
```

```
    texture = textureID;

}

void MeshRenderer::setScale(glm::vec3 _scale) {

    this->scale = _scale;

}


void MeshRenderer::setPosition(glm::vec3 _position) {

    this->position = _position;

}


void MeshRenderer::setProgram(GLuint _program) {

    this->program = _program;

}
```

Creating the TextureLoader class

We created the `MeshRenderer` class, but we still need to load the texture and set the texture ID, which can be passed to the `MeshRendered` object. For this, we will create a `TextureLoader` class that will be responsible for loading the textures. Let's see how to do this.

We first need to create the new `.h` and `.cpp` file called `TextureLoader`.

To load the JPEG or PNG image, we will use a header-only library called STB. This can be downloaded from `https://github.com/nothings/stb`. Clone or download the source from the link and place the `stb-master` folder in the `Dependencies` folder.

In the `TextureLoader` class, add the following:

```
#include <string>
#include <GL/glew.h>

class TextureLoader
{
public:
    TextureLoader();

    GLuint getTextureID(std::string  texFileName);
```

```
~TextureLoader();
};
```

We will then use the `string` and `glew.h` libraries, as we will be passing the location of the file where the JPEG is located and `STB` will load the file from there. We will add a constructor and a destructor as they are required; otherwise, the compiler will give an error. We will then create a function called `getTextureID`, which takes a string as an input and returns `GLuint`, which will be the texture ID.

In the `TextureLoader.cpp` file, we include `TextureLoader.h`. We then add the following to include `STB`:

```
#define STB_IMAGE_IMPLEMENTATION
#include "Dependencies/stb-master/stb_image.h"
```

We add `#define` as it is required in a `TextureLoader.cpp` file, navigate to `stb_image.h`, and include it in the project. We then add the constructor and destructor as follows:

```
TextureLoader::TextureLoader(){

}

TextureLoader::~TextureLoader(){

}
```

Next, we create the `getTextureID` function as follows:

```
GLuint TextureLoader::getTextureID(std::string texFileName){

}
```

In the `getTextureID` function, we will first create three `int` variables to store the width, height, and number of channels. An image usually only has three channels: red, green, and blue. However, it could have a fourth channel, the alpha channel, which is used for transparency. JPEG pictures have only three channels, but the PNG file could have three or four channels.

In our game, we will only be using a JPEG file, so the `channels` parameter will always be three, as shown in the following code:

```
int width, height, channels;
```

We will use the `stbi_load` function to load the image data to an unsigned char pointer, as follows:

```
stbi_uc* image = stbi_load(texFileName.c_str(), &width, &height,
                           &channels, STBI_rgb);
```

The function takes five parameters. The first is the string of the location of the file/filename. Then, it returns the width, height, and number of channels as the second, third, and fourth parameters, and in the fifth parameter, you set the required components. In this case, we want just the r, g, and b channels, so we specify `STBI_rgb`.

We then have to generate and bind the texture as follows:

```
GLuint mtexture;
glGenTextures(1, &mtexture);
glBindTexture(GL_TEXTURE_2D, mtexture);
```

First, a texture ID called `mtexture` of the `GLuint` type is created. Then, we call the `glGenTextures` function, pass in the number of objects we want to create, and pass in the array names, which is `mtexture`. We also have to bind the texture type by calling `glBindTexture` and pass in the texture type, which is `GL_TEXTURE_2D`, specifying that it is a 2D texture and stating the texture ID.

Next, we have to set the texture wrapping. Texture wrapping dictates what happens when the texture coordinate is greater or less than 1 in x and y.

Textures can be wrapped in one of four ways: `GL_REPEAT`, `GL_MIRRORED_REPEAT`, `GL_CLAMP_TO_EDGE`, or `GL_CLAMP_TO_BORDER`.

If we imagine a texture applied to a quad, then the positive *s*-axis runs horizontally and the *t*-axis runs vertically, starting at the origin (the bottom-left corner), as shown in the following screenshot:

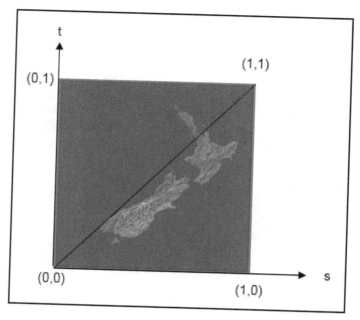

Let's look at the different ways that the textures can be wrapped, as shown in the following list:

- `GL_REPEAT` just repeats the texture when applied to a quad.
- `GL_MIRRORER_REPEAT` repeats the texture, but also mirrors the texture the next time.
- `GL_CLAMP_TO_EDGE` takes the `rgb` value at the edge of the texture and repeats the value for the entire object. In the following screenshot, the red border pixels are repeated.
- `GL_CLAMP_TO_BORDER` takes a user-specific value and applies it to the end of the object instead of applying the edge color, as shown in the following screenshot:

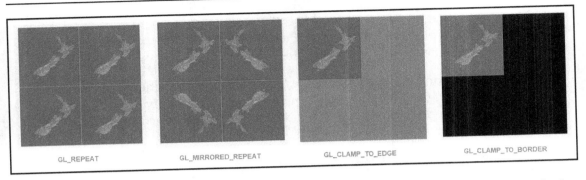

| GL_REPEAT | GL_MIRRORED_REPEAT | GL_CLAMP_TO_EDGE | GL_CLAMP_TO_BORDER |

For our purposes, we need `GL_REPEAT`, which is set as the default anyway, but if you had to set it, you will need to add the following:

```
glTexParameteri(GL_TEXTURE_2D, GL_TEXTURE_WRAP_S, GL_REPEAT);
glTexParameteri(GL_TEXTURE_2D, GL_TEXTURE_WRAP_T, GL_REPEAT);
```

You use the `glTexParameteri` function, which takes three parameters. The first is the texture type, which is `GL_TEXTURE_2D`. The next parameter is the direction in which you want the wrapping to apply, which is `S` or `T`. The `S` direction is the same as x and `T` is the same as y. The last parameter is the wrapping parameter itself.

Next, we can set the texture filtering. Sometimes, when you apply a low-quality texture to a big quad, if you zoom in closer, the texture will be pixelated, as shown in the left-hand picture in the following screenshot:

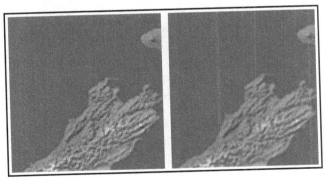

The picture on the left is the output of setting the texture filtering to `GL_NEAREST`, and the picture on the right is the result of applying texture filtering to `GL_LINEAR`. The `GL_LINEAR` wrapping linearly interpolates with the texel value of the surrounding values to give a much smoother result when compared to `GL_NEAREST`.

When the texture is magnified, it is better to set the value to GL_LINEAR to get a smoother picture, and when the picture is minimized, it can then be set to GL_NEAREST, as the texels (which are texture elements) will be so small that we won't be able to see them anyway.

To set the texture filtering, we use the same glTexParameteri function, but instead of passing in the wrapping direction as the second parameter we specify GL_TEXTURE_MIN_FILTER and GL_TEXTURE_MAG_FILTER as the second parameter and pass in GL_NEAREST or GL_LINEAR as the third parameter, as follows:

```
glTexParameteri(GL_TEXTURE_2D, GL_TEXTURE_MIN_FILTER, GL_NEAREST);
glTexParameteri(GL_TEXTURE_2D, GL_TEXTURE_MAG_FILTER, GL_LINEAR);
```

It doesn't make sense to load a huge image with the object so far away that you can't even see it, so for optimization purposes, you can create mipmaps. Mipmaps basically take the texture and converts it to a lower resolution. This will automatically change the image to a lower resolution image when the texture is too far away from the camera. It will also change to a higher resolution image when the camera is closer.

Here is the mipmap chain for the texture we are using:

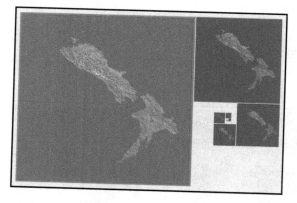

The mipmap quality can be set using the glTexParameteri function again. This basically replaces GL_NEAREST with either GL_NEAREST_MIPMAP_NEAREST, GL_LINEAR_MIPMAP_NEAREST, GL_NEAREST_MIPMAP_LINEAR, or GL_LINEAR_ MIPMAP_LINEAR.

The best option is GL_LINEAR_MIPMAP_LINEAR because it linearly interpolates the value of the texel between two mipmaps, as well as samples, by linearly interpolating between the surrounding texels (a texel is the lowest unit of an image in the same way that a pixel is the smallest unit of a screen to represent a color at a location on the screen. If a 1080p picture is shown on a 1080p screen, then 1 texel is mapped to 1 pixel).

So, we will use the following as our new filtering/mipmap values:

```
glTexParameteri(GL_TEXTURE_2D, GL_TEXTURE_MIN_FILTER,
    GL_LINEAR_MIPMAP_LINEAR);
glTexParameteri(GL_TEXTURE_2D, GL_TEXTURE_MAG_FILTER, GL_LINEAR);
```

Once this has been set, we can finally create the texture using the `glTexImage2D` function, as follows:

```
glTexImage2D(GL_TEXTURE_2D, 0, GL_RGB, width, height, 0,GL_RGB,
    GL_UNSIGNED_BYTE, image);
```

The `glTexImage2D` function takes nine parameters. These are described as follows:

- The first is the texture type, which is `GL_TEXTURE_2D`.
- The second is the mipmap level. If we want to use a lower quality picture, we can set this value to 1, 2, or 3. For our purposes, we will leave this value as 0, which is the base level.
- For the third parameter, we will specify which all-color channels we want to store from the image. Since we want to store all three channels, we specify `GL_RGB`.
- The fourth and fifth parameters that we specify are the width and height of the picture.
- The next parameter has to be set to 0, as specified in the documentation (which can be found at `https://www.khronos.org/registry/OpenGL-Refpages/gl4/html/glTexImage2D.xhtml`).
- The next parameter that we specify is the data format of the image source.
- The next parameter is the type of data that is passed in, which is `GL_UNSIGNED_BYTE`.
- Finally, we set the image data.

Now that the texture is created, we call `glGenerateMipmap` and pass in the `GL_TEXTURE_2D` texture type, as follows:

```
glGenerateMipmap(GL_TEXTURE_2D);
```

We then unbind the texture, free the picture, and finally return the `textureID` function like so:

```
glBindTexture(GL_TEXTURE_2D, 0);
stbi_image_free(image);

    return mtexture;
```

With all that done, we call finally add our texture to the game object.

In the source.cpp, include MeshRenderer.h and TextureLoader.h by going through the following steps:

1. At the top, create a MeshRenderer pointer object called a sphere as follows:

```
Camera* camera;
LightRenderer* light;
MeshRenderer* sphere;
```

2. In the init function, create a new shader program called texturedShaderProgram of the GLuint type as follows:

```
GLuint flatShaderProgram = shader.CreateProgram(
                           "Assets/Shaders/FlatModel.vs",
                           "Assets/Shaders/FlatModel.fs");
GLuint texturedShaderProgram = shader.CreateProgram(
                           "Assets/Shaders/TexturedModel.vs",
                           "Assets/Shaders/TexturedModel.fs");
```

3. We will now load the two shaders called TexturedModel.vs and TexturedModel.fs as follows:

   • Here is the TexturedModel.vs shader:

```
#version 450 core
layout (location = 0) in vec3 position;
layout (location = 1) in vec2 texCoord;

out vec2 TexCoord;

uniform mat4 vp;
uniform mat4 model;


void main(){

   gl_Position = vp * model *vec4(position, 1.0);

   TexCoord = texCoord;
}
```

The only difference between this and FlatModel.vs is that here, the second location is a vec2 called texCoord. We create an out vec2 called TexCoord, into which we will store this value in the main function.

- Here is the `TexturedModel.fs` shader:

```
#version 450 core

in vec2 TexCoord;

out vec4 color;

// texture
uniform sampler2D Texture;


void main(){
        color = texture(Texture, TexCoord);
}
```

We create a new `vec2` called `TexCoord` to receive the value from the vertex shader.

We then create a new uniform type called `sampler2D` and call it `Texture`. The texture is received through a sampler that will be used to sample the texture depending upon the wrap and filtering parameters we set while creating the texture.

Then, the color is set depending upon the sampler and texture coordinates using the `texture` function. This function takes sampler and texture coordinates as parameters. The texel at a texture coordinate is sampled based on the sampler, and that color value is returned and assigned to the object at that texture coordinate.

Let's continue creating the `MeshRenderer` object. Load the `globe.jpg` texture file using the `getTextureID` function of the `TextureLoader` class and set it to a `GLuint` called `sphereTexture` as follows:

```
TextureLoader tLoader;
GLuint sphereTexture = tLoader.getTextureID("Assets/Textures/globe.jpg");
```

Create the sphere `MeshRederer` object, set the mesh type, and pass the camera. Set the program, texture, position, and scale as follows:

```
sphere = new MeshRenderer(MeshType::kSphere, camera);
sphere->setProgram(texturedShaderProgram);
sphere->setTexture(sphereTexture);
sphere->setPosition(glm::vec3(0.0f, 0.0f, 0.0f));
sphere->setScale(glm::vec3(1.0f));
```

In the `renderScene` function, draw the `sphere` object as follows:

```
void renderScene(){

    glClear(GL_COLOR_BUFFER_BIT | GL_DEPTH_BUFFER_BIT);
    glClearColor(1.0, 1.0, 0.0, 1.0);

    sphere->draw();

}
```

You should now see the textured globe when you run the project, as shown in the following screenshot:

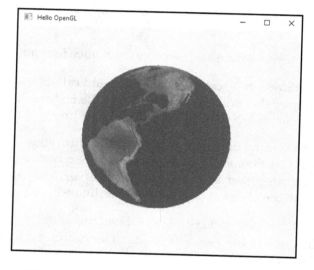

The camera is created as follows, and is set at the z position of four units:

```
camera = new Camera(45.0f, 800, 600, 0.1f, 100.0f, glm::vec3(0.0f,
    0.0f, 4.0f));
```

Adding Bullet Physics

To add physics to our game, we will be using the Bullet Physics engine. This is an open source project that is widely used in AAA games and movies. It is used for collision detection as well as soft- and rigid-body dynamics. The library is free for commercial use.

Download the source from `https://github.com/bulletphysics/bullet3`, and using CMake you will need to build the project for the release version of x64. For your convenience, the header and `lib` files are included in the project for the chapter. You can take the folder and paste it into the `dependencies` folder.

Now that we have the folder, let's take a look at how to add Bullet Physics by following these steps:

1. Add the `include` folder in **C/C++ | General | Additional Include Directories** as shown in the following screenshot:

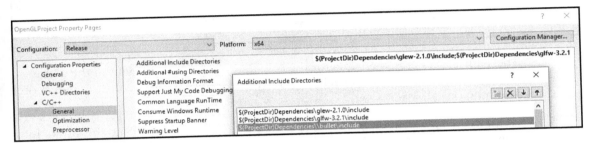

2. Add the `lib/win64/Rls` folder in **Linker | General | Additional Library Directories**:

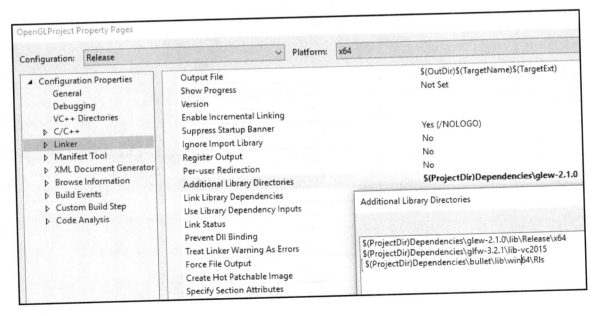

3. Add `BulletCollision.lib`, `BulletDynamics.lib`, and `LinearMath.lib` to **Linker | Input | Additional Dependencies**, as shown in the following screenshot:

These libraries are responsible for the calculation of the movement of the game objects based on conditions such as gravity and external force, collision detection, and memory allocation.

4. With the prep work out of the way, we can start adding physics to the game. In the `source.cpp` file, include `btBulletDynamicsCommon.h` at the top of the file, as follows:

```
#include "Camera.h"
#include "LightRenderer.h"
#include "MeshRenderer.h"
#include "TextureLoader.h"

#include <btBulletDynamicsCommon.h>
```

5. After this, create a new pointer object to `btDiscreteDynamicsWorld` as follows:

```
btDiscreteDynamicsWorld* dynamicsWorld;
```

6. This object keeps track of all the physics settings and objects in the current scene.

However, before we create `dynamicWorld`, the Bullet Physics library requires some objects to be initialized first.

These required objects are listed as follows:

- `btBroadPhaseInerface`: Collision detection is actually done in two phases: `broadphase` and `narrowphase`. In the `broadphase`, the physics engine eliminates all the objects that are unlikely to collide. This check is done using the objects' bounding boxes. Then, in the `narrowphase`, the actual shape of the object is used to check the likelihood of a collision. Pairs of objects are created with a strong likelihood of collision. In the following screenshot, the red box around the sphere is used for `broadphase` collision and the white wiremesh of the sphere is used for `narrowphase` collision:

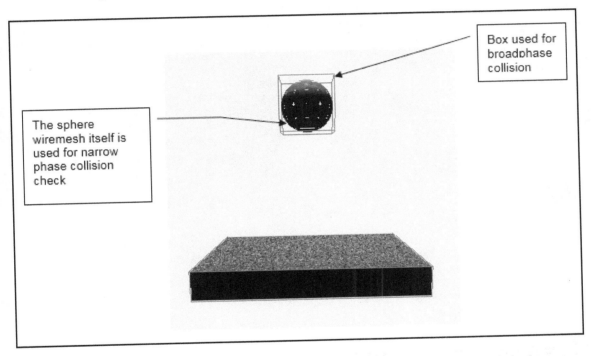

- `btDefaultColliusion` **configuration**: This is used for setting up default memory.
- `btCollisionDispatcher`: A pair of objects that have a strong likelihood of colliding are tested for collision using actual shapes. This is used for getting details of the collision detection, such as which object collided with which other object.

- btSequentialImpulseConstraintSolver: You can create constraints, such as a hinge constraint or slider constraint, which can restrict the motion or rotation of one object about another object. For example, if there is a hinge joint between the wall and the door, then the door can only rotate around the joint and cannot be moved about, as it is fixed at the hinge joint. The constraint solver is responsible for calculating this correctly. The calculation is repeated a number of times to get close to the optimal solution.

In the init function, before we create the sphere object, we will initialize these objects as follows:

```
//init physics
btBroadphaseInterface* broadphase = new btDbvtBroadphase();
btDefaultCollisionConfiguration* collisionConfiguration =
    new btDefaultCollisionConfiguration();
btCollisionDispatcher* dispatcher =
    new btCollisionDispatcher(collisionConfiguration);
btSequentialImpulseConstraintSolver* solver =
    new btSequentialImpulseConstraintSolver();
```

7. Then, we will create a new dynamicWorld by passing the dispatcher, broadphase, solver, and collisionConfiguration as parameters to the btDiscreteDynamicsWorld function, as follows:

```
dynamicsWorld = new btDiscreteDynamicsWorld(dispatcher, broadphase,
    solver, collisionConfiguration);
```

8. Now that our physics world is created, we can set the parameters for our physics. The basic parameter is gravity. We set its value to real-world conditions, as follows:

```
dynamicsWorld->setGravity(btVector3(0, -9.8f, 0));
```

Adding rigid bodies

Now we can create rigid bodies or soft bodies and watch them interact with other rigid or soft bodies. A rigid body is an animate or inanimate object that doesn't change its shape or physical properties. Soft bodies, on the other hand, can be squishy and made to change shape.

In the following example, we will focus on the creation of a rigid body.

To create a rigid body, we have to specify the shape of the object and the motion state, and then set the mass and inertia of the objects. Shapes are defined using btCollisionShape. An object can have different shapes, or sometimes even a combination of shapes, called a compound shape. We use btBoxShape to create cubes and cuboids and btSphereShape to create spheres. We can also create other shapes, such as btCapsuleShape, btCylinderShape, and btConeShape, which will be used for narrowphase collision by the library.

In our case, we are going to create a sphere shape and see our Earth sphere bounce around. So, let's begin:

1. Using the following code, create a btSphere for creating a sphere shape and set the radius as 1.0, which is the radius of our rendered sphere as well:

```
btCollisionShape* sphereShape = new btSphereShape(1.0f);
```

2. Next, set the btDefaultMotionState, where we specify the rotation and position of the sphere, as follows:

```
btDefaultMotionState* sphereMotionState = new
btDefaultMotionState(btTransform(btQuaternion(0, 0, 0, 1),
btVector3(0, 10.0f, 0)));
```

We set the rotation to 0 and set the position of the rigid body to a distance of 10.0f along the *y*-axis. We should also set the mass and inertia and calculate the inertia of the sphereShape as follows:

```
btScalar mass = 10.0;
btVector3 sphereInertia(0, 0, 0);
sphereShape->calculateLocalInertia(mass, sphereInertia);
```

3. To create the rigid body, we first have to create btRiigidBodyConstructionInfo and pass the variables to it as follows:

```
btScalar mass = 10.0;
btVector3 sphereInertia(0, 0, 0);
sphereShape->calculateLocalInertia(mass, sphereInertia);

btRigidBody::btRigidBodyConstructionInfo sphereRigidBodyCI(mass,
sphereMotionState, sphereShape, sphereInertia);
```

4. Now, create the rigid body object by passing btRiigidBodyConstructionInfo into it using the following code:

```
btRigidBody* sphereRigidBody = new btRigidBody(sphereRigidBodyCI);
```

5. Now, set the physical properties of the rigid body, including friction and restitution, using the following code:

```
sphereRigidBody->setRestitution(1.0f);
sphereRigidBody->setFriction(1.0f);
```

These values are between `0.0f` and `1.0.0.0`, meaning that the object is really smooth and has no friction, and has no restitution or bounciness. The `1.0` figure, on the other hand, means that the object is rough on the outside and extremely bouncy, like a bouncy ball.

6. After these necessary parameters are set, we need to add the rigid body to the `dynamicWorld` we created as follows, using the `addRigidBody` function of the `dynamicsWorld`:

```
dynamicsWorld->addRigidBody(sphereRigidBody);
```

Now, for our sphere mesh to actually behave like the sphere body, we have to pass the rigid body to the sphere mesh class and make some minor changes. Open the `MeshRenderer.h` and `.cpp` files. In the `MeshRenderer.h` file, include the `btBulletDynamicsCommon.h` header and add a local `btRigidBody` called `rigidBody` to the `private` section. You should also change the constructor to take a rigid body, as follows:

```
#include <btBulletDynamicsCommon.h>

    class MeshRenderer{
public:
MeshRenderer(MeshType modelType, Camera* _camera, btRigidBody*
_rigidBody);
        .
        .
    private:
        .
        .
            btRigidBody* rigidBody;
};
```

7. In the `MeshRenderer.cpp` file, change the constructor to take a `rigidBody` variable and set the local `rigidBody` variable to it as follows:

```
MeshRenderer::MeshRenderer(MeshType modelType, Camera* _camera,
btRigidBody* _rigidBody) {

    rigidBody = _rigidBody;
    camera = _camera;
```

```
    .
    .
    .
}
```

8. Then, in the `draw` function, we have to replace the code where we set the `modelMatrix` variable with the code where we get the sphere rigid body value, as follows:

    ```
    btTransform t;

    rigidBody->getMotionState()->getWorldTransform(t);
    ```

9. We use the `btTransform` variable to get the transformation from the rigid body's `getMotionState` function and then get the `WorldTransform` variable and set it to our `brTransform` variable t, as follows:

    ```
    btQuaternion rotation = t.getRotation();
    btVector3 translate = t.getOrigin();
    ```

10. We create two new variables of the `btQuaternion` type to store rotation and `btVector3` to store the translation values using the `getRotation` and `getOrigin` functions of the `btTransform` class, as follows:

    ```
    glm::mat4 RotationMatrix = glm::rotate(glm::mat4(1.0f),
    rotation.getAngle(),glm::vec3(rotation.getAxis().getX(),rotation.ge
    tAxis().getY(), rotation.getAxis().getZ())));

    glm::mat4 TranslationMatrix = glm::translate(glm::mat4(1.0f),
                             glm::vec3(translate.getX(),
                             translate.getY(), translate.getZ())));

    glm::mat4 scaleMatrix = glm::scale(glm::mat4(1.0f), scale);
    ```

11. Next, we create three `glm::mat4` variables, called `RotationMatrix`, `TranslationMatrix`, and `ScaleMatrix`, and set the values of rotation and translation using the `glm::rotate` and `glm::translation` functions. We then pass in the rotation and translation values we stored earlier, as shown in the following code. We will keep the `ScaleMatrix` variable as is:

    ```
    modelMatrix = TranslationMatrix * RotationMatrix * scaleMatrix;
    ```

    The new `modelMatrix` variable will be the multiplication of the scale, rotation, and translation matrices in that order. The rest of the code will remain the same in the `draw` function.

12. In the `init` function, change the code to reflect the modified `MeshRenderer` constructor:

```
// Sphere Mesh

sphere = new MeshRenderer(MeshType::kSphere, camera,
        sphereRigidBody);
sphere->setProgram(texturedShaderProgram);
sphere->setTexture(sphereTexture);
sphere->setScale(glm::vec3(1.0f));
```

13. We don't have to set the position, as that will be set by the rigid body. Set the camera as shown in the following code so that we can see the sphere:

```
camera = new Camera(45.0f, 800, 600, 0.1f, 100.0f, glm::vec3(0.0f,
        4.0f, 20.0f));
```

14. Now, run the project. We can see the sphere being drawn, but it is not moving. That's because we have to update the physics bodies.
15. We have to use the `dynamicsWorld` and `stepSimulation` functions to update the simulation every frame. To do this, we have to calculate the delta time between the previous and current frames.
16. At the top of the `source.cpp`, include `<chrono>` so that we can calculate the tick update. Now, we have to make changes to the `main` function and the `while` loop as follows:

```
auto previousTime = std::chrono::high_resolution_clock::now();

while (!glfwWindowShouldClose(window)){

        auto currentTime = std::chrono::
                        high_resolution_clock::now();
        float dt = std::chrono::duration<float, std::::
                chrono::seconds::period>(currentTime -
                previousTime).count();

        dynamicsWorld->stepSimulation(dt);

        renderScene();

        glfwSwapBuffers(window);
        glfwPollEvents();

        previousTime = currentTime;
    }
```

Just before the `while` loop, we create a variable called `previousTime` and initialize it with the current time. In the `while` loop, we get the current time and store it in the variable. Then, we calculate the delta time between the previous time and the current time by subtracting the two. We have the delta time now, so we call the `stepSimulation` and pass in the delta time. Then we render the scene and swap the buffer and poll for events as usual. Finally, we set the current time as the previous time.

Now, when we run the project, we can see the sphere falling down, which is pretty cool. However, the sphere doesn't interact with anything.

Let's add a box rigid body at the bottom and watch the sphere bounce off it. After the sphere `MeshRenderer` object, add the following code to create a box rigid body:

```
btCollisionShape* groundShape = new btBoxShape(btVector3(4.0f,
                                0.5f, 4.0f));
btDefaultMotionState* groundMotionState = new
  btDefaultMotionState(btTransform(btQuaternion
  (0, 0, 0, 1), btVector3(0, -2.0f, 0)));
btRigidBody::btRigidBodyConstructionInfo
  groundRigidBodyCI(0.0f, new btDefaultMotionState(),
  groundShape, btVector3(0, 0, 0));


btRigidBody* groundRigidBody = new btRigidBody(
                              groundRigidBodyCI);


groundRigidBody->setFriction(1.0);
groundRigidBody->setRestitution(0.9);
groundRigidBody->setCollisionFlags(btCollisionObject
  ::CF_STATIC_OBJECT);

dynamicsWorld->addRigidBody(groundRigidBody);
```

Here, we first create a shape of the btBoxShape type with the length, height, and depth set as 4.0, 0.5, and 4.0 respectively. Next, we will set the motion state, where we set the rotation to zero and the position at -2.0 in the *y*-axis and 0 along the *x*- and *z*-axis. For the construction information, we set the mass and intertia to 0. We also set the default motion state and pass in the shape. Next, we create the rigid body by passing the rigid body information into it. Once the rigid body is created, we set the restitution and friction value. Next, we use the setCollisionFlags function of rigidBody to set the rigid body type as static. This means that it will be like a brick wall or won't move and be affected by forces from other rigid bodies, but other bodies will still be affected by it.

Finally, we add the ground rigid body to the world so that the box rigid body will be part of the physics simulation as well. We now have to create a MeshRenderer cube to render the ground rigid body. Create a new MeshRenderer object called Ground at the top, under which you created the sphere MeshRenderer object. In the init function, under which we added the code for the ground rigid body, add the following:

```
// Ground Mesh
GLuint groundTexture = tLoader.getTextureID(
                    "Assets/Textures/ground.jpg");
ground = new MeshRenderer(MeshType::kCube, camera,
        groundRigidBody);
ground->setProgram(texturedShaderProgram);
ground->setTexture(groundTexture);
ground->setScale(glm::vec3(4.0f, 0.5f, 4.0f));
```

We will create a new texture by loading ground.jpg, so make sure you add it to the Assets/ Textures directory. Call the constructor and set the meshtype to cube, and then set the camera and pass in the ground rigid body. We then set the shader program, texture, and scale of the object.

17. In the renderScene function, draw the ground MeshRenderer object as follows:

```
void renderScene(){

    glClear(GL_COLOR_BUFFER_BIT | GL_DEPTH_BUFFER_BIT);
    glClearColor(1.0, 1.0, 0.0, 1.0);

    sphere->draw();
    ground->draw();
}
```

18. Now, when you run the project, you will see the sphere bouncing on the ground box:

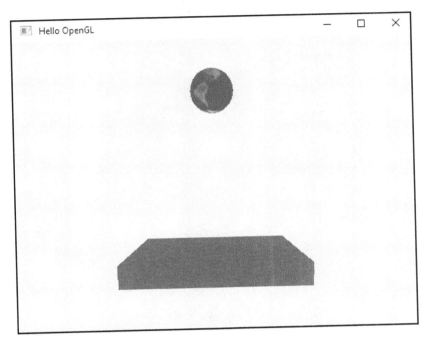

Summary

In this chapter, we created a new class called MeshRenderer, which will be used to render textured 3D objects to our scene. We created a texture-loaded class, which will be used to load the textures from the images provided. Then, we added physics to the object by adding the Bullet Physics library. We then initialized the physics world and created and added the rigid body to the mesh renderer by adding the body itself to the world, causing the rendered object to be affected by physics.

In the next chapter, we will add a gameplay loop, as well as scoring and text rendering to display the score on the viewport. We will also add lighting to our world.

8
Enhancing Your Game with Collision, Loops, and Lighting

In this chapter, we will learn how to add collision to detect contact between the ball and the enemy; this will determine the lose condition. We will also check the contact between the ball and the ground to find out whether the player can jump or not. Then, we will finalize the gameplay loop.

Once the gameplay loop is complete, we will be able to add text rendering to show the player their score. To display the necessary text, we will use the FreeType library. This will load in the characters from the font file.

We will also add some basic lighting to the objects in the scene. Lighting will be calculated using the Phong lighting model, and we will cover how this is implemented in practice. To finish the gameplay loop, we will have to add an enemy.

In this chapter, we will cover the following topics:

- Adding a `RigidBody` name
- Adding an enemy
- Moving the enemy
- Checking collision
- Adding keyboard controls
- Gameloop and scoring
- Text rendering
- Adding lighting

Adding a RigidBody name

To identify the different rigid bodies we are going to be adding to the scene, we will add a property to the `MeshRenderer` class that will specify each object being rendered. Let's look at how to do this:

1. In the `MeshRenderer.h` class, which can be found within the `MeshRenderer` class, change the constructor of the class to take in a string as the name for the object, as follows:

   ```
   MeshRenderer(MeshType modelType, std::string _name, Camera *
       _camera, btRigidBody* _rigidBody)
   ```

2. Add a new public property called `name` of the `std::string` type and initialize it, as follows:

   ```
   std::string name = "";
   ```

3. Next, in the `MeshRenderer.cpp` file, modify the constructor implementation, as follows:

   ```
   MeshRenderer::MeshRenderer(MeshType modelType, std::string _name,
       Camera* _camera, btRigidBody* _rigidBody){
       name = _name;
   ...
   ...

   }
   ```

We have successfully added the `name` property to the `MeshRenderer` class.

Adding an enemy

Before we add an enemy to the scene, let's clean up our code a little bit and create a new function called `addRigidBodies` in `main.cpp` so that all the rigid bodies will be created in a single function. To do so, follow these steps:

1. In the source of the `main.cpp` file, create a new function called `addRigidBodies` above the `main()` function.

2. Add the following code to the `addRigidBodies` function. This will add the sphere and ground. We are doing this instead of putting all the game code in the `main()` function:

```
// Sphere Rigid Body

btCollisionShape* sphereShape = new btSphereShape(1);
btDefaultMotionState* sphereMotionState = new
    btDefaultMotionState(btTransform(btQuaternion(0, 0, 0, 1),
    btVector3(0, 0.5, 0)));

btScalar mass = 13.0f;
btVector3 sphereInertia(0, 0, 0);
sphereShape->calculateLocalInertia(mass, sphereInertia);

btRigidBody::btRigidBodyConstructionInfo sphereRigidBodyCI(mass,
    sphereMotionState, sphereShape, sphereInertia);

btRigidBody* sphereRigidBody = new btRigidBody(
                                    sphereRigidBodyCI);

sphereRigidBody->setFriction(1.0f);
sphereRigidBody->setRestitution(0.0f);

sphereRigidBody->setActivationState(DISABLE_DEACTIVATION);

dynamicsWorld->addRigidBody(sphereRigidBody);

// Sphere Mesh

sphere = new MeshRenderer(MeshType::kSphere, "hero", camera,
            sphereRigidBody);
sphere->setProgram(texturedShaderProgram);
sphere->setTexture(sphereTexture);
sphere->setScale(glm::vec3(1.0f));

sphereRigidBody->setUserPointer(sphere);

// Ground Rigid body

btCollisionShape* groundShape = new btBoxShape(btVector3(4.0f,
                                    0.5f, 4.0f));
btDefaultMotionState* groundMotionState = new
    btDefaultMotionState(btTransform(btQuaternion(0, 0, 0, 1),
    btVector3(0, -1.0f, 0)));

btRigidBody::btRigidBodyConstructionInfo groundRigidBodyCI(0.0f,
    groundMotionState, groundShape, btVector3(0, 0, 0));
```

```
btRigidBody* groundRigidBody = new btRigidBody(
                           groundRigidBodyCI);

groundRigidBody->setFriction(1.0);
groundRigidBody->setRestitution(0.0);

groundRigidBody->setCollisionFlags(
    btCollisionObject::CF_STATIC_OBJECT);

dynamicsWorld->addRigidBody(groundRigidBody);

// Ground Mesh
ground = new MeshRenderer(MeshType::kCube, "ground", camera,
        groundRigidBody);
ground->setProgram(texturedShaderProgram);
ground->setTexture(groundTexture);
ground->setScale(glm::vec3(4.0f, 0.5f, 4.0f));

groundRigidBody->setUserPointer(ground);
```

Note that some of the values have been changed to suit our game. We have also disabled deactivation on the sphere because, if we don't, then the sphere will be unresponsive when we want it to jump for us.

To access the name of the rendered mesh, we can set this instance as a property of the rigid body by using the `setUserPointer` property of the `RigidBody` class. `setUserPointer` takes a void pointer, so any kind of data can be passed into it. For the sake of convenience, we are just passing the instance of the `MeshRenderer` class itself. In this function, we will also add the enemy's rigid body to the scene, as follows:

```
// Enemy Rigid body

btCollisionShape* shape = new btBoxShape(btVector3(1.0f, 1.0f,
1.0f));
btDefaultMotionState* motionState = new
btDefaultMotionState(btTransform(btQuaternion(0, 0, 0, 1),
btVector3(18.0, 1.0f, 0)));
btRigidBody::btRigidBodyConstructionInfo rbCI(0.0f, motionState,
shape, btVector3(0.0f, 0.0f, 0.0f));

  btRigidBody* rb = new btRigidBody(rbCI);

rb->setFriction(1.0);
rb->setRestitution(0.0);
```

```
//rb->setCollisionFlags(btCollisionObject::CF_KINEMATIC_OBJECT);

rb->setCollisionFlags(btCollisionObject::CF_NO_CONTACT_RESPONSE);

    dynamicsWorld->addRigidBody(rb);

    // Enemy Mesh
    enemy = new MeshRenderer(MeshType::kCube, "enemy", camera, rb);
    enemy->setProgram(texturedShaderProgram);
    enemy->setTexture(groundTexture);
    enemy->setScale(glm::vec3(1.0f, 1.0f, 1.0f));

    rb->setUserPointer(enemy);
```

3. Add the enemy in the same way that we added the sphere and the ground. Since the shape of the enemy object is a cube, we use btBoxShape to set the shape of the box for the rigid body. We set the location to 18 units' distance in the X-axis and one unit's distance in the Y-axis. Then, we set the friction and restitution values.

   For the type of the rigid body, we set its collision flag to NO_CONTACT_RESPONSE instead of KINEMATIC_OBJECT. We could have set the type to KINEMATIC_OBJECT, but then the enemy object would exert force on other objects, such as the sphere, when it comes in contact with it. To avoid this, we use NO_CONTACT_RESPONSE, which will just check if there was an overlap between the enemy rigid body and another body, instead of applying force to it.

   You can uncomment the KINEMATIC_OBJECT line of code and comment on the NO_CONTACT_RESPONSE line of code to see how using either changes the way the object behaves in the physics simulation.

4. Once we have created the rigid body, we add the rigid body to the world, set the mesh renderer for the enemy object, and name it **enemy**.

Moving the enemy

To update the enemy's movement, we will add a tick function that will be called by the rigid body world. In this tick function, we will update the position of the enemy so that the enemy cube moves from the right of the screen to the left. We will also check whether the enemy has gone beyond the left-hand side of the screen.

If it has, then we will reset its position to the right of the screen. To do so, follow these steps:

1. In this update function, we will also update our gameplay logic and scoring, as well as how we check for contact between the sphere and the enemy and the sphere and the ground. Add the tick function callback prototype to the top of the `Main.cpp` file, as follows:

```
void myTickCallback(btDynamicsWorld *dynamicsWorld,
    btScalar timeStep);
```

2. In the `TickCallback` function, update the position of the enemy, as follows:

```
void myTickCallback(btDynamicsWorld *dynamicsWorld, btScalar
timeStep) {

        // Get enemy transform
        btTransform t(enemy->rigidBody->getWorldTransform());

        // Set enemy position
        t.setOrigin(t.getOrigin() + btVector3(-15, 0, 0) *
        timeStep);

        // Check if offScreen
        if(t.getOrigin().x() <= -18.0f) {
            t.setOrigin(btVector3(18, 1, 0));
        }
        enemy->rigidBody->setWorldTransform(t);
        enemy->rigidBody->getMotionState()->setWorldTransform(t);
}
```

In the `myTickCallback` function, we get the current transform and store it in a variable, `t`. Then, we set the origin, which is the position of the transform, by getting the current position, moving it 15 units to the left, and multiplying it by the current timestep (which is the difference between the previous and current time).

Once we get the updated location, we check that the current location is less than 18 units. If it is, then the current location is beyond the screen bounds on the left of the screen. Consequently, we set the current location back to the right of the viewport and make the object wrap around the screen.

Then, we update the location of the object itself to this new location by updating the `worldTransform` of the rigid body and the motion state of the object.

3. Set the tick function as the default `TickCallback` of the dynamic world in the `init` function, as follows:

```
dynamicsWorld = new btDiscreteDynamicsWorld(dispatcher, broadphase,
                solver, collisionConfiguration);
dynamicsWorld->setGravity(btVector3(0, -9.8f, 0));
dynamicsWorld->setInternalTickCallback(myTickCallback);
```

4. Build and run the project to see the cube enemy spawn at the right of the screen, followed by it passing through the sphere and moving toward the left of the screen. When the enemy goes offscreen, it will be looped around to the right of the screen, as shown in the following screenshot:

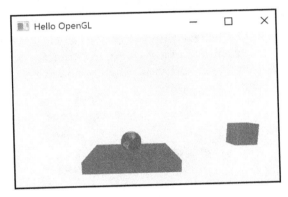

5. If we set the `collisionFlag` of the enemy to `KINEMATIC_OBJECT`, you will see that the enemy doesn't go through the sphere but pushes it off the ground, as follows:

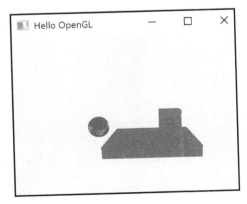

6. This is not what we want as we don't want the enemy to physically interact with any objects. Change the collision flag of the enemy back to NO_CONTACT_RESPONSE to amend this.

Checking collision

In the tick function, we need to check for collision between the sphere and the enemy, as well as the sphere and the ground. Follow these steps to do so:

1. To check the number of contacts between objects, we will use the getNumManifolds property of the dynamic world object. The manifold will contain information regarding all the contacts in the scene per update cycle.

2. We need to check whether the number of contacts is greater than zero. If it is, then we check which pairs of objects were in contact with each other. After updating the enemy object, add the following code to check for contact between the hero and the enemy:

```
int numManifolds = dynamicsWorld->getDispatcher()->
   getNumManifolds();

   for (int i = 0; i < numManifolds; i++) {

       btPersistentManifold *contactManifold = dynamicsWorld->
       getDispatcher()->getManifoldByIndexInternal(i);

       int numContacts = contactManifold->getNumContacts();

       if (numContacts > 0) {

           const btCollisionObject *objA = contactManifold->
           getBody0();
           const btCollisionObject *objB = contactManifold->
           getBody1();

           MeshRenderer* gModA = (MeshRenderer*)objA->
           getUserPointer();
           MeshRenderer* gModB = (MeshRenderer*)objB->
           getUserPointer();

               if ((gModA->name == "hero" && gModB->name ==
                   "enemy") || (gModA->name == "enemy" && gModB->
                   name == "hero")) {
                       printf("collision: %s with %s \n",
                       gModA->name, gModB->name);
```

```
                    if (gModB->name == "enemy") {
                        btTransform b(gModB->rigidBody-
                        >getWorldTransform());
                        b.setOrigin(btVector3(18, 1, 0));
                        gModB->rigidBody-
                        >setWorldTransform(b);
                        gModB->rigidBody->
                        getMotionState()-
                        >setWorldTransform(b);
                    }else {
                        btTransform a(gModA->rigidBody->
                        getWorldTransform());
                        a.setOrigin(btVector3(18, 1, 0));
                        gModA->rigidBody->
                        setWorldTransform(a);
                        gModA->rigidBody->
                        getMotionState()->
                        setWorldTransform(a);
                    }

                }

                if ((gModA->name == "hero" && gModB->name ==
                    "ground") || (gModA->name == "ground" &&
                    gModB->name == "hero")) {
                    printf("collision: %s with %s \n",
                    gModA->name, gModB->name);

                }
            }
        }
```

3. First, we get the number of contact manifolds or contact pairs. Then, for each contact manifold, we check whether the number of contacts is greater than zero. If it is greater than zero, then it means there has been a contact in the current update.

4. Then, we get both collision objects and assign them to `ObjA` and `ObjB`. After this, we get the user pointer for both objects and typecast it to `MeshRenderer` to access the name of the objects we assigned. When checking for contact between two objects, object A can be in contact with object B or the other way around. If there has been contact between the sphere and the enemy, we set the position of the enemy back to the right of the viewport. We also check for contact between the sphere and the ground. If there is contact, we just print out that there has been contact.

Adding keyboard controls

Let's add some keyboard controls so that we can interact with the sphere. We will set it so that, when we press the up key on the keyboard, the sphere jumps. We will add the jump feature by applying an impulse to the sphere. To do so, follow these steps:

1. First, we'll use GLFW, which has a keyboard callback function so that we can add interaction with the keyboard for the game. Before we begin with the `main()` function, we will set this keyboard callback function:

```
void updateKeyboard(GLFWwindow* window, int key, int scancode, int
action, int mods){

    if (glfwGetKey(window, GLFW_KEY_ESCAPE) == GLFW_PRESS) {
        glfwSetWindowShouldClose(window, true);
    }

    if (key == GLFW_KEY_UP && action == GLFW_PRESS) {
            if (grounded == true) {
                    grounded = false;
sphere->rigidBody->applyImpulse(btVector3(0.0f,
    100.0f, 0.0f), btVector3(0.0f, 0.0f, 0.0f));
                    printf("pressed up key \n");
            }
        }
}
```

The two main parameters that we are concerned with are the key and action. With key, we get which key is pressed, and with action, we can retrieve what action was performed on that key. In the function, we check whether the *Esc* key was pressed using the `glfwGetKey` function. If so, then we close the window using the `glfwSetWindowShouldClose` function by passing true as the second parameter.

To make the sphere jump, we check whether the up key was pressed. If it was, we create a new Boolean member variable called grounded, which describes a state if the sphere is touching the ground. If this is true, we set the Boolean value to false and apply an impulse of 100 units on the sphere's rigid body origin in the Y direction by calling the applyImpulse function of rigidbody.

2. In the tick function, before we get the number of manifolds, we set the grounded Boolean to false, as follows:

```
grounded = false;

int numManifolds = dynamicsWorld->getDispatcher()->
                    getNumManifolds();
```

3. We set the grounded Boolean value to true when there is contact between the sphere and the ground, as follows:

```
if ((gModA->name == "hero" && gModB->name == "ground") ||
    (gModA->name == "ground" && gModB->name == "hero")) {

//printf("collision: %s with %s \n", gModA->name, gModB->name);

    grounded = true;

}
```

4. In the main function, set updateKeyboard as the callback using glfwSetKeyCallback, as follows:

```
int main(int argc, char **argv) {
...
    glfwMakeContextCurrent(window);
    glfwSetKeyCallback(window, updateKeyboard);
    ...
}
```

5. Now, build and run the application. Press the up key to see the sphere jump, but only when it is grounded, as follows:

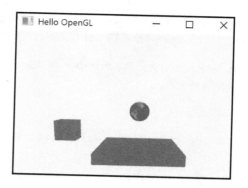

Game loop and scoring

Let's wrap this up by adding scoring and finishing the game loop:

1. Along with the grounded Boolean, add another Boolean and check for gameover. After doing this, add an int called score and initialize it to 0 at the top of the main.cpp file, as follows:

```
GLuint sphereTexture, groundTexture;

bool grounded = false;
bool gameover = true;
int score = 0;
```

2. Next, in the tick function, the enemy should only move when the game is not over. So we wrap the update for the position of the enemy inside an **if** statement to check whether or not the game is over. If the game is not over, then we update the position of the enemy, as follows:

```
void myTickCallback(btDynamicsWorld *dynamicsWorld, btScalar
timeStep) {

    if (!gameover) {

        // Get enemy transform
        btTransform t(enemy->rigidBody->getWorldTransform());
```

```
// Set enemy position

t.setOrigin(t.getOrigin() + btVector3(-15, 0, 0) *
timeStep);

// Check if offScreen

if (t.getOrigin().x() <= -18.0f) {

        t.setOrigin(btVector3(18, 1, 0));
        score++;
        label->setText("Score: " + std::to_string(score));

    }

    enemy->rigidBody->setWorldTransform(t);
    enemy->rigidBody->getMotionState()->setWorldTransform(t);

}
...
}
```

3. We also increment the score if the enemy goes beyond the left of the screen. Still in the tick function, if there is contact between the sphere and the enemy, we set the score to 0 and set gameover to true, as follows:

```
if ((gModA->name == "hero" && gModB->name == "enemy") ||
        (gModA->name == "enemy" && gModB->name ==
        "hero")) {

        if (gModB->name == "enemy") {
            btTransform b(gModB->rigidBody->
            getWorldTransform());
            b.setOrigin(btVector3(18, 1, 0));
            gModB->rigidBody->
            setWorldTransform(b);
            gModB->rigidBody->getMotionState()->
            setWorldTransform(b);
            }else {
            btTransform a(gModA->rigidBody->
            getWorldTransform());
            a.setOrigin(btVector3(18, 1, 0));
            gModA->rigidBody->
            setWorldTransform(a);
            gModA->rigidBody->getMotionState()->
            setWorldTransform(a);
            }
```

```
                  gameover = true;
                  score = 0;

         }
```

4. In the update keyboard function, when the up keyboard key is pressed, we check whether the game is over. If it is, we set the `gameover` Boolean to false, which will start the game. Now, when the player presses the up key again, the character will jump. This way, the same key can be used for starting the game and also making the character jump.

5. Make the required changes to the `updateKeyboard` function, as follows:

```
void updateKeyboard(GLFWwindow* window, int key, int scancode, int
action, int mods){

    if (glfwGetKey(window, GLFW_KEY_ESCAPE) == GLFW_PRESS) {
        glfwSetWindowShouldClose(window, true);
    }

    if (key == GLFW_KEY_UP && action == GLFW_PRESS) {

        if (gameover) {
            gameover = false;
        } else {
            if (grounded == true) {

                grounded = false;
sphere->rigidBody->applyImpulse(btVector3(0.0f, 100.0f, 0.0f),
    btVector3(0.0f, 0.0f, 0.0f));
                printf("pressed up key \n");
            }
        }
    }
}
```

6. Although we are calculating the score, the user still cannot see what the score is, so let's add text rendering to the game.

Text rendering

For rendering text, we will use a library called FreeType, load in the font, and read the characters from it. FreeType can load a popular font format called TrueType. TrueType fonts have a .ttf extension.

TTFs contain vector information called glyphs that can be used to store any data. One use case is, of course, to represent characters with them.

So, when we want to render a particular glyph, we load the character glyph by specifying its size; the character will be generated without there being a loss in quality.

 The source of the FreeType library can be downloaded from their website at https://www.freetype.org/ and the library can be built from it. The precompiled libraries can also be downloaded from https://github.com/ubawurinna/freetype-windows-binaries.

Let's add the library to our project. Since we are developing for the 64-bit OS, we are interested in the include directory and the win64 directory; they contain the freetype.lib and freetype.dll files for our version of the project:

1. Create a folder called freetype in your dependencies folder and extract the files into it, as follows:

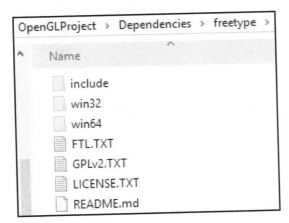

2. Open the project's properties and, under **C/C++** in **Additional Include Directory**, add the `freetype` include directory location, as follows:

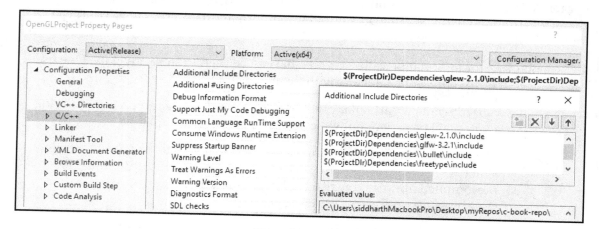

3. Under **Configuration Properties | Linker | General | Additional Library Directories**, add the freetype `win64` directory, as follows:

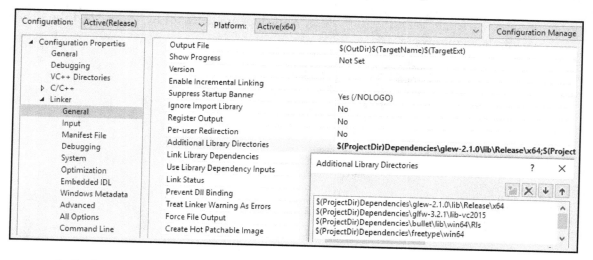

4. In the project directory, copy the `Freetype.dll` file from the `win64` directory and paste it here:

With the prep work out of the way, we can start working on the project.

5. Create a class called `TextRenderer`, as well as a file called `TextRenderer.h` and a file called `TextRenderer.cpp`. We will add the functionality for text rendering to these files. In `TextRenderer.h`, include the usual include headers for GL and glm as b, as follows:

```
#include <GL/glew.h>

#include "Dependencies/glm/glm/glm.hpp"
#include "Dependencies/glm/glm/gtc/matrix_transform.hpp"
#include "Dependencies/glm/glm/gtc/type_ptr.hpp"
```

6. Next, we will include the headers for `freetype.h`, as follows:

```
#include <ft2build.h>
#include FT_FREETYPE_H
```

7. The `FT_FREETYPE_H` macro just includes `freetype.h` in the `freetype` directory. Then, we will `include <map>` as we will have to map each character's location, size, and other information. We will also `include <string>` and pass a string into the class to be rendered, as follows:

```
#include <string>
```

8. For each glyph, we will need to keep track of certain properties. For this, we will create a `struct` called `Character`, as follows:

```
struct Character {
    GLuint      TextureID;  // Texture ID of each glyph texture
    glm::ivec2 Size;        // glyph Size
    glm::ivec2 Bearing;     // baseline to left/top of glyph
    GLuint      Advance;    // id to next glyph
};
```

For each glyph, we will store the texture ID of the texture we create for each character. We store the size of it, the bearing, which is the distance from the top left corner of the glyph from the baseline of the glyph, and the ID of the next glyph in the font file.

9. This is what a font file looks like when it has all the character glyphs in it:

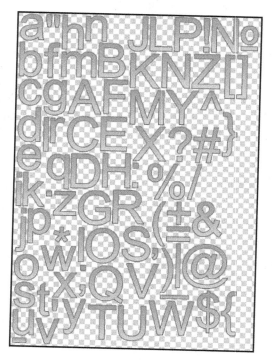

Information regarding each character is stored in relation to the character adjacent to it, as follows:

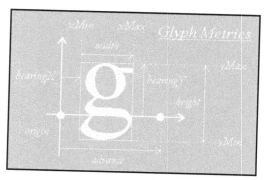

Each of these properties can be accessed on a per glyph basis after we load the font face of the `FT_Face` type. The width and height of each glyph can be accessed using the glyph property per font face, that is, `face->glyph` as `face->glyph->bitmap.width` and `face->glyph->bitmap.rows`.

The image data is available per glyph using the `bitmap.buffer` property, which we will be using when we create the texture for each glyph. The following code shows how all of this is implemented.

The next glyph in the font file can be accessed using the `advance.x` property of the glyph if the font is horizontally aligned.

 That's enough theory about the library. If you are interested in finding out more, the necessary documentation is available on FreeType's website: `https://www.freetype.org/freetype2/docs/tutorial/step2.html#section-1`.

Let's continue with the `TextRenderer.h` file and create the `TextRenderer` class, as follows:

```
class TextRenderer{

public:
    TextRenderer(std::string text, std::string font, int size,
        glm::vec3 color, GLuint  program);
    ~TextRenderer();

    void draw();
    void setPosition(glm::vec2 _position);
    void setText(std::string _text);

private:
    std::string text;
    GLfloat scale;
    glm::vec3 color;
    glm::vec2 position;

    GLuint VAO, VBO, program;
    std::map<GLchar, Character> Characters;

};
```

In the class under the public section, we add the constructor and destructor. In the constructor, we pass in the string we want to draw, the file we want to use, the size and color of the text we want to draw in, and pass in a shader program to use while drawing the font.

Then, we have the `draw` function to draw the text, a couple of setters to set the position, and a `setText` function to set a new string to draw if needed. In the private section, we have local variables for the text string, scale, color, and position. We also have member variables for VAO, VBO, and `program` so that we can draw the text string. At the end of the class, we create a map to store all the loaded characters and assign each GLchar to a character `struct` in the map. This is all we need to do for the `TextRenderer.h` file.

In the `TextRenderer.cpp` file, include the `TextRenderer.h` file at the top of the file and perform the following steps:

1. Add the `TextRenderer` constructor implementation, as follows:

```
TextRenderer::TextRenderer(std::string text, std::string font, int
size, glm::vec3 color, GLuint program){

}
```

In the constructor, we will add the functionally for loading all the characters and prep the class for drawing the text.

2. Let's initialize the local variables, as follows:

```
this->text = text;
this->color = color;
this->scale = 1.0;
this->program = program;
this->setPosition(position);
```

3. Next, we need to set the projection matrix. For text, we specify the orthographic projection since it doesn't have any depth, as follows:

```
glm::mat4 projection = glm::ortho(0.0f, static_cast<GLfloat>
                        (800), 0.0f, static_cast<GLfloat>(600));
glUseProgram(program);
glUniformMatrix4fv(glGetUniformLocation(program, "projection"),
    1, GL_FALSE, glm::value_ptr(projection));
```

The projection is created using the `glm::ortho` function, which takes origin x, window width, origin y, and window height as the parameters for creating the orthographic projection matrix. We will use the current program and pass the value for the projection matrix to a location called projection, and then pass this on to the shader. Since this value will never change, it is called and assigned once in the constructor.

4. Before we load the font itself, we have to initialize the FreeType library, as follows:

```
// FreeType
FT_Library ft;

// Initialise freetype
if (FT_Init_FreeType(&ft))
std::cout << "ERROR::FREETYPE: Could not init FreeType Library"
        << std::endl;
```

5. Now, we can load the font face itself, as follows:

```
// Load font
FT_Face face;
if (FT_New_Face(ft, font.c_str(), 0, &face))
    std::cout << "ERROR::FREETYPE: Failed to load font"
                << std::endl;
```

6. Now, set the font size in pixels and disable the byte alignment restriction. If we don't restrict the byte alignment, the font will be drawn jumbled, so don't forget to add this:

```
// Set size of glyphs
FT_Set_Pixel_Sizes(face, 0, size);

// Disable byte-alignment restriction
glPixelStorei(GL_UNPACK_ALIGNMENT, 1);
```

7. Then, we will load the first 128 characters into the font we loaded and create and assign the texture ID, size, bearing, and advance. After, we will store the font in the characters map, as follows:

```
for (GLubyte i = 0; i < 128; i++){

    // Load character glyph
    if (FT_Load_Char(face, i, FT_LOAD_RENDER)){
        std::cout << "ERROR::FREETYTPE: Failed to
                        load Glyph" << std::endl;

        continue;
```

```
        }

        // Generate texture
        GLuint texture;
        glGenTextures(1, &texture);
        glBindTexture(GL_TEXTURE_2D, texture);
        glTexImage2D(
                GL_TEXTURE_2D,
                0,
                GL_RED,
                face->glyph->bitmap.width,
                face->glyph->bitmap.rows,
                0,
                GL_RED,
                GL_UNSIGNED_BYTE,
                face->glyph->bitmap.buffer
                );

        // Set texture filtering options
        glTexParameteri(GL_TEXTURE_2D, GL_TEXTURE_WRAP_S,
        GL_CLAMP_TO_EDGE);
        glTexParameteri(GL_TEXTURE_2D, GL_TEXTURE_WRAP_T,
        GL_CLAMP_TO_EDGE);
        glTexParameteri(GL_TEXTURE_2D, GL_TEXTURE_MIN_FILTER,
        GL_LINEAR);
        glTexParameteri(GL_TEXTURE_2D, GL_TEXTURE_MAG_FILTER,
        GL_LINEAR);
        // Create a character
        Character character = {
                texture,
                glm::ivec2(face->glyph->bitmap.width,
                        face->glyph->bitmap.rows),
                glm::ivec2(face->glyph->bitmap_left,
          face->glyph->bitmap_top),
                face->glyph->advance.x
        };
        // Store character in characters map
        Characters.insert(std::pair<GLchar, Character>(i,
        character));
    }
```

8. Once the characters have been loaded, we can unbind the texture and destroy the font face and FreeType library, as follows:

```
glBindTexture(GL_TEXTURE_2D, 0);

// Destroy FreeType once we're finished
FT_Done_Face(face);
FT_Done_FreeType(ft);
```

9. Each character will be drawn as a texture on a separate quad, so set the VAO/VBO for a quad, create a position attribute, and enable it, as follows:

```
glGenVertexArrays(1, &VAO);
glGenBuffers(1, &VBO);

glBindVertexArray(VAO);
glBindBuffer(GL_ARRAY_BUFFER, VBO);
glBufferData(GL_ARRAY_BUFFER, sizeof(GLfloat) * 6 * 4, NULL,
    GL_DYNAMIC_DRAW);
glEnableVertexAttribArray(0);
glVertexAttribPointer(0, 4, GL_FLOAT, GL_FALSE, 4 *
    sizeof(GLfloat), 0);
```

10. Now, we need to unbind VBO and VAO, as follows:

```
glBindBuffer(GL_ARRAY_BUFFER, 0);
glBindVertexArray(0);
```

That's all for the constructor. Now, we can move on to the draw function. Let's take a look:

1. First, create the draw function's implementation, as follows:

```
void TextRenderer::draw(){
}
```

2. We will add the functionality for drawing to this function. First, we'll get the position where the text needs to start drawing, as follows:

```
glm::vec2 textPos = this->position;
```

3. Then, we have to enable blending. If we don't enable blending, the whole quad for the text will be colored instead of just the area where the text is present, as shown in the image on the left:

In the image on the left, where the S is supposed to be, we can see the whole quad colored in red, including the pixels where it is supposed to be transparent.

By enabling blending, we set the final color value as a pixel using the following equation:

$$Color_{final} = Color_{Source} * Alpha_{Source} + Color_{Destination} * 1 - Alpha_{Source}$$

Here, source color and source alpha are the color and alpha values of the text at a certain pixel location, while the destination color and alpha are the values of the color and alpha at the color buffer.

In this example, since we draw the text later, the destination color will be yellow, and the source color, which is the text, will be red. The destination alpha value is 1.0 while the yellow color is opaque. For the text, if we take a look at the S glyph, for example, within the S, which is the red area, it is opaque, but it is transparent.

Using this formula, let's calculate the final pixel color around the S where it is transparent using the following equation:

$$Color_{final} = (1.0f, 0.0f, 0.0f, 0.0f) * 0.0 + (1.0f, 1.0f, 0.0f, 1.0f) * (1.0f - 0.0f)$$
$$= (1.0f, 1.0f, 0.0f, 1.0f);$$

This is just the yellow background color.

Conversely, within the S glyph, it is not transparent, so the alpha value is 1 at that pixel location. So, when we apply the same formula, we get the final color, as follows:

$$Color_{final} = (1.0f, 0.0f, 0.0f, 1.0f) * 1.0 + (1.0f, 1.0f, 0.0f, 1.0f) * (1.0f - 1.0f)$$
$$= (1.0f, 0.0f, 0.0f, 1.0f)$$

This is just the red text color, as shown in the following diagram:

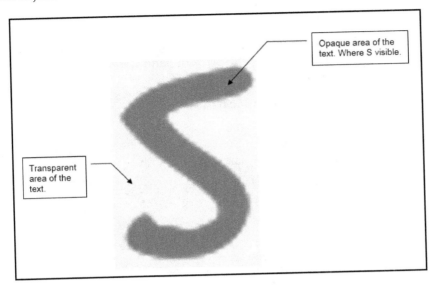

Let's see how this is implemented in practice.

4. The `blend` function is as follows:

```
glEnable(GL_BLEND);
```

Now, we need to set the source and destination blending factors, that is, GL_SRC_ALPHA. For the source pixel, we use its alpha value as-is, whereas, for the destination, we set the alpha to GL_ONE_MINUS_SRC_ALPHA, which is the source alpha minus one, as follows:

```
glBlendFunc(GL_SRC_ALPHA, GL_ONE_MINUS_SRC_ALPHA);
```

By default, the value source and destination values are added. You can subtract, add, and divide as well.

5. Now, we need to call the `glUSeProgram` function to set the program, set the text color to the uniform location, and set the default texture, as follows:

```
glUseProgram(program);
glUniform3f(glGetUniformLocation(program, "textColor"),
    this->color.x, this->color.y, this->color.z);
glActiveTexture(GL_TEXTURE0);
```

6. Next, we need to bind the VAO, as follows:

```
glBindVertexArray(VAO);
```

7. Let's go through all the characters in the text we want to draw and get their size, the bearing, so that we can set the position, and the texture ID of each glyph we want to draw, as follows:

```
std::string::const_iterator c;

for (c = text.begin(); c != text.end(); c++){

    Character ch = Characters[*c];

    GLfloat xpos = textPos.x + ch.Bearing.x * this->scale;
    GLfloat ypos = textPos.y - (ch.Size.y - ch.Bearing.y) *
    this->scale;

    GLfloat w = ch.Size.x * this->scale;
    GLfloat h = ch.Size.y * this->scale;
    // Per Character Update VBO
    GLfloat vertices[6][4] = {
            { xpos,     ypos + h,   0.0, 0.0 },
            { xpos,     ypos,       0.0, 1.0 },
            { xpos + w, ypos,       1.0, 1.0 },

            { xpos,     ypos + h,   0.0, 0.0 },
            { xpos + w, ypos,       1.0, 1.0 },
            { xpos + w, ypos + h,   1.0, 0.0 }
    };

    // Render glyph texture over quad
    glBindTexture(GL_TEXTURE_2D, ch.TextureID);
    // Update content of VBO memory
    glBindBuffer(GL_ARRAY_BUFFER, VBO);
    // Use glBufferSubData and not glBufferData
    glBufferSubData(GL_ARRAY_BUFFER, 0, sizeof(vertices),
    vertices);

    glBindBuffer(GL_ARRAY_BUFFER, 0);
    // Render quad
    glDrawArrays(GL_TRIANGLES, 0, 6);
    // Now advance cursors for next glyph (note that advance
    is number of 1/64 pixels)
    // Bitshift by 6 to get value in pixels (2^6 = 64 (divide
    amount of 1/64th pixels by 64 to get amount of pixels))
    textPos.x += (ch.Advance >> 6) * this->scale;
}
```

We will now bind the VBO and pass in the vertex data for all the quads to be drawn using glBufferSubData. Once bound, the quads are drawn using glDrawArrays and we pass in 6 for the number of vertices to be drawn.

Then, we calculate textPos.x, which will determine where the next glyph will be drawn. We get this distance by multiplying the advance of the current glyph by the scale and adding it to the current text position's x component. A bit shift of 6 is done to advance, to get the value in pixels.

8. At the end of the draw function, we unbind the vertex array and the texture, and then disable blending, as follows:

```
glBindVertexArray(0);
glBindTexture(GL_TEXTURE_2D, 0);

glDisable(GL_BLEND);
```

9. Finally, we add the implementation of the setPOsiton and setString functions, as follows:

```
void TextRenderer::setPosition(glm::vec2 _position){

    this->position = _position;
}


void TextRenderer::setText(std::string _text){
    this->text = _text;
}
```

We're finally done with the TextRenderer class. Now, let's learn how we can display the text in our game:

1. In the main.cpp file, includeTextRenderer.h at the top of the file and create a new object of the class called label, as follows:

```
#include "TextRenderer.h"

TextRenderer* label;
```

2. Create a new GLuint for the text shader program, as follows:

```
GLuint textProgram
```

3. Then, create the new shaded program for the text, as follows:

```
textProgram = shader.CreateProgram("Assets/Shaders/text.vs",
"Assets/Shaders/text.fs");
```

4. The `text.vs` and `text.fs` files are placed in the `Assets` directory under `Shaders.text.vs`, as follows:

```
#version 450 core
layout (location = 0) in vec4 vertex;
uniform mat4 projection;

out vec2 TexCoords;

void main(){
    gl_Position = projection * vec4(vertex.xy, 0.0, 1.0);
    TexCoords = vertex.zw;
}
```

We get the vertex position as an attribute and the projection matrix as a uniform. The texture coordinate is set in the main function and is sent out to the next shader stage. The position of the vertex of the quad is set by multiplying the local coordinates by the orthographic projection matrix in the `main()` function.

5. Next, we'll move on to the fragment shader, as follows:

```
#version 450 core

in vec2 TexCoords;

uniform sampler2D text;
uniform vec3 textColor;

out vec4 color;

void main(){
vec4 sampled = vec4(1.0, 1.0, 1.0, texture(text, TexCoords).r);
color = vec4(textColor, 1.0) * sampled;
}
```

We get the texture coordinate from the vertex shader and the texture and color as uniforms. A new out vec4 is created called color to send out color information. In the main() function, we create a new vec4 called sampled and store the r, g, and b values as 1. We also store the red color as the alpha value to draw only the opaque part of the text. Then, a new vec4 called color is created, in which the white color is replaced with the color we want the text to be drawn in, and we assign the color variable.

6. Let's continue with the text label implementation. After the addRigidBody function in the init function, initialize the label object, as follows:

```
label = new TextRenderer("Score: 0", "Assets/fonts/gooddog.ttf",
         64, glm::vec3(1.0f, 0.0f, 0.0f), textProgram);
    label->setPosition(glm::vec2(320.0f, 500.0f));
```

In the constructor, we set the string we want to render, pass in the location of the font file, and pass in the text height, the text color, and the text program. Then, we use the setPosition function to set the position of the text.

7. Next, in the tick function, where we update the score, we update the text as well, as follows:

```
if (t.getOrigin().x() <= -18.0f) {

    t.setOrigin(btVector3(18, 1, 0));
    score++;
    label->setText("Score: " + std::to_string(score));
}
```

8. In the tick function, we reset the string when the game is over, as follows:

```
gameover = true;
score = 0;
label->setText("Score: " + std::to_string(score));
```

9. In the render function, we call the draw function to draw the text, as follows:

```
void renderScene(float dt){

    glClear(GL_COLOR_BUFFER_BIT | GL_DEPTH_BUFFER_BIT);
    glClearColor(1.0, 1.0, 0.0, 1.0);

    // Draw Objects

    //light->draw();
```

```
        sphere->draw();
        enemy->draw();
        ground->draw();

        label->draw();
    }
```

Because of alpha blending, the text has to be drawn at the end, after all the other objects have been drawn.

10. Finally, make sure the font file has been added to the `Assets` folder under `Fonts`, as follows:

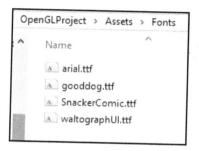

A few font files have been provided that you can experiment with. More free fonts can be downloaded from `https://www.1001freefonts.com/` and `https://www.dafont.com/`. Build and run the game to see the text being drawn and updated:

Adding lighting

Finally, let's add some lighting to the objects in the scene, just to make the objects more interesting to look at. We'll do this by allowing the light renderer to be drawn in the scene. Here, the light is originating from the center of this sphere. Using the position of the light source, we will calculate whether a pixel is lit or not, as follows:

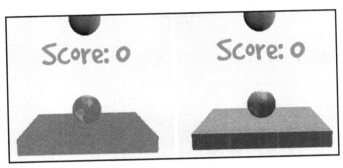

The picture on the left shows the scene unlit. In contrast, the scene on the right is lit with the earth sphere and the ground is affected by the light source. The surface that is facing the light is brightest, for example, at the top of the sphere. This creates a **Specular** at the top of the sphere. Since the surface is farther from/at an angle to the light source, those pixel values slowly diffuse. Then, there are surfaces that are not facing the light source at all, such as the side of the ground facing us. However, they are still not completely black as they are still being lit by the light from the source, which bounces around and becomes part of the ambient light. **Ambient, Diffuse,** and **Specular** become major parts of the lighting model when we wish to light up an object. Lighting models are used to simulate lighting in computer graphics because, unlike the real world, we are limited by the processing power of our hardware.

The formula for the final color of the pixel according to the Phong shading model is as follows:

$$C = ka* Lc+ Lc * max(0, n\ l) + ks * Lc * max(0, v\ r)\ p$$

Here, we have the following attributes:

- k_a is the ambient strength.
- L_c is the light color.
- n is the surface normal.
- l is the light direction.

- k_s is the specular strength.
- v is the view direction.
- r is the reflected light direction about the normal of the surface.
- p is the Phong exponent, which will determine how shiny a surface is.

For the **n, l, v** and **r** vectors, refer to the following diagram:

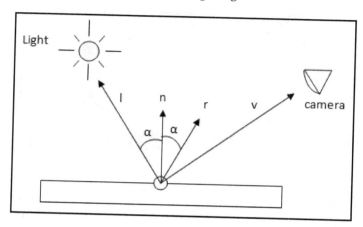

Let's look at how to implement this in practice:

1. All the lighting calculations are done in the fragment shader of the object, since this affects the final color of the object, depending on the light source and camera position. For each object to be lit, we also need to pass in the light color, diffuse, and specular strength. In the MeshRenderer.h file, change the constructor so that it takes the light source, diffuse, and specular strengths, as follows:

```
MeshRenderer(MeshType modelType, std::string _name, Camera *
    _camera, btRigidBody* _rigidBody, LightRenderer* _light, float
    _specularStrength, float _ambientStrength);
```

2. Include lightRenderer.h at the top of the file, as follows:

```
#include "LightRenderer.h"
```

3. In the private section of the class, add an object for LightRenderer and floats to store the ambient and specular strength, as follows:

```
GLuint vao, vbo, ebo, texture, program;
LightRenderer* light;
float ambientStrength, specularStrength;
```

4. In the `MeshRenderer.cpp` file, change the implementation of the constructor and assign the variables that were passed into the local variables, as follows:

```
MeshRenderer::MeshRenderer(MeshType modelType, std::string _name,
    Camera* _camera, btRigidBody* _rigidBody, LightRenderer* _light,
    float _specularStrength, float _ambientStrength) {
    name = _name;
    rigidBody = _rigidBody;
    camera = _camera;
    light = _light;
    ambientStrength = _ambientStrength;
    specularStrength = _specularStrength;
    ...
}
```

5. In the constructor, we also need to add a new normal attribute, as we will need the surface normal information for lighting calculations, as follows:

```
glEnableVertexAttribArray(0);
glVertexAttribPointer(0, 3, GL_FLOAT, GL_FALSE, sizeof(Vertex),
    (GLvoid*)0);

glEnableVertexAttribArray(1);
glVertexAttribPointer(1, 2, GL_FLOAT, GL_FALSE, sizeof(Vertex),
    (void*)(offsetof(Vertex, Vertex::texCoords)));
glEnableVertexAttribArray(2);
glVertexAttribPointer(2, 3, GL_FLOAT, GL_FALSE, sizeof(Vertex),
    (void*)(offsetof(Vertex, Vertex::normal)));
```

6. In the `Draw` function, we pass the camera position, light position, light color, specular strength, and ambient strength as uniforms to the shader, as follows:

```
// Set Texture
glBindTexture(GL_TEXTURE_2D, texture);

// Set Lighting
GLuint cameraPosLoc = glGetUniformLocation(program,
                        "cameraPos");
glUniform3f(cameraPosLoc, camera->getCameraPosition().x,
camera-> getCameraPosition().y, camera->getCameraPosition().z);

GLuint lightPosLoc = glGetUniformLocation(program, "lightPos");
glUniform3f(lightPosLoc, this->light->getPosition().x,
    this-> light->getPosition().y, this->light->getPosition().z);

GLuint lightColorLoc = glGetUniformLocation(program,
                        "lightColor");
glUniform3f(lightColorLoc, this->light->getColor().x,
```

```
                this-> light->getColor().y, this->light->getColor().z);

        GLuint specularStrengthLoc = glGetUniformLocation(program,
                                        "specularStrength");
        glUniform1f(specularStrengthLoc, specularStrength);

        GLuint ambientStrengthLoc = glGetUniformLocation(
                                program, "ambientStrength");
        glUniform1f(ambientStrengthLoc, ambientStrength);


        glBindVertexArray(vao);
        glDrawElements(GL_TRIANGLES, indices.size(),
            GL_UNSIGNED_INT, 0);
        glBindVertexArray(0);
```

7. We also need to create new vertex and fragment shaders for the effect to take place. Let's create a new vertex shader called `LitTexturedModel.vs`, as follows:

```
#version 450 core
layout (location = 0) in vec3 position;
layout (location = 1) in vec2 texCoord;
layout (location = 2) in vec3 normal;

out vec2 TexCoord;
out vec3 Normal;
out vec3 fragWorldPos;

uniform mat4 vp;
uniform mat4 model;

void main(){

    gl_Position = vp * model *vec4(position, 1.0);
    TexCoord = texCoord;
    fragWorldPos = vec3(model * vec4(position, 1.0));
    Normal = mat3(transpose(inverse(model))) * normal;
}
```

8. We add the new location layout in order to receive the normal attribute.

9. Create a new out `vec3` so that we can send the normal information to the fragment shader. We will also create a new out `vec3` to send the world coordinates of a fragment. In the `main()` function, we calculate the world position of the fragment by multiplying the local position by the world matrix and store it in the `fragWorldPos` variable. The normal is also converted into world space. Unlike how we multiplied the local position, the model matrix that's used to convert into the normal world space needs to be treated differently. The normal is multiplied by the inverse of the model matrix and is stored in the normal variable. That's all for the vertex shader. Now, let's look at `LitTexturedModel.fs`.

10. In the fragment shader, we get the texture coordinate, normal, and fragment world position. Next, we get the camera position, light position and color, specular and ambient strength uniforms, and the texture as uniform as well. The final pixel value will be stored in the out `vec4` called color, as follows:

```
#version 450 core

in vec2 TexCoord;
in vec3 Normal;
in vec3 fragWorldPos;

uniform vec3 cameraPos;
uniform vec3 lightPos;
uniform vec3 lightColor;

uniform float specularStrength;
uniform float ambientStrength;

// texture
uniform sampler2D Texture;

out vec4 color;
```

11. In the `main()` function of the shader, we add the lighting calculation, as shown in the following code:

```
void main(){
        vec3 norm = normalize(Normal);
        vec4 objColor = texture(Texture, TexCoord);

        //**ambient
        vec3 ambient = ambientStrength * lightColor;
        //**diffuse
        vec3 lightDir = normalize(lightPos - fragWorldPos);
        float diff = max(dot(norm, lightDir), 0.0);
```

```
vec3 diffuse = diff * lightColor;
//**specular
vec3 viewDir = normalize(cameraPos - fragWorldPos);
vec3 reflectionDir = reflect(-lightDir, norm);
float spec = pow(max(dot(viewDir,
            reflectionDir),0.0),128);
vec3 specular = specularStrength * spec * lightColor;
// lighting shading calculation
vec3 totalColor = (ambient + diffuse + specular) *
objColor.rgb;

color = vec4(totalColor, 1.0f);
}
```

12. We get the normal and object color first. Then, as per the formula equation, we calculate the ambient part of the equation by multiplying the ambient strength and light color and store it in a `vec3` called ambient. For the diffuse part of the equation, we calculate the light direction from the position of the pixel in the world space by subtracting the two positions. The resulting vector is normalized and saved in `vec3 lightDir`. Then, we get the dot product of the normal and light directions.

13. After this, we get the resultant value or 0, whichever is bigger, and store it in a float called `diff`. This is multiplied by the light color and stored in `vec3` to get the diffuse color. For the specular part of the equation, we calculate the view direction by subtracting the camera position from the fragment world position.

14. The resulting vector is normalized and stored in `vec3 specDir`. Then, the reflected light vector regarding the surface normal is calculated by using the reflect `glsl` intrinsic function and passing in the `viewDir` and surface normal.

15. Then, the dot product of the view and reflected vector is calculated. The bigger value of the calculated value and 0 is chosen. The resulting float value is raised to the power of 128. The value can be from *0 to 256*. The bigger the value, the shinier the object will appear. The specular value is calculated by multiplying the specular strength, the calculated spec value, and the light color stored in the specular `vec3`.

16. Finally, the total shading is calculated by adding the three ambient, diffuse, and specular values together and then multiplying this by the object color. The object color is a `vec4`, so we convert it into a `vec3`. The total color is assigned to the color variable by converting `totalColor` into a `vec4`. To implement this in the project, create a new shader program called `litTexturedShaderProgram`, as follows:

```
GLuint litTexturedShaderProgram;
Create the shader program and assign it to it in the init function
in main.cpp.
    litTexturedShaderProgram = shader.CreateProgram(
                        "Assets/Shaders/LitTexturedModel.vs",
"Assets/Shaders/LitTexturedModel.fs");
```

17. In the add `rigidBody` function, change the shaders for the sphere, ground, and enemy, as follows:

```
// Sphere Rigid Body

btCollisionShape* sphereShape = new btSphereShape(1);
btDefaultMotionState* sphereMotionState = new
    btDefaultMotionState(btTransform(btQuaternion(0, 0, 0, 1),
    btVector3(0, 0.5, 0)));

btScalar mass = 13.0f;
btVector3 sphereInertia(0, 0, 0);
sphereShape->calculateLocalInertia(mass, sphereInertia);

btRigidBody::btRigidBodyConstructionInfo
    sphereRigidBodyCI(mass, sphereMotionState, sphereShape,
    sphereInertia);

btRigidBody* sphereRigidBody = new btRigidBody
                        (sphereRigidBodyCI);

sphereRigidBody->setFriction(1.0f);
sphereRigidBody->setRestitution(0.0f);

sphereRigidBody->setActivationState(DISABLE_DEACTIVATION);

dynamicsWorld->addRigidBody(sphereRigidBody);

// Sphere Mesh

sphere = new MeshRenderer(MeshType::kSphere, "hero",
        camera, sphereRigidBody, light, 0.1f, 0.5f);
sphere->setProgram(litTexturedShaderProgram);
```

```cpp
sphere->setTexture(sphereTexture);
sphere->setScale(glm::vec3(1.0f));

sphereRigidBody->setUserPointer(sphere);

// Ground Rigid body

btCollisionShape* groundShape = new btBoxShape(btVector3(4.0f,
                      0.5f, 4.0f));
btDefaultMotionState* groundMotionState = new
  btDefaultMotionState(btTransform(btQuaternion(0, 0, 0, 1),
   btVector3(0, -1.0f, 0)));

btRigidBody::btRigidBodyConstructionInfo
   groundRigidBodyCI(0.0f, groundMotionState, groundShape,
   btVector3(0, 0, 0));

btRigidBody* groundRigidBody = new btRigidBody
                            (groundRigidBodyCI);

groundRigidBody->setFriction(1.0);
groundRigidBody->setRestitution(0.0);

groundRigidBody->setCollisionFlags(
   btCollisionObject::CF_STATIC_OBJECT);

dynamicsWorld->addRigidBody(groundRigidBody);

// Ground Mesh
ground = new MeshRenderer(MeshType::kCube, "ground",
        camera, groundRigidBody, light, 0.1f, 0.5f);
ground->setProgram(litTexturedShaderProgram);
ground->setTexture(groundTexture);
ground->setScale(glm::vec3(4.0f, 0.5f, 4.0f));

groundRigidBody->setUserPointer(ground);

// Enemy Rigid body

btCollisionShape* shape = new btBoxShape(btVector3(1.0f,
                      1.0f, 1.0f));
btDefaultMotionState* motionState = new btDefaultMotionState(
    btTransform(btQuaternion(0, 0, 0, 1),
    btVector3(18.0, 1.0f, 0)));
btRigidBody::btRigidBodyConstructionInfo rbCI(0.0f,
   motionState, shape, btVector3(0.0f, 0.0f, 0.0f));

btRigidBody* rb = new btRigidBody(rbCI);
```

```
rb->setFriction(1.0);
rb->setRestitution(0.0);

//rb->setCollisionFlags(btCollisionObject::CF_KINEMATIC_OBJECT);

rb->setCollisionFlags(btCollisionObject::CF_NO_CONTACT_RESPONSE);

dynamicsWorld->addRigidBody(rb);

// Enemy Mesh
enemy = new MeshRenderer(MeshType::kCube, "enemy",
        camera, rb, light, 0.1f, 0.5f);
enemy->setProgram(litTexturedShaderProgram);
enemy->setTexture(groundTexture);
enemy->setScale(glm::vec3(1.0f, 1.0f, 1.0f));

rb->setUserPointer(enemy);
```

18. Build and run the project to see the lighting shader take effect:

 As an exercise, try adding a texture to the background, just like we did in the SFML game.

Summary

In this chapter, we saw how we can add collision detection between the game objects, and then we finished the game loop by adding controls and scoring. Using the font loading library FreeType, we loaded the TrueType font into our game to add scoring text to the game. Finally, to top it all off, we added lighting to the scene by adding the Phong lighting model to the objects.

There is still a lot that can be added graphically to add more realism to our game, such as framebuffers that add postprocessing effects. We could also add particle effects such as dust and rain. To find out more, I would highly recommend `learnopengl.com`, as it is an amazing source if you wish to learn more about OpenGL.

In the next chapter, we will start exploring the Vulkan Rendering API and look at how it is different from OpenGL.

Section 4: Rendering 3D Objects with Vulkan

4

Using the knowledge of 3D graphics programming that we gained in the previous section, we can now build on it to develop a basic project with Vulkan. OpenGL is a high-level graphics library. There are a lot things that OpenGL does in the background that the user is generally not aware of. With Vulkan, we will see the inner workings of a graphics library. We will see the why and the how of creating SwapChains, image views, renderpasses, Framebuffers, command buffers, as well as rendering and presenting objects to a scene.

The following chapters are in this section:

Getting Started with Vulkan

9

In the previous three chapters, we did our rendering using OpenGL. Although OpenGL is good for developing prototypes and getting your rendering going faster, it does have its weaknesses. For one, OpenGL is very driver-dependent, which makes it slower and less predictable when it comes to performance, which is why we prefer Vulkan for rendering.

In this chapter, we will cover the following topics:

- About Vulkan
- Configuring Visual Studio
- Vulkan validation layers and extensions
- Vulkan instances
- The Vulkan Context class
- Creating the window surface
- Picking a physical device and creating a logical device

About Vulkan

With OpenGL, developers have to depend on vendors such as NVIDIA, AMD, and Intel to release appropriate drivers so that they can increase the performance of their games before they are released. This is only possible if the developer is working closely with the vendor. If not, the vendor will only be able to release optimized drivers after the release of the game, and it could take a couple of days to release the new drivers.

Furthermore, if you want to port your PC game to a mobile platform and you are using OpenGL as your renderer, you will need to port the renderer to OpenGLES, which is a subset of OpenGL, where the ES stands for Embedded Systems. Although there are a lot of similarities between OpenGL and OpenGLES, there is still additional work to be done to get it to work on other platforms. To alleviate these issues, Vulkan was introduced. Vulkan gives the developer more control by reducing driver impact and providing explicit developer control to make the game perform better.

Vulkan has been developed from the ground up and therefore is not backward compatible with OpenGL. When using Vulkan, you have complete access to the GPU.

With complete GPU access, you also have complete responsibility for implementing the rendering API. Consequently, the downside of using Vulkan is that you have to specify everything when you're developing with it.

All in all, this makes Vulkan a very verbose API where you have to specify everything. However, this also makes it easy to create extensions of the API specifications for Vulkan when GPUs add newer features.

Configuring Visual Studio

Vulkan is just a rendering API, so we need to create a window and do math. For both, we will use GLFW and GLM, like we did when we created an OpenGL project. To do this, follow these steps:

1. Create a new Visual Studio C++ project and call it `VulkanProject`.
2. Copy the `GLFW` and `GLM` folders from the OpenGL project and place them inside the `VulkanProject` folder, under a folder named `Dependencies`.
3. Download the Vulkan SDK. Go to `https://vulkan.lunarg.com/sdk/home` and download the Windows version of the SDK, as shown in the following screenshot:

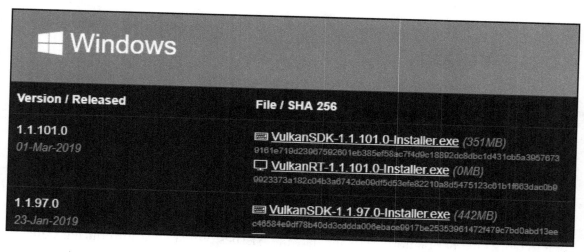

4. Install the SDK, as shown in the following screenshot:

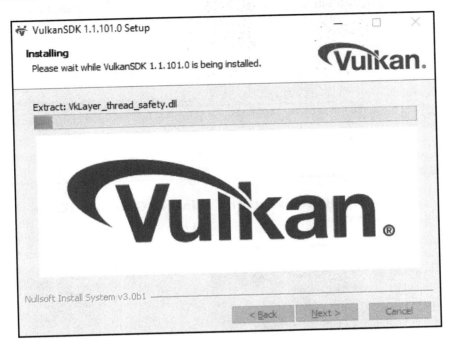

5. In the `Dependencies` directory, create a new folder called `Vulkan`. Copy and paste the `Lib` and include the folder from the Vulkan SDK folder in `C:\` drive, as shown in the following screenshot:

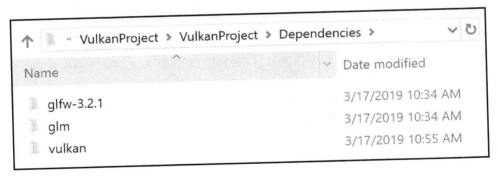

6. In the Visual Studio project, create a new blank `source.cpp` file. Open up the **Vulkan Project properties** and add the `include` directory to **C/C+ | General | Additional Include Directory**.

7. Make sure that **All Configurations** and **All Platforms** are selected in the **Configuration** and **Platform** drop-down lists, as shown in the following screenshot:

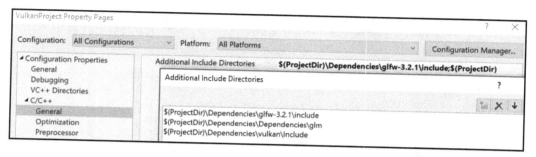

8. Add the **Library Directories** under the **Linker | General** section, as shown in the following screenshot:

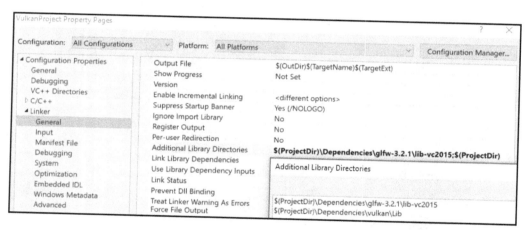

9. In **Linker | Input**, set the libraries that you want to use, as shown in the following screenshot:

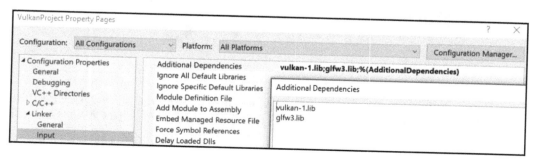

With this prep work out of the way, let's check whether our window creation works properly:

1. In source.cpp, add the following code:

```
#defineGLFW_INCLUDE_VULKAN
#include<GLFW/glfw3.h>

int main() {

    glfwInit();

    glfwWindowHint(GLFW_CLIENT_API, GLFW_NO_API);
    glfwWindowHint(GLFW_RESIZABLE, GLFW_FALSE);

    GLFWwindow* window = glfwCreateWindow(1280, 720, "HELLO VULKAN
", nullptr, nullptr);

    while (!glfwWindowShouldClose(window)) {


        glfwPollEvents();
    }

    glfwDestroyWindow(window);
    glfwTerminate();

    return 0;
}
```

First, we include glfw3.h and ask GLFW to include some Vulkan-related headers. Then, in the main function, we initialize GLFW by calling glfwInit(). Then, we call the glfwWindowHint functions. The first glfwWindowHint function doesn't create the OpenGL context since it is created by Glfw by default. In the next function, we disable resizing for the window we are about to create.

Then, we create the 1,280 x 720 window in a similar way to when we created the window in the OpenGL project. We create a while loop that checks whether the window should be closed. If the window doesn't need to be closed, we will poll the system events. Once this is done, we will destroy the window, terminate glfw, and return 0.

2. This should give us a window to work with. Run the application in **debug** mode as an **x64** executable to see the window being displayed and saying **HELLO VULKAN**, as shown in the following screenshot:

Vulkan validation layers and extensions

Before we jump into creating the Vulkan application, we have to check for application validation layers and extensions. Let's go over these in more detail:

- **Validation layers**: Since so much control is given to developers, it is also possible for the developers to implement the Vulkan applications in an incorrect manner. The Vulkan validation layers check for such errors and tell the developer that they are doing something wrong and need to fix it.
- **Extensions**: Over the course of the development of the Vulkan API, new features may be introduced to newer GPUs. To keep Vulkan up to date, we need to extend its functionality by adding extensions.

One example of this is the introduction of Ray Tracing in the RTX series of GPUs. In Vulkan, a new extension was created to support this change in the hardware by NVIDIA, that is, `Vk_NV_ray_tracing`. If our game uses this extension, we can check whether the hardware supports it.

Similar extensions can be added and checked at the application level as well. One such extension is the Debug report extension, which we can generate if something goes wrong when we're implementing Vulkan. Our first class will add this functionality to the application to check for application validation layers and extensions.

Let's start creating our first class. Create a new class called `AppValidationLayersAndExtensions`. In `AppValidationLayersAndExtensions.h`, add the following code:

```
#pragmaonce

#include<vulkan\vulkan.h>
#include<vector>
#include<iostream>
```

```cpp
#defineGLFW_INCLUDE_VULKAN
#include<GLFW\glfw3.h>

classAppValidationLayersAndExtensions {
public:
   AppValidationLayersAndExtensions();
   ~AppValidationLayersAndExtensions();

   const std::vector<constchar*> requiredValidationLayers = {
         "VK_LAYER_LUNARG_standard_validation"
   };

   bool checkValidationLayerSupport();
   std::vector<constchar*>getRequiredExtensions
     (boolisValidationLayersEnabled);


   // Debug Callback
   VkDebugReportCallbackEXT callback;

   void setupDebugCallback(boolisValidationLayersEnabled,
      VkInstancevkInstance);
   void destroy(VkInstanceinstance, boolisValidationLayersEnabled);


   // Callback

 * pCreateInfo, VkResultcreateDebugReportCallbackEXT(
        VkInstanceinstance,
        constVkDebugReportCallbackCreateInfoEXT
        constVkAllocationCallbacks* pAllocator,
        VkDebugReportCallbackEXT* pCallback) {

          auto func = (PFN_vkCreateDebugReportCallbackEXT)
                    vkGetInstanceProcAddr(instance,
                    "vkCreateDebugReportCallbackEXT");

          if (func != nullptr) {
               return func(instance, pCreateInfo, pAllocator, pCallback);
          }
          else {
               returnVK_ERROR_EXTENSION_NOT_PRESENT;
          }

   }

   void DestroyDebugReportCallbackEXT(
        VkInstanceinstance,
```

```
    VkDebugReportCallbackEXTcallback,
    constVkAllocationCallbacks* pAllocator) {

    auto func = (PFN_vkDestroyDebugReportCallbackEXT)
            vkGetInstanceProcAddr(instance,
            "vkDestroyDebugReportCallbackEXT");
    if (func != nullptr) {
        func(instance, callback, pAllocator);
    }
}

};
```

We include `vulkan.h`, `iostream`, `vector`, and `glfw`. Then, we create a vector called `requiredValidationLayers`; this is where we pass `VK_LAYER_LUNARG _standard_validation`. For our application, we will need the standard validation layer, which has all the validation layers in it. If we only need specific validation layers, then we can specify them individually as well. Next, we create two functions: one for checking the support for validation layers and one for getting the required extensions.

To generate a report in case an error occurs, we need a debug callback. We will add two functions to it: one to set up the debug callback and one to destroy it. These functions will call the `debug`, `create`, and `destroy` functions; they will call `vkGetInstanceProcAddr` to get the pointers for the `vkCreateDebugReportCallbackEXT` and `vkDestroyDebugReportCallbackEXT` pointer functions so that we can call them.

It would be better if it were less confusing to generate a debug report, but unfortunately, this is how it must be done. However, we only have to do this once. Let's move on to implementing `AppValidationLayersAndExtentions.cpp`:

1. First, we add the constructor and destructor, as follows:

```
AppValidationLayersAndExtensions::AppValidationLayersAndExtensions(){}


AppValidationLayersAndExtensions::~AppValidationLayersAndExtensions(){}
Then we add the implementation to checkValidationLayerSupport().

bool AppValidationLayersAndExtensions::checkValidationLayerSupport() {

    uint32_t layerCount;

    // Get count of validation layers available
    vkEnumerateInstanceLayerProperties(&layerCount, nullptr);

    // Get the available validation layers names
```

```
std::vector<VkLayerProperties>availableLayers(layerCount);
vkEnumerateInstanceLayerProperties(&layerCount,
availableLayers.data());

for (const char* layerName : requiredValidationLayers) { //layers we
require

        // boolean to check if the layer was found
        bool layerFound = false;

        for (const auto& layerproperties : availableLayers) {

                // If layer is found set the layar found boolean to true
                if (strcmp(layerName, layerproperties.layerName) == 0) {
                        layerFound = true;
                        break;
                }
        }

        if (!layerFound) {
                return false;
        }

        return true;

    }

}
```

To check the supported validation layers, call the vkEnumerateInstanceLayerProperties function twice. We call it the first time to get the number of validation layers that are available. Once we have the count, we call it again to populate it with the names of the layers.

We create an int called layerCount and pass it in the first time we call vkEnumerateInstanceLayerProperties. The function takes two parameters: the first is the count and the second is initially kept null. Once the function is called, we will know how many validation layers are available. For the names of the layers, we create a new vector called availableLayers of the VkLayerProperties type and initialize it with layerCount. Then, the function is called again, and this time we pass in layerCount and the vector as parameters to store the information. After, we make a check between the required layers and the available layers. If the validation layer was found, the function will return true. If not, it will return false.

2. Next, we need to add the `getRequiredInstanceExtentions` function, as follows:

```
std::vector<constchar*>AppValidationLayersAndExtensions::getRequire
dExtensions(boolisValidationLayersEnabled) {

    uint32_t glfwExtensionCount = 0;
    constchar** glfwExtensions;

    // Get extensions
    glfwExtensions = glfwGetRequiredInstanceExtensions
                        (&glfwExtensionCount);

    std::vector<constchar*>extensions(glfwExtensions, glfwExtensions
      + glfwExtensionCount);

    //debug report extention is added.

    if (isValidationLayersEnabled) {
        extensions.push_back("VK_EXT_debug_report");
    }

    return extensions;
}
```

The `getRequiredInstanceExtensions` phrase will get all the extensions that are supported by GLFW. It takes a Boolean to check whether the validation layers are enabled and returns a vector with the names of the supported extensions. In this function, we create a `unint32_t` called `glfwExtensionCount` and a `const char` for storing the names of the extensions. We call `glfwGetRequiredExtentions`, pass in `glfwExtentionCount`, and set it so that it's equal to `glfwExtensions`. This will store all the required extensions in `glfwExtensions`.

We create a new extensions vector and store the `glfwExtention` names. If we have enabled the validation layer, then we can add an additional extension layer called `VK_EXT_debug_report`, which is the extension for generating a debug report. This extension vector is returned at the end of the function.

3. Then, we add the debug report callback function, which will generate a report message whenever there is an error, as follows:

```
staticVKAPI_ATTRVkBool32VKAPI_CALL debugCallback(
  VkDebugReportFlagsEXTflags,
  VkDebugReportObjectTypeEXTobjExt,
  uint64_tobj,
```

```
size_tlocation,
int32_tcode,
constchar* layerPrefix,
constchar* msg,
void* userData) {

    std::cerr <<"validation layer: "<<msg<< std::endl << std::endl;

    returnfalse;

}
```

4. Next, we need to create the `setupDebugCallback` function, which will call the `createDebugReportCallbackExt` function, as follows:

```
voidAppValidationLayersAndExtensions::setupDebugCallback(boolisVali
dationLayersEnabled, VkInstancevkInstance) {

    if (!isValidationLayersEnabled) {
        return;
    }

    printf("setup call back \n");

    VkDebugReportCallbackCreateInfoEXT info = {};

    info.sType = VK_STRUCTURE_TYPE_DEBUG_REPORT
                _CALLBACK_CREATE_INFO_EXT;
    info.flags = VK_DEBUG_REPORT_ERROR_BIT_EXT |
                VK_DEBUG_REPORT_WARNING_BIT_EXT;
    info.pfnCallback = debugCallback; // callback function

    if (createDebugReportCallbackEXT(vkInstance, &info, nullptr,
      &callback) != VK_SUCCESS) {

        throw std::runtime_error("failed to set debug callback!");

    }

}
```

This function takes a Boolean, which will check that the validation layer is enabled. It also takes a Vulkan instance, which we will create after this class.

When creating a Vulkan object, we usually have to populate a struct with the required parameters. So, to create DebugReportCallback, we have to populate the VkDebugReportCallbackCreateInfoExt struct first. In the struct, we pass in sType, which specifies the structure type. We also pass in any flags for error and warning reporting. Finally, we pass in the callback function itself. Then, we call the createDebugReportCallbackExt function and pass in the instance, the struct, a null pointer for memory allocation, and the callback function. Even though we pass in a null pointer for memory allocation, Vulkan will take care of memory allocation by itself. This function is available if you have a memory allocation function of your own.

5. Now, let's create the destroy function so that we can destroy the debug report callback function, as follows:

```
voidAppValidationLayersAndExtensions::destroy(VkInstanceinstance,
boolisValidationLayersEnabled) {

    if (isValidationLayersEnabled) {
        DestroyDebugReportCallbackEXT(instance, callback,
nullptr);
    }

}
```

Vulkan instances

To use the AppValidationLayerAndExtension class, we have to create a Vulkan instance. To do so, follow these steps:

1. We will create another class called VulkanInstance. In VulkanInstance.h, add the following code:

```
#pragmaonce
#include<vulkan\vulkan.h>

#include"AppValidationLayersAndExtensions.h"


classVulkanInstance
{
public:
    VulkanInstance();
    ~VulkanInstance();
```

```
VkInstance vkInstance;

void createAppAndVkInstance(,boolenableValidationLayers
    AppValidationLayersAndExtentions *valLayersAndExtentions);

};
```

We're including `vulkan.h` and `AppValidationLayersAndExtentions.h` since we will need the required validation layers and extensions when we create the Vulkan instance. We add the constructor, destructor, and instance of `VkInstance`, as well as a function called `ceeateAppAndVkInstance`. This function takes a Boolean that checks whether the validation layers are enabled, as well as `AppValidationLayersAndExtentions`. That's it for the header.

2. In the `.cpp` file, add the following code:

```
#include"VulkanInstance.h"

VulkanInstance::VulkanInstance(){}

VulkanInstance::~VulkanInstance(){}
```

3. Then add the `createAppAndVkInstance` function, which will allow us to create the Vulkan instance, as follows:

```
voidVulkanInstance::createAppAndVkInstance(boolenableValidationLaye
rs, AppValidationLayersAndExtensions *valLayersAndExtensions) {

    // links the application to the Vulkan library

    VkApplicationInfo appInfo = {};
    appInfo.sType = VK_STRUCTURE_TYPE_APPLICATION_INFO;
    appInfo.pApplicationName = "Hello Vulkan";
    appInfo.applicationVersion = VK_MAKE_VERSION(1, 0, 0);
    appInfo.pEngineName = "SidTechEngine";
    appInfo.engineVersion = VK_MAKE_VERSION(1, 0, 0);
    appInfo.apiVersion = VK_API_VERSION_1_0;


    VkInstanceCreateInfo vkInstanceInfo = {};
    vkInstanceInfo.sType = VK_STRUCTURE_TYPE_INSTANCE_CREATE_INFO;
    vkInstanceInfo.pApplicationInfo = &appInfo;

    // specify extensions and validation layers
    // these are global meaning they are applicable to whole program
       not just the device
```

```
    auto extensions = valLayersAndExtentions->
                 getRequiredExtensions(enableValidationLayers);

    vkInstanceInfo.enabledExtensionCount = static_cast<uint32_t>
        (extensions.size());;
    vkInstanceInfo.ppEnabledExtensionNames = extensions.data();


    if (enableValidationLayers) {
      vkInstanceInfo.enabledLayerCount = static_cast<uint32_t>
      (valLayersAndExtentions->requiredValidationLayers.size());
      vkInstanceInfo.ppEnabledLayerNames =
      valLayersAndExtentions->requiredValidationLayers.data();
    }
    else {
        vkInstanceInfo.enabledLayerCount = 0;
    }
  if (vkCreateInstance(&vkInstanceInfo, nullptr, &vkInstance) !=
  VK_SUCCESS) {
    throw std::runtime_error("failed to create vkInstance ");
  }
    }
```

In the preceding function, we have to populate `VkApplicationInfostruct`, which will be required when we create `VkInstance`. Then, we create the `appInfo` struct. Here, the first parameter we specify is the `struct` type, which is of the `VK_STRUCTURE_TYPE_APPLICATION_INFO` type. The next parameter is the application name itself and is where we specify the application version, which is 1.0. Then, we specify the engine name and version. Finally, we specify the Vulkan API version to use.

Once the application `struct` has been populated, we can create the `vkInstanceCreateInfo` struct, which will create the Vulkan instance. In the struct instance we created – just like all the structs before this – we have to specify the struct with the `struct` type, which is `VK_STRUCTURE_TYPE_INSTANCE_CREATE_INFO`.

Then, we have to pass in the application info struct. We have to specify the Vulkan extension and validation layers and counts. This information is retrieved from the `AppValidationLayersAndExtensions` class. The validation layers are only enabled if the class is in debug mode; otherwise, it is not enabled.

Now, we can create the Vulkan instance by calling the `vkCreateInstance` function. This takes three parameters: the create info instance, an allocator, and the instance variable that's used to store the Vulkan instance. For allocation, we specify `nullptr` and let Vulkan take care of memory allocation. If the Vulkan instance wasn't created, a runtime error will be printed to the console to say that the function failed to create the Vulkan instance.

In order to use this `ValidationAndExtensions` class and the Vulkan instance class, we will create a new Singleton class called `VulkanContext`. We're doing this because we'll need access to some of the Vulkan objects in this class when we create our `ObjectRenderer`.

The Vulkan Context class

The Vulkan Context class will include all the functionality we need so that we can create our Vulkan renderer. In this class, we will create the validation layer, create the Vulkan application and instance, select the GPU we want to use, create the swapchain, create render targets, create the render pass, and add the command buffers so that we can send our draw commands to the GPU.

We will also add two new functions: `drawBegin` and `drawEnd`. In the `drawBegin` function, we will add the functionality for the preparation stages of drawing. The `drawEnd` function will be called after we have drawn an object and prepared it so that it can be presented to the viewport.

Create a new `.h` class and `.cpp` file. In the `.h` file, include the following code:

```
#defineGLFW_INCLUDE_VULKAN
#include<GLFW\glfw3.h>

#include<vulkan\vulkan.h>

#include"AppValidationLayersAndExtensions.h"
#include"VulkanInstance.h"
```

Next, we will create a Boolean called `isValidationLayersEnabled`. This will be set to `true` if the application is running in **debug** mode and `false` if it's running in **release** mode:

```
#ifdef _DEBUG
boolconstbool isValidationLayersEnabled = true;
#else
constbool isValidationLayersEnabled = false;
#endif
```

Next, we create the class itself, as follows:

```
classVulkanContext {

public:
staticVulkanContextn* instance;
```

```
staticVulkanContext* getInstance();

    ~VulkanContext();

    void initVulkan();


private:

    // My Classes
    AppValidationLayersAndExtensions *valLayersAndExt;
    VulkanInstance* vInstance;


};
```

In the `public` section, we create a static instance and the `getInstance` variable and function, which sets and gets the instance of this class. We add the destructor and add an `initVulkan` function, which will be used to initialize the Vulkan context. In the `private` section, we create an instance of the `AppValidationLayersAndExtentions` and `VulkanInstance` classes. In the `VulkanContext.cpp` file, we set the instance variable to null, and, in the `getInstance` function, we check whether the instance was created. If it was not created, we create a new instance, return it, and add the destructor:

```
#include"VulkanContext.h"

VulkanContext* VulkanContext::instance = NULL;


VulkanContext* VulkanContext::getInstance() {

    if (!instance) {
         instance = newVulkanContext();
    }
    return instance;
}

VulkanContext::~VulkanContext(){
```

Then, we add the functionality for the `initVulkan` function, as follows:

```
voidVulkanContext::initVulkan() {


    // Validation and Extension Layers
    valLayersAndExt = newAppValidationLayersAndExtensions();
```

```
if (isValidationLayersEnabled && !valLayersAndExt->
  checkValidationLayerSupport()) {
    throw std::runtime_error("Validation Layers
      Not Available !");
}

// Create App And Vulkan Instance()
vInstance = newVulkanInstance();
vInstance->createAppAndVkInstance(isValidationLayersEnabled,
  valLayersAndExt);

// Debug CallBack
valLayersAndExt->setupDebugCallback(isValidationLayersEnabled,
  vInstance->vkInstance);



}
```

First, we create a new `AppValidationLayersAndExtensions` instance. Then, we check whether the validation layers are enabled and check whether the validation layers are supported. If `ValidationLayers` is not available, a runtime error is sent out, saying that the validation layers are not available.

If the validation layers are supported, a new instance of the `VulkanInstance` class is created and the `createAppAndVkInstance` function is called, which creates a new `vkInstance`.

Once this is complete, we call the `setupDebugCallBack` function by passing in the Boolean and `vkInstance`. In the `source.cpp` file, include the `VulkanContext.h` file and call `initVulkan` after the window is created, as follows:

```
#defineGLFW_INCLUDE_VULKAN
#include<GLFW/glfw3.h>

#include"VulkanContext.h"

int main() {

  glfwInit();

  glfwWindowHint(GLFW_CLIENT_API, GLFW_NO_API);
  glfwWindowHint(GLFW_RESIZABLE, GLFW_FALSE);

  GLFWwindow* window = glfwCreateWindow(1280, 720, "HELLO VULKAN ",
                    nullptr, nullptr);

  VulkanContext::getInstance()->initVulkan();
```

```
while (!glfwWindowShouldClose(window)) {

    glfwPollEvents();
}

glfwDestroyWindow(window);
glfwTerminate();

return 0;
}
```

Hopefully, you won't get any errors in the console window when you build and run the application. If you do get errors, go through each line of code and make sure there are no spelling mistakes:

```
setup call back
```

Creating the window surface

We need an interface for the window we created for the current platform so that we can present the images we will render. We use the VKSurfaceKHR property to get access to the window surface. To store the surface information that the OS supports, we will call the glfw function, glfwCreateWindowSurface, to create the surface that's supported by the OS.

In VulkanContext.h, add a new variable of the VkSurfaceKHR type called surface, as follows:

```
private:

    //surface
    VkSurfaceKHR surface;
```

Since we need access to the window instance we created in source.cpp, change the initVulkan function so that it accepts a GLFWwindow, as follows:

```
void initVulkan(GLFWwindow* window);
```

In `VulkanContext.cpp`, change the `initVulkan` implementation as follows and call the `glfwCreateWindowSurface` function, which takes in the Vulkan instance and the window. Next, pass in `null` for the allocator and the surface to create the surface object:

```
void VulkanContext::initVulkan(GLFWwindow* window) {

    // -- Platform Specific

    // Validation and Extension Layers
    valLayersAndExt = new AppValidationLayersAndExtensions();

    if (isValidationLayersEnabled && !valLayersAndExt->
        checkValidationLayerSupport()) {
            throw std::runtime_error("Requested Validation Layers
                Not Available !");
    }

    // Create App And Vulkan Instance()
    vInstance = new VulkanInstance();
    vInstance->createAppAndVkInstance(isValidationLayersEnabled,
      valLayersAndExt);

    // Debug CallBack
    valLayersAndExt->setupDebugCallback(isValidationLayersEnabled,
      vInstance->vkInstance);

    // Create Surface
    if (glfwCreateWindowSurface(vInstance->vkInstance, window,
        nullptr, &surface) != VK_SUCCESS) {

            throw std::runtime_error(" failed to create window
                surface !");
    }
}
```

Finally, in `source.cpp`, change the `initVulkan` function, as follows:

```
GLFWwindow* window = glfwCreateWindow(WIDTH, HEIGHT,
                        "HELLO VULKAN ", nullptr, nullptr);


VulkanContext::getInstance()->initVulkan(window);
```

Picking a physical device and creating a logical device

Now, we will create the `Device` class, which will be used to go through the different physical devices we have. We will choose one to render our application. To check whether your GPU is compatible with Vulkan, check the compatibility list on your GPU vendor's site or go to `https://en.wikipedia.org/wiki/Vulkan_(API)`.

Basically, any NVIDIA GPU from the Geforce 600 series and AMD GPU from the Radeon HD 2000 series and later should be supported. To access the physical device and create a logical device, we will create a new class that will allow us to access it whenever we want. Create a new class called `Device`. In `Device.h`, add the following includes:

```
#include<vulkan\vulkan.h>
#include<stdexcept>

#include<iostream>
#include<vector>
#include<set>

#include"VulkanInstance.h"
#include"AppValidationLayersAndExtensions.h"
```

We will also add a couple of structs for the sake of convenience. The first is called `SwapChainSupportDetails`; it has access to `VkSurfaceCapabilitiesKHR`, which contains all the required details about the surface. We'll also add the `surfaceFormats` vector of the `VkSurfaceFormatKHR` type, which keeps track of all the different image formats the surface supports, and the `presentModes` vector of the `VkPresentModeKHR` type, which stores the presentation modes that the GPU supports.

Rendered images will be sent to the window surface and displayed. This is how we are able to see the final rendered image using a renderer, such as OpenGL or Vulkan. Now, we can show these images to the window one at a time, which is fine if we want to look at a still image forever. However, when we run a game that is updated every 16 milliseconds (60 times in a second), there may be cases where the image has not been fully rendered, but it would be time to display it. At this point, we will see half-rendered images, which leads to screen tearing.

To avoid this, we use double buffering. This allows us to render the image so that it has two different images, known as the front buffer and the back buffer, and ping-pong between them. Then, we present the buffer that has finished rendering and display it to the viewport while the next frame is still being rendered, as shown in the following diagram. There are different ways to present the image as well. We will look at these different presentation modes when we create the swapchain:

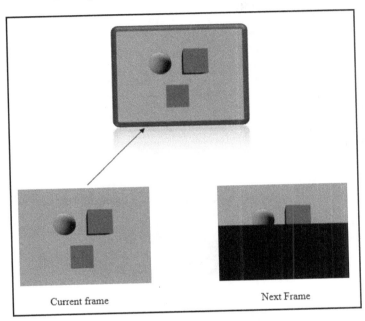

Current frame   Next Frame

We need to create a struct to track the surface properties, format, and presentation modes, as follows:

```
struct SwapChainSupportDetails {

    VkSurfaceCapabilitiesKHR surfaceCapabilities; // size and images
                                                  //    in swapchain
    std::vector<VkSurfaceFormatKHR> surfaceFormats;
    std::vector<VkPresentModeKHR> presentModes;
};
```

A GPU also has what is called `QueueFamilies`. Commands are sent to the GPU and then executed using queues. There are separate queues for different kinds of work. Render commands are sent to render queues, compute commands are sent to compute queues, and there are also presentation queues for presenting images. We also need to know which queues the GPU supports and how many of the queues are present.

The renderer, compute, and presentation queues can be combined and are known as queue families. These queues can be combined in different ways to form a number of queue families. This means that there can be a combination of render and presentation queues that forms one queue family, while another family may just contain compute queues. Therefore, we have to check whether we have at least one queue family with graphics and presentation queues. This is because we need a graphics queue to pass our rendering commands into and a presentation queue to present the image after we render it.

We will add one more struct to check for both, as follows:

```
structQueueFamilyIndices {

    int graphicsFamily = -1;
    int presentFamily = -1;

    bool arePresent() {
        return graphicsFamily >= 0 && presentFamily >= 0;
    }
};
```

Now, we will create the `Device` class itself. After creating the class, we add the constructor and destructor, as follows:

```
{

public:
    Device();
    ~Device();
```

Then, we need to add some variables so that we can store the physical device, the `SwapChainSupportDetails`, and the `QueueFamilyIndices`, as follows:

```
VkPhysicalDevice physicalDevice;
SwapChainSupportDetails swapchainSupport;
QueueFamilyIndices queueFamiliyIndices;
```

To create double buffering, we have to check that the device supports it. This is done using the `VK_KHR_SWAPCHAIN_EXTENSION_NAME` extension, which checks for a swapchain. First, we create a vector of the `char*` const and pass in the extension name, as follows:

```
std::vector<constchar*>deviceExtensions = { VK_KHR_SWAPCHAIN_EXTENSION_NAME
};
```

Then, we add the `pickPhysicalDevice` function, which will be selected depending on whether the device is suitable. While checking for suitability, we will check whether the selected device supports the swapchain extension, get the swapchain support details, and get the queue family indices, as follows:

```
void pickPhysicalDevice (VulkanInstance* vInstance,
    VkSurfaceKHR surface);

bool isDeviceSuitable(VkPhysicalDevice device,
    VkSurfaceKHR surface);

bool checkDeviceExtensionSupported(VkPhysicalDevice device) ;
SwapChainSupportDetails querySwapChainSupport (VkPhysicalDevice
    device, VkSurfaceKHR surface);
QueueFamilyIndices findQueueFamilies (VkPhysicalDevice device,
    VkSurfaceKHR surface);
```

We will also add a getter function to get the queue families of the current device, as follows:

```
QueueFamilyIndicesgetQueueFamiliesIndicesOfCurrentDevice();
```

Once we have the physical device we want to use, we will create an instance of the logical device. The logical device is an interface for the physical device itself. We will use the logical device to create buffers and so on. We will also store the current device graphics and present a queue so that we can send the graphics and presentation commands. Finally, we will add a `destroy` function, which is used to destroy the physical and logical devices we created, as follows:

```
// +++++++++++++
// Logical device
// +++++++++++++

void createLogicalDevice(VkSurfaceKHRsurface,
    boolisValidationLayersEnabled, AppValidationLayersAndExtensions
    *appValLayersAndExtentions);
VkDevice logicalDevice;

// handle to the graphics queue from the queue families of the gpu
VkQueue graphicsQueue; // we can also have seperate queue for
                        compute, memory transfer, etc.
VkQueue presentQueue; // queue for displaying the framebuffer


void destroy();
}; // End of Device class
```

That's all for the `Device.h` file. Let's move on to `Device.cpp`. First, we include `Device.h` and add the constructor and the destructor, as follows:

```cpp
#include"Device.h"
Device::Device(){}

Device::~Device(){

}
```

Now, the real work begins. We need to create the `pickPhysicalDevice` function, which takes a Vulkan instance and the `VkSurface`, as follows:

```cpp
voidDevice::pickPhysicalDevice(VulkanInstance* vInstance,
VkSurfaceKHRsurface) {
   uint32_t deviceCount = 0;

   vkEnumeratePhysicalDevices(vInstance->vkInstance, &deviceCount,
      nullptr);

   if (deviceCount == 0) {
       throw std::runtime_error("failed to find GPUs with vulkan
          support !");
   }

   std::cout <<"Device Count: "<< deviceCount << std::endl;

   std::vector<VkPhysicalDevice>devices(deviceCount);
   vkEnumeratePhysicalDevices(vInstance->vkInstance, &deviceCount,
      devices.data());


   std::cout << std::endl;
   std::cout <<"DEVICE PROPERTIES"<< std::endl;
   std::cout <<"================="<< std::endl;

   for (constauto& device : devices) {

       VkPhysicalDeviceProperties  deviceProperties;

       vkGetPhysicalDeviceProperties(device, &deviceProperties);
       std::cout << std::endl;
       std::cout <<"Device name: "<< deviceProperties.deviceName
              << std::endl;

       if (isDeviceSuitable(device, surface))
           physicalDevice = device;
```

```
        break;

    }

    if (physicalDevice == VK_NULL_HANDLE) {
        throw std::runtime_error("failed to find suitable GPU !");
    }

}
```

Here, we are creating an `int32` to store the count of the number of physical devices. We get the number of available GPUs using `vkEnumeratePhysicalDevices` and pass the Vulkan instance, the count, and `null` for the third parameter. This will retrieve the number of available devices. If `deviceCount` is zero, this means that there are no GPUs available. Then, we print the available number of devices to the console.

To get the physical devices themselves, we create a vector called `devices`, which will store the `VkPhysicalDevice` data type; this will store the devices for us. We will call the `vkEnumeratePhysicalDevices` function again, but this time – apart from passing in the Vulkan instance and the device count – we will also store the device information in the vector that we passed in as the third parameter. Then, we will print out the number of devices with the `DEVICE PROPERTIES` heading.

To get the properties of the available devices, we will go through the number of devices and get their properties using `vkGetPhysicalDeviceProperties` before storing them in the variable of the `VkPhysicalDeviceProperties` type.

Now, we need to print out the name of the device and call `DeviceSuitable` on the device. If the device is suitable, we will store it as a `physicalDevice` and break out of the loop. Note that we set the first available device as the device we will be using.

If there is no suitable device, we throw a runtime error to say that a suitable device wasn't found. Let's take a look at the `DeviceSuitable` function:

```
bool Device::isDeviceSuitable(VkPhysicalDevice device, VkSurfaceKHR
    surface)  {

    // find queue families the device supports

    QueueFamilyIndices qFamilyIndices = findQueueFamilies(device,
                                        surface);

    // Check device extentions supported
    bool extensionSupported = checkDeviceExtensionSupported(device);
```

```
bool swapChainAdequate = false;

// If swapchain extension is present
// Check surface formats and presentation modes are supported
if (extensionSupported) {

    swapchainSupport = querySwapChainSupport(device, surface);
    swapChainAdequate = !swapchainSupport.surfaceFormats.empty()
                    && !swapchainSupport.presentModes.empty();

}

VkPhysicalDeviceFeatures supportedFeatures;
vkGetPhysicalDeviceFeatures(device, &supportedFeatures);

return qFamilyIndices.arePresent() && extensionSupported &&
    swapChainAdequate && supportedFeatures.samplerAnisotropy;

}
```

In this function, we get the queue family indices by calling `findQueueFamilies`. Then, we check whether `VK_KHR_SWAPCHAIN_EXTENSION_NAME` extension is supported. After this, we check for swapchain support on the device. If the surface formats and presentation modes are not empty, `swapChainAdequate` boolean is set to `true`. Finally, we get the physical device features by calling `vkGetPhysicalDeviceFeatures`.

Finally, we return `true` if the queue families are present, the swapchain extension is supported, the swapchain is adequate, and the device supports anisotropic filtering. Anisotropic filtering is a mode that makes the pixels in the distance clearer.

Anisotropic filtering is a mode that, when enabled, helps sharpen textures that are viewed from extreme angles.

In the following example, the image on the right has anisotropic filtering enabled and the image on the left has it disabled. In the image on the right, the white dashed line is still relatively visible further down the road. However, in the image on the left, the dashed line becomes blurry and pixelated. Therefore, anisotropic filtering is required:

(Taken from `https://i.imgur.com/jzCq5sT.jpg`)

Let's look at the three functions we called in the previous function. First, let's check out the `findQueueFamilies` function:

```cpp
QueueFamilyIndicesDevice::findQueueFamilies(VkPhysicalDevicedevice,
VkSurfaceKHRsurface) {

    uint32_t queueFamilyCount = 0;

    vkGetPhysicalDeviceQueueFamilyProperties(device, &queueFamilyCount,
        nullptr);

    std::vector<VkQueueFamilyProperties>queueFamilies(queueFamilyCount);

    vkGetPhysicalDeviceQueueFamilyProperties(device, &queueFamilyCount,
        queueFamilies.data());

    int i = 0;

    for (constauto& queueFamily : queueFamilies) {

            if (queueFamily.queueCount > 0 && queueFamily.queueFlags
              &VK_QUEUE_GRAPHICS_BIT) {
                    queueFamiliyIndices.graphicsFamily = i;
            }

            VkBool32 presentSupport = false;
            vkGetPhysicalDeviceSurfaceSupportKHR(device, i, surface,
              &presentSupport);

            if (queueFamily.queueCount > 0 && presentSupport) {
                    queueFamiliyIndices.presentFamily = i;
            }
```

```
        if (queueFamiliyIndices.arePresent()) {
            break;
        }

        i++;
    }


    return queueFamiliyIndices;
}
```

To get the queue family properties, we call the
vkGetPhysicalDeviceQueueFamilyProperties function; then, in the physical device,
we pass an int, which we use to store the number of queue families, and the null pointer.
This will give us the number of queue families that are available.

Next, for the properties themselves, we create a vector of
the VkQueueFamilyProperties type, called queueFamilies, to store the necessary
information. Then, we call vkGetPhysicalDeviceFamilyProperties and pass in the
physical device, the count, and queueFamilies itself to populate it with the required data.
We create an int, i, and initialize it to 0. This will store the index of the graphics and
presentation indices.

In the for loop, we check whether each of the queue families supports a graphics queue by
looking for VK_QUEUE_GRAPHICS_BIT. If they do, we set the graphics family index.

Then, we check for presentation support by passing in the index. This will check whether
the same family supports presentation as well. If it supports presentation, we
set presentFamily to that index.

If the queue family supports graphics and presentation, the graphics and presentation
index will be the same.

The following screenshot shows the number of queue families by device and the number of
queues in each queue family:

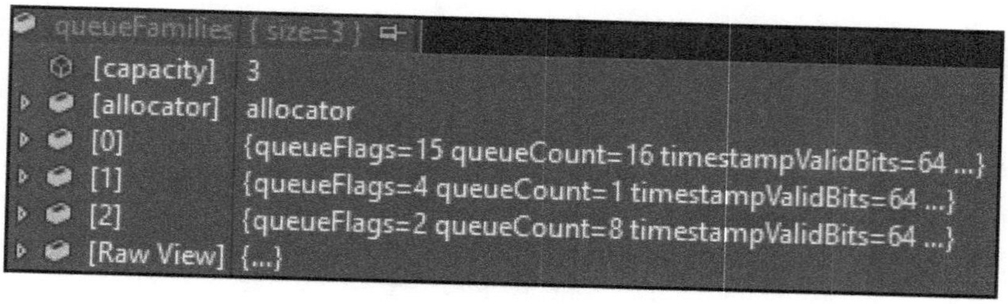

There are three queue families on my GPU. The first queue family at the 0th index has 16 queues, the second queue family at the 1st index has one queue, and the third queue family at the 2nd index has eight queues.

The queueFlags specify the queues in the queue family. The queues that are supported could be for graphics, compute, transfer, or sparse binding.

After this, we check that both the graphics and presentation indices were found, and then we break out of the loop. Finally, we return queueFamilyIndices. I am running the project on an Intel Iris Plus Graphics 650. This integrated intel GPU has one queue family that supports graphics and the presentation queue. Different GPUs have different queue families and each family may support more than one queue type. Next, let's look at the device extension that is supported. We can check this by using the checkDeviceExtensionSupported function, which takes in a physical device, as shown in the following code:

```cpp
boolDevice::checkDeviceExtensionSupported(VkPhysicalDevicedevice){

    uint32_t extensionCount;

    // Get available device extentions count
    vkEnumerateDeviceExtensionProperties(device, nullptr,
        &extensionCount, nullptr);

    // Get available device extentions
    std::vector<VkExtensionProperties>availableExtensions(extensionCount);

    vkEnumerateDeviceExtensionProperties(device, nullptr,
        &extensionCount, availableExtensions.data());

    // Populate with required device exentions we need
    std::set<std::string>requiredExtensions(deviceExtensions.begin(),
        deviceExtensions.end());

    // Check if the required extention is present
    for (constauto& extension : availableExtensions) {
        requiredExtensions.erase(extension.extensionName);
    }

    // If device has the required device extention then return
    return requiredExtensions.empty();
}
```

We get the number of extensions that are supported by the device by calling `vkEnumerateDeviceExtensionProperties` and passing in the physical device, the null pointer, an `int` to store the count in it, and `null`. The actual properties are stored inside the `availableExtensions` vector, which stores the `VkExtensionProperties` data type. By calling `vkEnumerateDeviceExtensionProperties` again, we get the device's extension properties.

We populate the `requiredExtensions` vector with the extension we require. Then, we check the available extension vector with the required extensions. If the required extension is found, we remove it from the vector. This means that the device supports the extension and returns the value from the function, as shown in the following code:

```
availableExtensions ( size=73 )
  [capacity]   73
  [allocator]  allocator
  [0]          {extensionName=0x000001fc8c7b6ee0 "VK_KHR_8bit_storage" specVersion=1 }
  [1]          {extensionName=0x000001fc8c7b6fe4 "VK_KHR_16bit_storage" specVersion=1 }
  [2]          {extensionName=0x000001fc8c7b70e8 "VK_KHR_bind_memory2" specVersion=1 }
  [3]          {extensionName=0x000001fc8c7b71ec "VK_KHR_create_renderpass2" specVersion=1 }
  [4]          {extensionName=0x000001fc8c7b72f0 "VK_KHR_dedicated_allocation" specVersion=3 }
  [5]          {extensionName=0x000001fc8c7b73f4 "VK_KHR_descriptor_update_template" specVersion=1 }
  [6]          {extensionName=0x000001fc8c7b74f8 "VK_KHR_device_group" specVersion=3 }
  [7]          {extensionName=0x000001fc8c7b75fc "VK_KHR_draw_indirect_count" specVersion=1 }
  [8]          {extensionName=0x000001fc8c7b7700 "VK_KHR_driver_properties" specVersion=1 }
  [9]          {extensionName=0x000001fc8c7b7804 "VK_KHR_external_fence" specVersion=1 }
  [10]         {extensionName=0x000001fc8c7b7908 "VK_KHR_external_fence_win32" specVersion=1 }
  [11]         {extensionName=0x000001fc8c7b7a0c "VK_KHR_external_memory" specVersion=1 }
  [12]         {extensionName=0x000001fc8c7b7b10 "VK_KHR_external_memory_win32" specVersion=1 }
```

The device I am running has 73 available extensions, as shown in the following code. You can set a breakpoint and take a look at the device extension properties to view the supported extension of the device. The third function we will look at is the `querySwapChainSupport` function, which populates the surface capabilities, surface formats, and presentation modes that are available:

```
SwapChainSupportDetailsDevice::querySwapChainSupport
    (VkPhysicalDevicedevice, VkSurfaceKHRsurface) {

    SwapChainSupportDetails details;

    vkGetPhysicalDeviceSurfaceCapabilitiesKHR(device, surface,
        &details.surfaceCapabilities);

    uint32_t formatCount;
    vkGetPhysicalDeviceSurfaceFormatsKHR(device, surface, &formatCount,
```

```
        nullptr);

    if (formatCount != 0) {
            details.surfaceFormats.resize(formatCount);
            vkGetPhysicalDeviceSurfaceFormatsKHR(device, surface,
                &formatCount, details.surfaceFormats.data());
    }

    uint32_t presentModeCount;
    vkGetPhysicalDeviceSurfacePresentModesKHR(device, surface,
        &presentModeCount, nullptr);

    if (presentModeCount != 0) {

            details.presentModes.resize(presentModeCount);
            vkGetPhysicalDeviceSurfacePresentModesKHR(device, surface,
                &presentModeCount, details.presentModes.data());
    }

    return details;
}
```

To get the surface capabilities, we call vkGetPhysicalDeviceSurfaceCapabilitiesKHR and pass in the device, that is, surface, to get the surface capabilities. To get the surface format and presentation modes, we call vkGetPhysicalDeviceSurfaceFormatKHR and vkGetPhysicalDeviceSurfacePresentModeKHR twice.

The first time we call the vkGetPhysicalDeviceSurfacePresentModeKHR function, we get the number of formats and modes that are present; we call it a second time to get the formats and the modes that have been populated and stored in the vectors of the struct.

Here are the capabilities of my device surface:

details.surfaceCapabilities {minImageCount=2 maxImageCount=8 currentExtent	
minImageCount	2
maxImageCount	8
currentExtent	{width=1280 height=720 }
minImageExtent	{width=1280 height=720 }
maxImageExtent	{width=1280 height=720 }
maxImageArrayLayers	1
supportedTransforms	1
currentTransform	VK_SURFACE_TRANSFORM_IDENTITY_BIT_KHR (1)
supportedCompositeAlpha	1
supportedUsageFlags	159

So, the minimum image count is two, meaning that we can add double buffering. These are the surface formats and the color space that my device supports:

```
details.surfaceFormats { size=2 }
   [capacity]    2
   [allocator]   allocator
   [0]           {format=VK_FORMAT_B8G8R8A8_UNORM (44) colorSpace=VK_COLOR_SPACE_SRGB_NONLINEAR_KHR (0) }
   [1]           {format=VK_FORMAT_B8G8R8A8_SRGB (50) colorSpace=VK_COLOR_SPACE_SRGB_NONLINEAR_KHR (0) }
   [Raw View]    {...}
```

Here are the presentation modes that are supported by my device:

```
details.presentModes { size=3 }
   [capacity]    3
   [allocator]   allocator
   [0]           VK_PRESENT_MODE_FIFO_KHR (2)
   [1]           VK_PRESENT_MODE_FIFO_RELAXED_KHR (3)
   [2]           VK_PRESENT_MODE_MAILBOX_KHR (1)
   [Raw View]    {...}
```

So, it seems that my device only supports the immediate mode. We will see the use of this in the ahead chapters. After getting the physical device properties, we set the getter function for the `queueFamiliyIndices`, as follows:

```
QueueFamilyIndicesDevice::getQueueFamiliesIndicesOfCurrentDevice() {

    return queueFamiliyIndices;
}
```

Now, we can create the logical device by using the `createLogicalDevice` function.

To create the logical device, we have to populate the `VkDeviceCreateInfo` struct, which requires the `queueCreateInfo` struct. Let's get started:

1. Create a vector so that we can store `VkDeviceQueueCreateInfo` and any necessary information for the graphics and presentation queues.
2. Create another vector of the `int` type so that we can store the indices of the graphics and presentation queues.

3. For each queue family, populate VkDeviceQueueCreateInfo. Create a local struct and pass in the struct type, the queue family index, the queue count, and priority (which is 1), and then push it into the queueCreateInfos vector, as shown in the following code:

```
void Device::createLogicalDevice(VkSurfaceKHRsurface,
boolisValidationLayersEnabled, AppValidationLayersAndExtensions
*appValLayersAndExtentions) {

    // find queue families like graphics and presentation
    QueueFamilyIndices indices = findQueueFamilies(physicalDevice,
            surface);

    std::vector<VkDeviceQueueCreateInfo> queueCreateInfos;

    std::set<int> uniqueQueueFamilies = { indices.graphicsFamily,
                                          indices.presentFamily };

    float queuePriority = 1.0f;

    for (int queueFamily : uniqueQueueFamilies) {

        VkDeviceQueueCreateInfo queueCreateInfo = {};
        queueCreateInfo.sType = VK_STRUCTURE_TYPE_DEVICE
                                _QUEUE_CREATE_INFO;
        queueCreateInfo.queueFamilyIndex = queueFamily;
        queueCreateInfo.queueCount = 1; // we only require 1 queue
        queueCreateInfo.pQueuePriorities = &queuePriority;
        queueCreateInfos.push_back(queueCreateInfo);

    }
```

4. To create the device, specify the device features that we will be using. For the device features, we will create a variable of the VkPhysicalDeviceFeatures type and set samplerAnisotropy to true, as follows:

```
//specify device features
    VkPhysicalDeviceFeatures deviceFeatures = {};

    deviceFeatures.samplerAnisotropy = VK_TRUE;
```

5. Create the `VkDeviceCreateInfo` struct, which we need in order to create the logical device. Set the type to `VK_STRUCTURE_TYPE_DEVICE_CREATE_INFO` and then set `queueCreateInfos`, the count, and the device features that are to be enabled.

6. Set the device extension count and names. If the validation layer is enabled, we set the validation layer's count and names. Create the `logicalDevice` by calling `vkCreateDevice` and passing in the physical device, the create device information, and `null` for the allocator. Then, create the logical device, as shown in the following code. If this fails, then we throw a runtime error:

```
VkDeviceCreateInfo createInfo = {};
createInfo.sType = VK_STRUCTURE_TYPE_DEVICE_CREATE_INFO;
createInfo.pQueueCreateInfos = queueCreateInfos.data();
createInfo.queueCreateInfoCount = static_cast<uint32_t>
                                    (queueCreateInfos.size());

createInfo.pEnabledFeatures = &deviceFeatures;
createInfo.enabledExtensionCount = static_cast<uint32_t>
   (deviceExtensions.size());
createInfo.ppEnabledExtensionNames = deviceExtensions.data();

if (isValidationLayersEnabled) {
    createInfo.enabledLayerCount =
static_cast<uint32_t>(appValLayersAndExtentions->requiredValidation
Layers.size());
    createInfo.ppEnabledLayerNames = appValLayersAndExtentions->
                             requiredValidationLayers.data();
}
else {
    createInfo.enabledLayerCount = 0;
}


//create logical device

if (vkCreateDevice(physicalDevice, &createInfo, nullptr,
   &logicalDevice) != VK_SUCCESS) {
    throw std::runtime_error("failed to create logical
       device !");
}
```

7. Get the device graphics and presentation queue, as shown in the following code. We are now done with the `Device` class:

```
//get handle to the graphics queue of the gpu
vkGetDeviceQueue(logicalDevice, indices.graphicsFamily, 0,
&graphicsQueue);

//get handle to the presentation queue of the gpu
vkGetDeviceQueue(logicalDevice, indices.presentFamily, 0,
&presentQueue);

}
```

8. This wraps up the `Device` class. Include the `Device.h` file in `VulkanContext.h` and add a new device object of the `Device` type to the `VulkanContext` class's private section, as follows:

```
// My Classes
    AppValidationLayersAndExtensions *valLayersAndExt;
    VulkanInstance* vInstance;
    Device* device;
```

9. In the `VulkanContext.cpp` file in the `VulkanInit` function, add the following code after creating the surface:

```
device = new Device();
device->pickPhysicalDevice(vInstance, surface);
device->createLogicalDevice(surface, isValidationLayersEnabled,
    valLayersAndExt);
```

10. This will create a new instance of the `device` class and we choose a device from the available physical devices. You will then be able to create the logical device. Run the application to see which device the application will run on. On my desktop, the following device count and name were found:

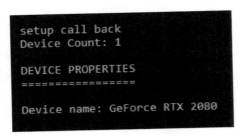

```
setup call back
Device Count: 1

DEVICE PROPERTIES
==================

Device name: GeForce RTX 2080
```

11. On my laptop, the application found one device with the following device name:

```
setup call back
Device Count: 1

DEVICE PROPERTIES
==================

Device name: Intel(R) Iris(R) Plus Graphics 650
```

12. Set breakpoints inside `findQueueFamilies`, `checkDeviceExtensionSupport`, and `querySwapChainSupport` to check for the number of queue family device extensions and for swapchain support for your GPUs.

Summary

We are about a quarter of the way through the process of seeing something being rendered to the viewport. In this chapter, we set the validation layers and the extension that we will need in order to set up Vulkan rendering. We created a Vulkan application and instance and then created a device class so that we can select the physical device. We also created the logical device so that we can interact with the GPU.

In the next chapter, we will create the swapchain itself so that we can swap between buffers, and we will create the render and the depth texture to draw the scene. We will create a render pass to set how the render textures are to be used and then create the draw command buffers, which will execute our draw commands.

Preparing the Clear Screen

10

In the last chapter, we enabled the Vulkan validation layers and extensions, created the Vulkan application and instance, chose the device, and created the logical device. In this chapter, we will continue the journey toward creating a clear screen picture and presenting it to the viewport.

Before drawing pictures, we first clear and erase the previous picture with a color value. If we don't do this, the new picture will be written on top of the previous picture, which will create a psychedelic effect.

Each picture is cleared and rendered and then presented on the screen. While the current one is being shown, the next picture is in the process of being drawn in the background. Once that is rendered, the current picture will be swapped with the new picture. This swapping of pictures is taken care of by the **SwapChain**.

In our case, each picture in the SwapChain we are drawing simply stores the color information. This target picture is rendered and, hence, it is called the render target. We can also have other target pictures. For example, we can have a depth target/picture, which will store the depth information of each pixel per frame. Consequently, we create these render targets as well.

Each of these target pictures per frame is set as an attachment and used to create the framebuffer. Since we have double buffering (meaning we have two sets of pictures to swap between), we create a framebuffer for each frame. Consequently, we will create two framebuffers—one for each frame—and we will add the picture as an attachment.

The commands that we give to the GPU—for example, the draw command—are sent to the GPU with each frame using a command buffer. The command buffer stores all the commands to be submitted to the GPU using the graphics queue of the device. So, for each frame, we create a command buffer to carry all our commands as well.

Once the commands are submitted and the scene is rendered, instead of presenting the drawn picture to the screen, we can save it and add any post-processing effects to it, such as motion blur. In the renderpass, we can specify how the render target is to be used. Although in our case, we are not going to add any post-processing effects, we still need to create a renderpass. Consequently, we create a renderpass, which will specify to the device how many swap chain pictures and buffers we will be using, what kind of buffers they are, and how they are to be used.

The different stages the picture will go through are as follows:

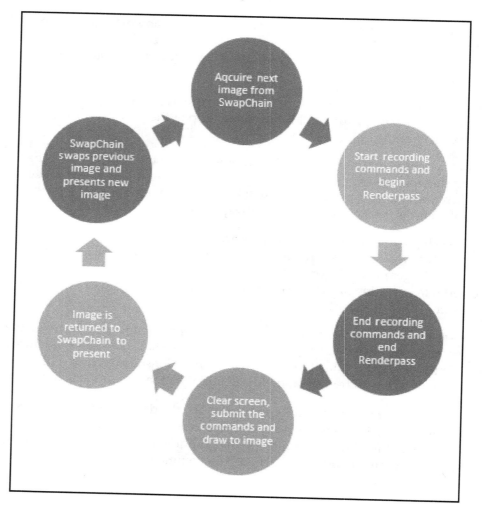

The topics covered in this chapter are as follows:

- Creating `SwapChain`
- Creating `Renderpass`
- Using render views and `Framebuffers`
- Creating `CommandBuffer`
- Beginning and ending `Renderpass`
- Creating the clear screen

Creating SwapChain

While the scene is rendered, the buffers are swapped and presented to the window surface. The surface is platform-dependent and, depending upon the operating system, we have to choose the surface format accordingly. For the scene to be presented properly, we create the `SwapChain`, depending upon the surface format, presentation mode, and the extent, meaning the width and height, of the picture that the window can support.

In `Chapter 10`, *Drawing Vulkan Objects*, when we chose the GPU device to use, we retrieved the properties of the device, such as the surface format and the presentation modes it supports. While we create the `SwapChain`, we match and check the surface format and the presentation that is available from the device, and that is also supported by the window to create the `SwapChain` object itself.

We create a new class called `SwapChain` and add the following includes to `SwapChain.h`:

```
#include <vulkan\vulkan.h>
#include <vector>
#include <set>
#include <algorithm>
```

We then create the class, as follows:

```
classSwapChain {
public:
    SwapChain();
    ~SwapChain();


    VkSwapchainKHR swapChain;
    VkFormat swapChainImageFormat;
    VkExtent2D swapChainImageExtent;
    std::vector<VkImage> swapChainImages;
```

```
VkSurfaceFormatKHRchooseSwapChainSurfaceFormat(
    const std::vector<VkSurfaceFormatKHR>&availableFormats);
VkPresentModeKHRchooseSwapPresentMode(
    const std::vector<VkPresentModeKHR>availablePresentModes);
VkExtent2DchooseSwapExtent(constVkSurfaceCapabilitiesKHR&capabilities);
void create(VkSurfaceKHRsurface);

void destroy();
}
```

In the public section of the class, we create the constructor and the destructor. Then, we create the variables of the VkSwapchainKHR, VkFormat, and VkExtent2D types to store the swapchain itself. When we create the surface, we store the format of the picture itself, which is supported, as well as the extent of the picture, which is the width and height of the viewport. This is because, when the viewport is stretched or changed, the size of the swapchain picture will also be changed accordingly.

We create a vector of the VkImage type, called swapChainImages, to store the SwapChain pictures. Three helper functions, chooseSwapChainSurfaceFormat, chooseSwapPresentMode, and chooseSwapExtent, are created to get the most suitable surface format, present mode, and SwapChain extent. Finally, the create function takes the surface in which we will create the swapchain itself. We also add a function to destroy and release the resources back to the system.

That is it for the SwapChain.h file. We will now move on to SwapChain.cpp to incorporate the implementation of the functions.

In the SwapChain.cpp file, add the following includes:

```
#include"SwapChain.h"
```

```
#include "VulkanContext.h"
```

We will need to include VulkanContext.h to get the device's SwapChainSupportDetails struct, which we populated in the last chapter when we selected the physical device and created the logical device. Before we create the swapchain, let's first look at the three helper functions and see how each is created.

The first of the three functions is `chooseSwapChainSurfaceFormat`. This function takes in a vector of `VkSurfaceFormatKHR`, which is the available format supported by the device. Using this function, we will choose the surface format that is most suitable. The function is created as follows:

```
VkSurfaceFormatKHRSwapChain::chooseSwapChainSurfaceFormat(const
std::vector<VkSurfaceFormatKHR>&availableFormats) {

    if (availableFormats.size() == 1 &&availableFormats[0].format ==
       VK_FORMAT_UNDEFINED) {
            return{VK_FORMAT_B8G8R8A8_UNORM,
               VK_COLOR_SPACE_SRGB_NONLINEAR_KHR };
    }

    for (constauto& availableFormat : availableFormats) {
            if (availableFormat.format == VK_FORMAT_B8G8R8A8_UNORM&&
               availableFormat.colorSpace ==
               VK_COLOR_SPACE_SRGB_NONLINEAR_KHR) {
                    return availableFormat;
            }
    }
    returnavailableFormats[0];
}
```

First, we check whether the available format is just 1 and whether it is undefined by the device. This means that there is no preferred format, so we choose the one that is most convenient for us.

The values returned are the color format and color space. The color format specifies the format of the color itself, VK_FORMAT_B8G8R8A8_UNORM, which tells us that we store 32 bits of information in each pixel. The colors are stored in the Blue, Green, Red, and Alpha channels, and in that order. Each channel is stored in 8 bits, so that means 2^8, which is 256 color values. UNORM suggests that each color value is normalized, so the color values, instead of being from 0-255, are normalized between 0 and 1.

We choose the SRGB color space as the second parameter, as we want more of a range of colors to be represented. If there is no preferred format, we go through the formats available and then check and return the ones that we need. We choose this color space, as most surfaces support this format because it is widely available. Otherwise, we just return the first available format.

The next function is `chooseSwapPresentMode`, which takes in a vector of `VkPresentModeKHR` called `availablePresentModes`. Presentation modes specify how the final rendered picture is presented to the viewport. Here are the available modes:

- `VK_PRESENT_MODE_IMMEDIATE_KHR`: In this case, the picture will be displayed as soon as a picture is available to present. Pictures are not queued to be displayed. This causes picture tearing.

- `VK_PRESENT_MODE_FIFO_KHR`: The acquired pictures to be presented are put in a queue. The size of the queue is one minus the swap chain size. At vsync, the first picture to be displayed gets displayed in the **First In First Out (FIFO)** manner. There is no tearing as pictures are displayed in the same order in which they were added to the queue and vsync is enabled. This mode needs to always be supported.

- `VK_PRESENT_MODE_FIFO_RELAXED_KHR`: This is a variation of the `FIFO` mode. In this mode, if the rendering is faster than the refresh rate of the monitor, it is fine, but if the drawing is slower than the monitor, there will be screen tearing as the next available picture is presented immediately.

- `VK_PRESENTATION_MODE_MAILBOX_KHR`: The presentation of the pictures is put in a queue, but it has just one element in it, unlike `FIFO`, which has more than one element in the queue. The next picture to be displayed will wait for the queue to be displayed and then the presentation engine will display the picture. This doesn't cause tearing.

With this information, let's create the `chooseSwapPresentMode` function:

```
VkPresentModeKHRSwapChain::chooseSwapPresentMode(
  const std::vector<VkPresentModeKHR>availablePresentModes) {

    VkPresentModeKHR bestMode = VK_PRESENT_MODE_FIFO_KHR;

    for (constauto& availablePresentMode : availablePresentModes) {

        if (availablePresentMode == VK_PRESENT_MODE_MAILBOX_KHR) {
            return availablePresentMode;
        }
        elseif (availablePresentMode == VK_PRESENT_MODE_IMMEDIATE_KHR) {
            bestMode = availablePresentMode;
        }

        return bestMode;
    }
}
```

Since the FIFO mode is our most preferred mode, we set it in the function so that we can compare it with the available modes of the device. If it is not available, we go for the next best mode, which is the MAILBOX mode, so that the presentation queue will have at least one more picture to avoid screen tearing. If neither mode is available, we go for the IMMEDIATE mode, which is least desirable.

The third function is the chooseSwapExtent function. In this function, we get the resolution of the window that we drew to set the resolution of the swapchain pictures. It is added as follows:

```
VkExtent2DSwapChain::chooseSwapExtent(constVkSurfaceCapabilitiesKHR&
    capabilities) {

    if (capabilities.currentExtent.width !=
std::numeric_limits<uint32_t>::max()) {
        returncapabilities.currentExtent;
    }
    else {

        VkExtent2D actualExtent = { 1280, 720 };

        actualExtent.width = std::max(capabilities.minImageExtent.
                            width, std::min(capabilities.
                            maxImageExtent. width,
                            actualExtent.width));
        actualExtent.height = std::max(capabilities.minImageExtent.
                            height, std::min(capabilities.
                            maxImageExtent.height,
                            actualExtent.height));

        return actualExtent;
    }
}
```

The resolution of this window should match the swapchain pictures. Some window managers allow the resolution to be different between the pictures and the window. This is indicated by setting the value to the maximum of uint32_t. If not, then in that case, we return the current extent that we retrieved by the capabilities of the hardware, or pick the resolution that best matches the resolution between the maximum and minimum values available, as compared to the actual resolution we set, which is 1,280 x 720.

Let's now look at the create function, in which we actually create the SwapChain itself. To create this function, we will add the functionality to create the SwapChain:

```
void SwapChain::create(VkSurfaceKHR surface) {
...
}
```

The first thing we do is get the device support details, which we retrieved for our device when we created the Device class:

```
SwapChainSupportDetails swapChainSupportDetails =
VulkanContext::getInstance()-> getDevice()->swapchainSupport;
```

Then, using the helper function we created, we get the surface format, present mode, and the extent:

```
VkSurfaceFormatKHR surfaceFormat = chooseSwapChainSurfaceFormat
    (swapChainSupportDetails.surfaceFormats);
VkPresentModeKHR presentMode = chooseSwapPresentMode
    (swapChainSupportDetails.presentModes);
VkExtent2D extent = chooseSwapExtent
    (swapChainSupportDetails.surfaceCapabilities);
```

We then set the minimum number of pictures required to make the swapchain:

```
uint32_t imageCount = swapChainSupportDetails.
                  surfaceCapabilities.minImageCount;
```

We should also make sure that we don't exceed the maximum available picture count, so if the imageCount is more than the maximum amount, we set imageCount to the maximum count:

```
if (swapChainSupportDetails.surfaceCapabilities.maxImageCount > 0 &&
    imageCount > swapChainSupportDetails.surfaceCapabilities.
  maxImageCount) {
        imageCount = swapChainSupportDetails.surfaceCapabilities.
                  maxImageCount;
}
```

To create the swapchain, we have to populate the VkSwapchainCreateInfoKHR struct first, so let's create it. Create a variable called createInfo and specify the type of the structure:

```
VkSwapchainCreateInfoKHR createInfo = {};
createInfo.sType = VK_STRUCTURE_TYPE_SWAPCHAIN_CREATE_INFO_KHR;
```

In this, we have to specify the surface to use, the minimum picture count, the picture format, the space, and the extent. We also need to specify the picture array layers. Since we are not going to create a stereoscopic application like a virtual reality game, in which there would be two surfaces, one for the left eye and one for the right eye, instead, we just set the value for it as 1. We also need to specify what the picture will be used for. Here, it will be used to show the color information using the color attachment:

```
createInfo.surface = surface;
createInfo.minImageCount = imageCount;
createInfo.imageFormat = surfaceFormat.format;
createInfo.imageColorSpace = surfaceFormat.colorSpace;
createInfo.imageExtent = extent;
createInfo.imageArrayLayers = 1; // this is 1 unless you are making
a stereoscopic 3D application
createInfo.imageUsage = VK_IMAGE_USAGE_COLOR_ATTACHMENT_BIT;
```

We now specify the graphics, presentation indices, and the count. We also specify the sharing mode. It is possible for the presentation and graphics family to be either the same or different.

If the presentation and graphics family is different, the sharing mode is said to be of the VK_SHARING_MODE_CONCURRENT type. This means that the picture can be used across multiple queue families. However, if the picture is in the same queue family, the sharing mode is said to be of the VK_SHARING_MODE_EXCLUSIVE type:

```
if (indices.graphicsFamily != indices.presentFamily) {

    createInfo.imageSharingMode = VK_SHARING_MODE_CONCURRENT;
    createInfo.queueFamilyIndexCount = 2;
    createInfo.pQueueFamilyIndices = queueFamilyIndices;

}
else {

    createInfo.imageSharingMode = VK_SHARING_MODE_EXCLUSIVE;
    createInfo.queueFamilyIndexCount = 0;
    createInfo.pQueueFamilyIndices = nullptr;

}
```

If we want, we can apply a pre-transform to the picture to either flip it or mirror it. In this case, we just keep the current transform. We can also alpha-blend the picture with other window systems, but we just keep it opaque and ignore the alpha channel, set the present mode, and set whether the pixel should be clipped if there is a window in front. We can also specify an old SwapChain if the current one becomes invalid when we resize the window. Since we don't resize the window, we don't have to specify an older swapchain.

After setting the info struct, we can create the swapchain itself:

```
if (vkCreateSwapchainKHR(VulkanContext::getInstance()->getDevice()->
    logicalDevice, &createInfo, nullptr, &swapChain) != VK_SUCCESS) {
        throw std::runtime_error("failed to create swap chain !");
    }
```

We create the swapchain using the `vkCreateSwapchainKHR` function, which takes the logical device, the `createInfo` struct, an allocator callback, and the swapchain itself. If it doesn't create the `SwapChain` because of an error, we will send out an error. Now that the swapchain is created, we will obtain the swapchain pictures.

Depending upon the picture count, we call the `vkGetSwapchainImagesKHR` function, which we use to first get the picture count and then call the function again to populate the `vkImage` vector with the pictures:

```
vkGetSwapchainImagesKHR(VulkanContext::getInstance()->getDevice()->
    logicalDevice, swapChain, &imageCount, nullptr);
swapChainImages.resize(imageCount);
vkGetSwapchainImagesKHR(VulkanContext::getInstance()->getDevice()->
    logicalDevice, swapChain, &imageCount, swapChainImages.data());
```

The creation of pictures is a bit more involved, but Vulkan automatically creates color pictures. We can set the picture format and extent as well:

```
swapChainImageFormat = surfaceFormat.format;
swapChainImageExtent= extent;
```

Then, we add the `destroy` function, which destroys the `SwapChain` by calling the `vkDestroySwapchainKHR` function:

```
void SwapChain::destroy(){

    // Swapchain
    vkDestroySwapchainKHR(VulkanContext::getInstance()-> getDevice()->
        logicalDevice, swapChain, nullptr);
}
```

In the `VulkanApplication.h` file, include the `SwapChain` header and create a new `SwapChain` instance in the `VulkanApplication` class. In `VulkanApplication.cpp`, in the `initVulkan` function, after creating the logical device, create the `SwapChain` as follows:

```
swapChain = new SwapChain();
swapChain->create(surface);
```

Build and run the application to make sure the SwapChain is created without any errors.

Creating Renderpass

After creating the SwapChain, we move on to the Renderpass. Here, we specify how many color attachments and depth attachments are present and how many samples to use for each of them for each framebuffer.

As mentioned at the start of this chapter, a framebuffer is a collection of target attachments. Attachments can be of type color, depth, and so on. The color attachment stores the color information that is presented to the viewport. There are other attachments that the end user doesn't see, but that are used internally. This includes depth, for example, which has all the depth information per pixel. In the render pass, apart from the type of attachments, we also specify how the attachments are used.

For this book, we will be presenting what is rendered in a scene to the viewport, so we will just use a single pass. If we add a post-processing effect, we will take the rendered picture and apply this effect to it, for which we will need to use multiple passes. We will create a new class called Renderpass, in which we will create the render pass.

In the Renderpass.h file, add the following includes and class:

```cpp
#include <vulkan\vulkan.h>
#include <array>

class Renderpass
{
public:
    Renderpass();
    ~Renderpass();

    VkRenderPass renderPass;

    void createRenderPass(VkFormat swapChainImageFormat);

    void destroy();
};
```

In the class, add the constructor, destructor, and the VkRenderPass and renderPass variables. Add a new function called createRenderPass to create the Renderpass itself, which takes in the picture format. Also, add a function to destroy the Renderpass object after use.

In the Renderpass.cpp file, add the following includes, as well as the constructor and destructor:

```
#include"Renderpass.h"
#include "VulkanContext.h"
Renderpass::Renderpass(){}


Renderpass::~Renderpass(){}
```

We now add the createRenderPass function, in which we will add the functionality to create the Renderpass for the current scene to be rendered:

```
voidRenderpass::createRenderPass(VkFormatswapChainImageFormat) {
...
}
```

When we create the render pass, we have to specify the number and the type of attachments that we are using. So, for our project, we want only color attachments as we will only be drawing color information. We could also have a depth attachment, which stores depth information. We need to provide subpasses, and if so, then how many, as we could be using subpasses for adding post-processing effects to the current frame.

For the attachments and subpasses, we have to populate structs to pass to them at the time of creating the render pass.

So, let's populate the structs. First, we create the attachments:

```
VkAttachmentDescription colorAttachment = {};
colorAttachment.format = swapChainImageFormat;
colorAttachment.samples = VK_SAMPLE_COUNT_1_BIT;
colorAttachment.loadOp = VK_ATTACHMENT_LOAD_OP_CLEAR;
colorAttachment.storeOp = VK_ATTACHMENT_STORE_OP_STORE;
colorAttachment.stencilLoadOp = VK_ATTACHMENT_LOAD_OP_DONT_CARE;
colorAttachment.stencilStoreOp = VK_ATTACHMENT_STORE_OP_DONT_CARE;

colorAttachment.initialLayout = VK_IMAGE_LAYOUT_UNDEFINED;
colorAttachment.finalLayout = VK_IMAGE_LAYOUT_PRESENT_SRC_KHR;
```

We create the struct and specify the format to be used, which is the same as the swapChainImage format. We have to provide the sample count as 1 as we are not going to be using multi-sampling. In loadOp and storeOp, we specify what to do with the data before and after rendering. We specify that at the time of loading the attachment, we will clear the data to a constant at the start. After the render process, we store the data so we can read from it later. We then decide what to do with the data before and after the stencil operation.

Since we are not using the stencil buffer, we specify DON'T CARE during loading and storing. We also have to specify the data layout before and after processing the picture. The previous layout of the picture doesn't matter, but after rendering, the picture needs to be changed to the layout in order for it to be ready for presenting.

Now we'll go through the subpass. Each subpass references the attachments that need to be specified as a separate structure:

```
VkAttachmentReference colorAttachRef = {};
colorAttachRef.attachment = 0;
colorAttachRef.layout = VK_IMAGE_LAYOUT_COLOR_ATTACHMENT_OPTIMAL;
```

In the subpass reference, we specify the attachment index, which is the 0th index and specify the layout, which is a color attachment with optimal performance. Next, we create the subpass structure:

```
VkSubpassDescription subpass = {};
subpass.pipelineBindPoint = VK_PIPELINE_BIND_POINT_GRAPHICS;
subpass.colorAttachmentCount = 1;
subpass.pColorAttachments = &colorAttachRef;
```

In the pipeline bind point, we specify that this is a graphics subpass, as it could have been a compute subpass. Specify the attachment count as 1 and provide the color attachment. Now, we can create the renderpass info struct:

```
std::array<VkAttachmentDescription, 1> attachments =
    { colorAttachment };

VkRenderPassCreateInfo rpCreateInfo = {};
rpCreateInfo.sType = VK_STRUCTURE_TYPE_RENDER_PASS_CREATE_INFO;
rpCreateInfo.attachmentCount = static_cast<uint32_t>
                                (attachments.size());
rpCreateInfo.pAttachments = attachments.data();
rpCreateInfo.subpassCount = 1;
rpCreateInfo.pSubpasses = &subpass;
```

We create an array of one element of the `VkAttachmentDescription` type, and then we create the info struct and pass in the type. The attachment count and the attachments are passed in, and then the subpass count and the subpass is passed in as well. Create the renderpass itself by calling `vkCreateRenderPass` and passing in the logical device, the create info, and the allocator callback to get the renderpass:

```
if (vkCreateRenderPass(VulkanContext::getInstance()->
    getDevice()->logicalDevice, &rpCreateInfo, nullptr, &renderPass)
    != VK_SUCCESS) {
        throw std::runtime_error(" failed to create renderpass !!");
    }
```

Finally, in the `destroy` function, we call `vkDestroyRenderPass` to destroy it after we are done:

```
voidRenderpass::destroy(){
    vkDestroyRenderPass(VulkanContext::getInstance()-> getDevice()->
        logicalDevice, renderPass, nullptr);

}
```

In `VulkanApplication.h`, include `RenderPass.h` and create a render pass object. In `VulkanApplication.cpp`, after creating the swapchain, create the renderpass:

```
renderPass = new Renderpass();
renderPass->createRenderPass(swapChain->swapChainImageFormat);
```

Now, build and run the project to make sure there are no errors.

Using render targets and framebuffers

To use a picture, we have to create an `ImageView`. The picture doesn't have any information, such as mipmap levels, and you can't access a portion of the picture. However, by now using picture views, we specify the type of the texture and whether it has mipmaps. In addition, in renderpass, we specified the attachments per frame buffer. We will create framebuffers here and pass in the picture views as attachments.

Create a new class called `RenderTexture`. In the `RenderTexture.h` file, add the following headers and then create the class itself:

```
#include <vulkan/vulkan.h>
#include<array>

class RenderTexture
```

```
{
public:
    RenderTexture();
    ~RenderTexture();
    std::vector<VkImage> _swapChainImages;
    VkExtent2D _swapChainImageExtent;

    std::vector<VkImageView> swapChainImageViews;
    std::vector<VkFramebuffer> swapChainFramebuffers;


    void createViewsAndFramebuffer(std::vector<VkImage> swapChainImages,
        VkFormat swapChainImageFormat, VkExtent2D swapChainImageExtent,
        VkRenderPass renderPass);

    void createImageViews(VkFormat swapChainImageFormat);
    void createFrameBuffer(VkExtent2D swapChainImageExtent,
        VkRenderPass renderPass);

    void destroy();

};
```

In the class, we add the constructor and destructor as usual. We will store `swapChainImages` and the extent to use it locally. We create two vectors to store the created ImageViews and framebuffers. To create the views and framebuffers, we will call the `createViewsAndFramebuffers` function, which takes the pictures, picture format, extent, and the renderpass as the input. This function intern will call `createImageViews` and `CreateFramebuffer` to create the views and buffers. We will add the `destroy` function, which destroys and releases the resources back to the system.

In the `RenderTexture.cpp` file, we will add the following includes as well as the constructor and destructor:

```
#include "RenderTexture.h"
#include "VulkanContext.h"
RenderTexture::RenderTexture(){}

RenderTexture::~RenderTexture(){}
```

Then, add the `createViewAndFramebuffer` function:

```
void RenderTexture::createViewsAndFramebuffer(std::vector<VkImage>
swapChainImages, VkFormat swapChainImageFormat,
VkExtent2D swapChainImageExtent,
VkRenderPass renderPass){
```

```
    _swapChainImages =  swapChainImages;
    _swapChainImageExtent = swapChainImageExtent;

    createImageViews(swapChainImageFormat);
    createFrameBuffer(swapChainImageExtent, renderPass);
}
```

We first assign the images and `imageExtent` to the local variables. Then, we call the `imageViews` function, followed by `createFramebuffer`, in order to create both of them. To create the image views, use the `createImageViews` function:

```
void RenderTexture::createImageViews(VkFormat swapChainImageFormat){

    swapChainImageViews.resize(_swapChainImages.size());

    for (size_t i = 0; i < _swapChainImages.size(); i++) {

        swapChainImageViews[i] = vkTools::createImageView
                                    (_swapChainImages[i],
            swapChainImageFormat,
            VK_IMAGE_ASPECT_COLOR_BIT);
    }
}
```

We specify the vector size depending upon the swapchain image count first. For each of the image counts, we create image views using the `createImageView` function in the `vkTool` namespace. The `createImageView` function takes in the image itself, the image format, and `ImageAspectFlag`. This will be `VK_IMAGE_ASPECT_COLOR_BIT` or `VK_IMAGE_ASPECT_DEPTH_BIT` depending on the kind of view that you want to create for the image. The `createImageView` function is created in the `Tools.h` file under the `vkTools` namespace. The `Tools.h` file is as follows:

```
#include <vulkan\vulkan.h>
#include <stdexcept>
#include <vector>

namespace vkTools {


    VkImageView createImageView(VkImage image, VkFormat format,
        VkImageAspectFlags aspectFlags);


}
```

The implementation of the function is created in the `Tools.cpp` file as follows:

```cpp
#include "Tools.h"
#include "VulkanContext.h"

namespace vkTools {
    VkImageView createImageView(VkImage image, VkFormat format,
VkImageAspectFlags aspectFlags) {

        VkImageViewCreateInfo viewInfo = {};
        viewInfo.sType = VK_STRUCTURE_TYPE_IMAGE_VIEW_CREATE_INFO;
        viewInfo.image = image;
        viewInfo.viewType = VK_IMAGE_VIEW_TYPE_2D;
        viewInfo.format = format;


        viewInfo.subresourceRange.aspectMask = aspectFlags;
        viewInfo.subresourceRange.baseMipLevel = 0;
        viewInfo.subresourceRange.levelCount = 1;
        viewInfo.subresourceRange.baseArrayLayer = 0;
        viewInfo.subresourceRange.layerCount = 1;

        VkImageView imageView;
        if (vkCreateImageView(VulkanContext::getInstance()->
            getDevice()->logicalDevice, &viewInfo, nullptr, &imageView)
            != VK_SUCCESS) {
                throw std::runtime_error("failed to create
                    texture image view !");
        }

        return imageView;
    }

}
```

To create the `imageView`, we have to populate the `VkImageViewCreateInfo` struct and then use the `vkCreateImageView` function to create the view itself. To populate the view info, we specify the structure type, the picture itself, the view type, which is `VK_IMAGE_VIEW_TYPE_2D`, and a 2D texture, and then specify the format. We pass in the aspectFlags for the aspect mask. We create the image view without any mipmap level or layers, so we set them to 0. We would only need multiple layers if we were making something like a VR game.

We then create an `imageView` of the `VkImage` type and create it using the `vkCreateImageView` function, which takes in the logical device, the view info struct, and then the picture view is created and returned. That's all for the Tools file.

We will use the Tools file and add more functions to it when we want functions that can be reused. Now, let's go back to the `RenderTexture.cpp` file and add in the function to create the framebuffer.

We will create framebuffers for each frame in the swapchain. `createFramebuffer` requires the picture extent and the renderpass itself:

```
void RenderTexture::createFrameBuffer(VkExtent2D swapChainImageExtent,
VkRenderPass renderPass){

    swapChainFramebuffers.resize(swapChainImageViews.size());

    for (size_t i = 0; i < swapChainImageViews.size(); i++) {

        std::array<VkImageView, 2> attachments = {
            swapChainImageViews[i]
        };

        VkFramebufferCreateInfo fbInfo = {};
        fbInfo.sType = VK_STRUCTURE_TYPE_FRAMEBUFFER_CREATE_INFO;
        fbInfo.renderPass = renderPass;
        fbInfo.attachmentCount = static_cast<uint32_t>
                                 (attachments.size());;
        fbInfo.pAttachments = attachments.data();;
        fbInfo.width = swapChainImageExtent.width;
        fbInfo.height = swapChainImageExtent.height;
        fbInfo.layers = 1;

        if (vkCreateFramebuffer(VulkanContext::getInstance()->
            getDevice()->logicalDevice, &fbInfo, NULL,
            &swapChainFramebuffers[i]) != VK_SUCCESS) {

            throw std::runtime_error(" failed to create
                framebuffers !!!");
        }
    }
}
```

For each frame that we create, the Framebuffer first populates the `framebufferInfo` struct and then calls `vkCreateFramebuffer` to create the Framebuffer itself. For each frame, we create a new info struct and specify the type of struct. We then pass the renderpass, the attachment count, and the attachment views, specify the width and height of the Framebuffer, and set the layers to 1.

Finally, we create the framebuffer by calling the `vkCreateFramebuffer` function:

```
void RenderTexture::destroy(){

    // image views
    for (auto imageView : swapChainImageViews) {

        vkDestroyImageView(VulkanContext::getInstance()->getDevice()->
            logicalDevice, imageView, nullptr);

    }


    // Framebuffers
    for (auto framebuffer : swapChainFramebuffers) {
        vkDestroyFramebuffer(VulkanContext::getInstance()->
            getDevice()->logicalDevice, framebuffer, nullptr);

    }

}
```

In the `destroy` function, we destroy each of the picture views and framebuffers we created by calling `vkDestroyImageView` and `vkDestroyFramebuffer`. And that is all for the `RenderTexture` class.

In `VulkanApplication.h`, include `RenderTexture.h` and create an instance of it called `renderTexture` in the `VulkanApplication` class. In the `VulkanApplication.cpp` file, include the `initVulkan` function and create a new `RenderTexture`:

```
renderTexture = new RenderTexture();
renderTexture->createViewsAndFramebuffer(swapChain->swapChainImages,
        swapChain->swapChainImageFormat,
        swapChain->swapChainImageExtent,
        renderPass->renderPass);
```

Creating CommandBuffer

In Vulkan, the drawing and other operations done on the GPU are performed using command buffers. The command buffers contain the draw commands, which are recorded and then executed. Draw commands are to be recorded and executed in every frame. To create a command buffer, we have to first create a command pool and then allocate command buffers from the command pool, and then the commands are recorded per frame.

Let's create a new class for creating the command buffer pool and then allocate the command buffers. We also create a function to start and stop recording and to destroy the command buffers. Create a new class, called `DrawCommandBuffer`, and `DrawCommandBuffer.h` as follows:

```
#include <vulkan\vulkan.h>
#include <vector>

class DrawCommandBuffer
{
public:
    DrawCommandBuffer();
    ~DrawCommandBuffer();

    VkCommandPool commandPool;
    std::vector<VkCommandBuffer> commandBuffers;

    void createCommandPoolAndBuffer(size_t imageCount);
    void beginCommandBuffer(VkCommandBuffer commandBuffer);
    void endCommandBuffer(VkCommandBuffer commandBuffer);

    void createCommandPool();
    void allocateCommandBuffers(size_t imageCount);

    void destroy();
};
```

In the class, we create the constructor and destructor. We create variables to store the command pool and a vector to store `VkCommandBuffer`. We create one function initially to create the command pool and allocate the command buffers. The next two functions, `beginCommandBuffer` and `endCommandBuffer`, will be called when we want to start and stop recording the command buffer. The `createCommandPool` and `allocateCommandBuffers` functions will be called by `createCommandPoolAndBuffer`.

We will create the `destroy` function to destroy the command buffers when we want the resources to be released to the system. In `CommandBuffer.cpp`, add the necessary includes and the constructor and destructor:

```
#include "DrawCommandBuffer.h"
#include "VulkanContext.h"

DrawCommandBuffer::DrawCommandBuffer(){}

DrawCommandBuffer::~DrawCommandBuffer(){}
```

Then, we add `createCommandPoolAndBuffer`, which takes in the picture count:

```
void DrawCommandBuffer::createCommandPoolAndBuffer(size_t imageCount){

    createCommandPool();
    allocateCommandBuffers(imageCount);
}
```

The `createCommandPoolAndBuffer` function will call the `createCommandPool` and `allocateCommandBuffers` functions. First, we create the `createCommandPool` function. Commands have to be sent to a certain queue. We have to specify the queue when we create the command pool:

```
void DrawCommandBuffer::createCommandPool() {

    QueueFamilyIndices qFamilyIndices = VulkanContext::
                                getInstance()->getDevice()->
    getQueueFamiliesIndicesOfCurrentDevice();

    VkCommandPoolCreateInfo cpInfo = {};

    cpInfo.sType = VK_STRUCTURE_TYPE_COMMAND_POOL_CREATE_INFO;
    cpInfo.queueFamilyIndex = qFamilyIndices.graphicsFamily;
    cpInfo.flags = VK_COMMAND_POOL_CREATE_RESET_COMMAND_BUFFER_BIT;

    if (vkCreateCommandPool(VulkanContext::getInstance()->
        getDevice()->logicalDevice, &cpInfo, nullptr, &commandPool)
        != VK_SUCCESS) {
            throw std::runtime_error(" failed to create command pool !!");
    }

}
```

To start, we get the queue family indices for the current device. To create the command pool, we have to populate the `VkCommandPoolCreateInfo` struct. As usual, we specify the type. Then, we set the queue family index in which the pool has to be created. After that, we set the `VK_COMMAND_POOL_CREATE_RESET_COMMAND_BUFFER_BIT` flags, which will reset the values of the command buffer every time. We then use the `vkCreateCommandPool` function by passing in the logical device and the info struct to get the command pool. Next, we create the `allocateCommandBuffers` function:

```
void DrawCommandBuffer::allocateCommandBuffers(size_t imageCount) {

    commandBuffers.resize(imageCount);

    VkCommandBufferAllocateInfo cbInfo = {};
```

```
cbInfo.sType = VK_STRUCTURE_TYPE_COMMAND_BUFFER_ALLOCATE_INFO;
cbInfo.commandPool = commandPool;
cbInfo.level = VK_COMMAND_BUFFER_LEVEL_PRIMARY;
cbInfo.commandBufferCount = (uint32_t)commandBuffers.size();

if (vkAllocateCommandBuffers(VulkanContext::getInstance()->
    getDevice()->logicalDevice, &cbInfo, commandBuffers.data())
    != VK_SUCCESS) {

    throw std::runtime_error(" failed to allocate
        command buffers !!");
}

}
```

We resize the `commandBuffers` vector. Then, to allocate the command buffers, we have to populate `VkCommandBufferAllocateInfo`. We first set the type of the struct and the command pool. Then, we have to specify the level of the command buffers. You can have a chain of command buffers, with the primary command buffer containing the secondary command buffer. For our use, we will set the command buffers as primary. We then set `commandBufferCount`, which is equal to the swapchain pictures.

Then, we allocate the command buffers using the `vkAllocateCommandBuffers` function. We pass in the logical device, the info struct, and the command buffers to allocate memory for the command buffers.

Then, we add `beginCommandBuffer`. This takes in the current command buffer to start recording commands in it:

```
void DrawCommandBuffer::beginCommandBuffer(VkCommandBuffer commandBuffer){

    VkCommandBufferBeginInfo cbBeginInfo = {};

    cbBeginInfo.sType = VK_STRUCTURE_TYPE_COMMAND_BUFFER_BEGIN_INFO;
    cbBeginInfo.flags = VK_COMMAND_BUFFER_USAGE_SIMULTANEOUS_USE_BIT;

    if (vkBeginCommandBuffer(commandBuffer, &cbBeginInfo) != VK_SUCCESS) {

        throw std::runtime_error(" failed to begin command buffer !!");
    }

}
```

To record command buffers, we also have to populate `VkCommandBufferBeginInfoStruct`. Once again, we specify the struct type and the `VK_COMMAND_BUFFER_USAGE_SIMULTANEOUS_USE_BIT` flag. This enables us to schedule the command buffer for the next frame while the last frame is still in use. `vkBeginCommandBuffer` is called to start recording the commands by passing in the current command buffer.

Next, we add in the `endCommandBuffer` function. This function just calls `vkEndCommandBuffer` to stop recording to the command buffer:

```
void DrawCommandBuffer::endCommandBuffer(VkCommandBuffer commandBuffer){

    if (vkEndCommandBuffer(commandBuffer) != VK_SUCCESS) {

        throw std::runtime_error(" failed to record command buffer");

    }

}
```

We can then destroy the command buffers and the pool using the `Destroy` function. Here, we just destroy the pool, which will destroy the command buffers as well:

```
void DrawCommandBuffer::destroy(){

    vkDestroyCommandPool(VulkanContext::getInstance()->
        getDevice()->logicalDevice, commandPool, nullptr);

}
```

In the `VulkanApplication.h` file, include `DrawCommandBuffer.h` and create an object of this class. In `VulkanApplication.cpp`, in the `VulkanInit` function, after creating `renderViewsAndFrameBuffers`, create `DrawCommandBuffer`:

```
renderTexture = new RenderTexture();
renderTexture->createViewsAndFramebuffer(swapChain->swapChainImages,
        swapChain->swapChainImageFormat,
        swapChain->swapChainImageExtent,
        renderPass->renderPass);

drawComBuffer = new DrawCommandBuffer();
drawComBuffer->createCommandPoolAndBuffer(swapChain->
    swapChainImages.size());
```

Beginning and ending Renderpass

Along with the commands being recorded in each frame, the renderpass is also processed for each frame where the color and the depth information is reset. So, since we only have color attachments in each frame, we have to clear the color information for each frame as well. Go back to the `Renderpass.h` file and add two new functions, called `beginRenderPass` and `endRenderPass`, in the class, as follows:

```
class Renderpass
{
public:
    Renderpass();
    ~Renderpass();


    VkRenderPass renderPass;

    void createRenderPass(VkFormat swapChainImageFormat);

    void beginRenderPass(std::array<VkClearValue, 1>
        clearValues, VkCommandBuffer commandBuffer, VkFramebuffer
        swapChainFrameBuffer, VkExtent2D swapChainImageExtent);
    void endRenderPass(VkCommandBuffer commandBuffer);

    void destroy();
};
```

In `RenderPass.cpp`, add the implementation of the `beginRenderPass` function:

```
void Renderpass::beginRenderPass(std::array<VkClearValue, 1> clearValues,
    VkCommandBuffer commandBuffer, VkFramebuffer swapChainFrameBuffer,
    VkExtent2D swapChainImageExtent) {

    VkRenderPassBeginInfo rpBeginInfo = {};
    rpBeginInfo.sType = VK_STRUCTURE_TYPE_RENDER_PASS_BEGIN_INFO;
    rpBeginInfo.renderPass = renderPass;
    rpBeginInfo.framebuffer = swapChainFrameBuffer;
    rpBeginInfo.renderArea.offset = { 0,0 };
    rpBeginInfo.renderArea.extent = swapChainImageExtent;

    rpBeginInfo.pClearValues = clearValues.data();
    rpBeginInfo.clearValueCount = static_cast<uint32_t>(clearValues.size());

    vkCmdBeginRenderPass(commandBuffer, &rpBeginInfo,
        VK_SUBPASS_CONTENTS_INLINE);
}
```

We then populate the `VkRenderPassBeginInfo` struct. In this, we specify the struct type, pass in the renderpass and the current framebuffer, set the render area as the whole viewport, and pass in the clear value and the count. The clear value is the color value we want to clear the screen with, and the count would be 1, as we would like to clear only the color attachment.

To begin the renderpass, we pass in the current command buffer, the info struct, and specify the third parameter as `VK_SUBPASS_CONTENTS_INLINE`, specifying that the renderpass commands are bound to the primary command buffer.

In the `endCommandBuffer` function, we finish the `Renderpass` for the current frame:

```
void Renderpass::endRenderPass(VkCommandBuffer commandBuffer){
    vkCmdEndRenderPass(commandBuffer);
}
```

To end the `Renderpass`, the `vkCmdEndRenderPass` function is called and the current command buffer is passed in.

We have the required classes to get the clear screen going. Now, let's go to the Vulkan Application class and add some lines of code to get it working.

Creating the clear screen

In the `VulkanApplication.h` file, we will add three new functions, called `drawBegin`, `drawEnd`, and `cleanup`. `drawBegin` will be called before we pass in any draw commands, and `drawEnd` will be called once the drawing is done and the frame is ready to be presented to the viewport. In the `cleanup` function, we will destroy all the resources.

We will also create two variables. The first is `uint32_t`, to get the current picture from the swapchain, and the second is `currentCommandBuffer` of the `VkCommandBuffer` type to get the current command buffer:

```
public:
    static VulkanApplication* getInstance();
    static VulkanApplication* instance;

    ~VulkanApplication();

    void initVulkan(GLFWwindow* window);

    void drawBegin();
    void drawEnd();
```

```
    void cleanup();

private:

    uint32_t imageIndex = 0;
    VkCommandBuffer currentCommandBuffer;

    //surface
    VkSurfaceKHR surface;
```

In the `VulkanApplication.cpp` file, we add the implementation of the `drawBegin` and `drawEnd` functions:

```
void VulkanApplication::drawBegin(){

    vkAcquireNextImageKHR(VulkanContext::getInstance()->
        getDevice()->logicalDevice,
            swapChain->swapChain,
            std::numeric_limits<uint64_t>::max(),
            NULL,
            VK_NULL_HANDLE,
            &imageIndex);

    currentCommandBuffer = drawComBuffer->commandBuffers[imageIndex];

    // Begin command buffer recording
    drawComBuffer->beginCommandBuffer(currentCommandBuffer);

    // Begin renderpass
    VkClearValue clearcolor = { 1.0f, 0.0f, 1.0f, 1.0f };

    std::array<VkClearValue, 1> clearValues = { clearcolor };

    renderPass->beginRenderPass(clearValues,
            currentCommandBuffer,
            renderTexture->swapChainFramebuffers[imageIndex],
            renderTexture->_swapChainImageExtent);


}
```

First, we acquire the next picture from the swap chain. This is done using the Vulkan `vkAcquireNextImageKHR` API call. To do this, we pass in the logical device, the swapchain instance. Next, we need to pass in the timeout, for which we pass in the maximum numerical value as we don't care about the time limit. The next two variables are kept as null. These require a semaphore and a fence, which we will discuss in a later chapter. Finally, we pass in the `imageIndex` itself.

Then, we get the current command buffer from the command buffers vector. We begin recording the command buffer by calling `beginCommandBuffer` and the commands will be stored in the `currentCommandBuffer` object. We now start the renderpass. In this, we pass the clear color value, which is the color purple, because *why not?* ! Pass in the current `commandbuffer`, the frame buffer, and the picture extent.

We can now implement the `drawEnd` function:

```
void VulkanApplication::drawEnd(){

    // End render pass commands
    renderPass->endRenderPass(currentCommandBuffer);

    // End command buffer recording
    drawComBuffer->endCommandBuffer(currentCommandBuffer);

    // submit command buffer
    VkSubmitInfo submitInfo = {};
    submitInfo.sType = VK_STRUCTURE_TYPE_SUBMIT_INFO;
    submitInfo.commandBufferCount = 1;
    submitInfo.pCommandBuffers = &currentCommandBuffer;

    vkQueueSubmit(VulkanContext::getInstance()->getDevice()->
        graphicsQueue, 1, &submitInfo, NULL);


    // Present frame
    VkPresentInfoKHR presentInfo = {};
    presentInfo.sType = VK_STRUCTURE_TYPE_PRESENT_INFO_KHR;
    presentInfo.swapchainCount = 1;
    presentInfo.pSwapchains = &swapChain->swapChain;
    presentInfo.pImageIndices = &imageIndex;

    vkQueuePresentKHR(VulkanContext::getInstance()->
        getDevice()->presentQueue, &presentInfo);
    vkQueueWaitIdle(VulkanContext::getInstance()->
        getDevice()->presentQueue);


}
```

We end the renderpass and stop recording to the command buffer. Then, we have to submit the command buffer and present the frame. To submit the command buffer, we create a `VkSubmitInfo` struct and populate it with the struct type, the buffer count, which is 1 per frame, and the command buffer itself. The command is submitted to the graphics queue by calling `vkQueueSubmit` and passing in the graphics queue, the submission count, and the submit info.

Once the frame is rendered, it is presented to the viewport using the present queue.

To present the scene once it is drawn, we have to create and populate the VkPresentInfoKHR struct. For presentation, the picture is sent back to the swapchain. When we create the info and set the type of the struct, we also have to set the swapchain, the image index, and the swapchain count, which is 1.

We then present the picture using vkQueuePresentKHR by passing in the present queue and the present info to the function. At the end, we wait for the host to finish the presentation operation of a given queue using the vkQueueWaitIdle function, which takes in the present queue. Also, it is better to clean up the resources when you are done with them, so add the cleanup function as well:

```
void VulkanApplication::cleanup() {
    vkDeviceWaitIdle(VulkanContext::getInstance()->
        getDevice()->logicalDevice);

    drawComBuffer->destroy();
    renderTexture->destroy();
    renderPass->destroy();
    swapChain->destroy();

    VulkanContext::getInstance()->getDevice()->destroy();

    valLayersAndExt->destroy(vInstance->vkInstance,
        isValidationLayersEnabled);

    vkDestroySurfaceKHR(vInstance->vkInstance, surface, nullptr);
    vkDestroyInstance(vInstance->vkInstance, nullptr);
}
    delete drawComBuffer;
    delete renderTarget;
    delete renderPass;
    delete swapChain;
    delete device;

    delete valLayersAndExt;
    delete vInstance;

    if (instance) {
     delete instance;
     instance = nullptr;
    }
```

When we are destroying the objects, we have to call `vkDeviceWaitIdle` to stop using the device. Then, we destroy the objects in reverse order. So, we destroy the command buffer first, then the render texture resources, then renderpass, and then the swapchain. We then destroy the device, validation layer, surface, and finally, the Vulkan instance. Finally, we also delete the class instances we created for `DrawCommandBuffer`, `RenderTarget`, `Renderpass`, `Swapchain`, `Device`, `ValidationLayersAndExtensions`, and `VulkanInstance`.

And finally, we also delete the instance of `VulkanContext` as well and set it to `nullptr` after deleting it.

In the `source.cpp` file, in the `while` loop, call the `drawBegin` and `drawEnd` functions. Then call the `cleanup` function after the loop:

```cpp
#define GLFW_INCLUDE_VULKAN
#include<GLFW/glfw3.h>

#include "VulkanApplication.h"

int main() {

    glfwInit();

    glfwWindowHint(GLFW_CLIENT_API, GLFW_NO_API);
    glfwWindowHint(GLFW_RESIZABLE, GLFW_FALSE);

    GLFWwindow* window = glfwCreateWindow(1280, 720,
                        "HELLO VULKAN ", nullptr, nullptr);

    VulkanApplication::getInstance()->initVulkan(window);

    while (!glfwWindowShouldClose(window)) {

        VulkanApplication::getInstance()->drawBegin();

        // draw command

        VulkanApplication::getInstance()->drawEnd();

        glfwPollEvents();
    }

    VulkanApplication::getInstance()->cleanup();

    glfwDestroyWindow(window);
```

```
    glfwTerminate();

    return 0;
}
```

You will see a purple viewport, as follows, when you build and run the command:

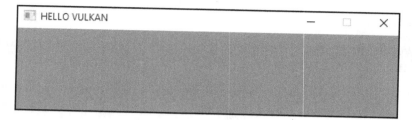

The screen looks OK, but if you look at the console, you will see the following error, which says that when we call `vkAcquireNextImageKHR`, the semaphore and fence cannot both be NULL:

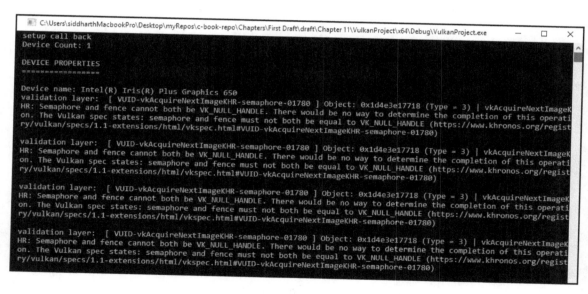

Summary

In this chapter, we looked at the creation of the swapchain, renderpass, render views, framebuffers, and the command buffers. We also looked at what each does and why they are important for rendering a clear screen.

In the next chapter, we will create the resources that will enable us to render geometry to the viewport. Once we have the object resources ready, we will render the objects. We will then explore semaphores and fences and why they are needed.

11
Creating Object Resources

In the previous chapter, we got our clear screen working and created the Vulkan instance. We also created the logical device, the swapchain, the render targets, and the views, as well as the draw command buffer, to record and submit commands to the GPU. Using it, we were able to have a purple clear screen. We haven't drawn any geometry yet, but we are now ready to do so.

In this chapter, we will get most of the things that we need ready to render the geometries. We have to create vertex, index, and uniform buffers. The vertex, index, and uniform buffers will have information regarding the vertex attributes, such as position, color, normal and texture coordinates; index information will have the indices of the vertices we want to draw, and uniform buffers will have information such as a novel view projection matrix.

We will need to create a descriptor set and layout, which will specify to which shader stage the uniform buffers are bound.

We also have to generate the shaders that will be used to draw the geometry.

To create both the object buffers and descriptor sets and layouts, we will create new classes so that they are compartmentalized and we can understand how they are related. Before we hop on the object buffer class, we will add the Mesh class that we created in the OpenGL project, and we will use the same class and add minor changes to it. The Mesh class has information regarding the vertex and index information for the different geometry shapes we want to draw.

We will cover the following topics in this chapter:

- Updating the Mesh class for Vulkan
- Creating the ObjectBuffers class
- Creating the Descriptor class
- Creating the SPIR-V shader binary

Updating the Mesh class for Vulkan

In the `Mesh.h` file, we just have to add a few lines of code to specify `InputBindingDescription` and `InputAttributeDescription`. In `InputBindingDescription`, we specify the binding location, the stride of the data itself, and the input rate, which specifies whether the data is per vertex or per instance. In the `Mesh.h` file in the OpenGL project, we will just add functions to the `Vertex` struct:

```
struct Vertex {

    glm::vec3 pos;
    glm::vec3 normal;
    glm::vec3 color;
  glm::vec2 texCoords;

};
```

So, in the `Vertex` struct, add the function to retrieve `AttributeDesciption`:

```
static VkVertexInputBindingDescription getBindingDescription() {

    VkVertexInputBindingDescription bindingDescription = {};

    bindingDescription.binding = 0;
    bindingDescription.stride = sizeof(Vertex);
    bindingDescription.inputRate = VK_VERTEX_INPUT_RATE_VERTEX;

    return bindingDescription;
}
```

In the function, `VertexInputBindingDescriptor` specifies that the binding is at the 0th index, the stride is equal to the size of the `Vertex` struct itself, and the input rate is `VK_VERTEX_INPUT_RATE_VERTEX`, which is per vertex. The function just returns the created binding description.

Since we have four attributes in the vertex struct, we have to create an attribute descriptor for each one. Add the following function to the `Vertex` struct as well, which returns an array of four input attribute descriptors. For each attribute descriptor, we have to specify the binding location, which is 0 as specified in the binding description, the layout location for each attribute, the format of the data type, and the offset from the start of the `Vertex` struct:

```
static std::array<VkVertexInputAttributeDescription, 4>
getAttributeDescriptions() {
```

```
std::array<VkVertexInputAttributeDescription, 4>
attributeDescriptions = {};

attributeDescriptions[0].binding = 0; // binding index, it is 0 as
                                           specified above
attributeDescriptions[0].location = 0; // location layout
// data format
attributeDescriptions[0].format = VK_FORMAT_R32G32B32_SFLOAT;
attributeDescriptions[0].offset = offsetof(Vertex, pos); // bytes
    since the start of the per vertex data

attributeDescriptions[1].binding = 0;
attributeDescriptions[1].location = 1;
attributeDescriptions[1].format = VK_FORMAT_R32G32B32_SFLOAT;
attributeDescriptions[1].offset = offsetof(Vertex, normal);

attributeDescriptions[2].binding = 0;
attributeDescriptions[2].location = 2;
attributeDescriptions[2].format = VK_FORMAT_R32G32B32_SFLOAT;
attributeDescriptions[2].offset = offsetof(Vertex, color);

attributeDescriptions[3].binding = 0;
attributeDescriptions[3].location = 3;
attributeDescriptions[3].format = VK_FORMAT_R32G32_SFLOAT;
attributeDescriptions[3].offset = offsetof(Vertex, texCoords);

    return attributeDescriptions;
}
```

We will also create a new struct in the `Mesh.h` file to organize the uniform data information. So, create a new struct called `UniformBufferObject`:

```
struct UniformBufferObject {

    glm::mat4 model;
    glm::mat4 view;
    glm::mat4 proj;

};
```

At the top of the `Mesh.h` file, we will also include two `define` statements to tell GLM to use radians instead of degrees, and to use the normalized depth value:

```
#define GLM_FORCE_RADIAN
#define GLM_FORCE_DEPTH_ZERO_TO_ONE
```

That is all for `Mesh.h`. The `Mesh.cpp` file doesn't get modified at all.

Creating the ObjectBuffers class

To create object-related buffers, such as vertex, index, and uniform, we will create a new class called `ObjectBuffers`. In the `ObjectBuffers.h` file, we will add the required `include` statements:

```
#include <vulkan\vulkan.h>
#include <vector>

#include "Mesh.h"
```

Then, we will create the class itself. In the public section, we will add the constructor and the destructor and add the required data types for creating vertex, index, and uniform buffers. We add a vector of the data vertex to set the vertex information of the geometry, create a `VkBuffer` instance called `vertexBuffer` to store the vertex buffer, and create a `VkDeviceMemory` instance called `vertexBufferMemory`:

- `VkBuffer`: This is the handle to the object buffer itself.
- `VkDeviceMemory`: Vulkan operates on memory data in the device's memory through the `DeviceMemory` object.

Similarly, we create a vector to store indices, and create an `indexBuffer` and an `indexBufferMemory` object, just as we did for vertex.

For the uniform buffer, we only create `uniformBuffer` and `uniformBuffer` memory as a vector is not required.

We add a `createVertexIndexUniformBuffers` function that takes in a `Mesh` type, and the vertices and indices will be set based on it.

We also add a destroy function to destroy the Vulkan object we created.

In the private section, we add three functions, which `createVertexIndexUniformBuffers` will call to create the buffers. That is all for the `ObjectBuffers.h` file. So, the `ObjectBuffers` class should be like this:

```
class ObjectBuffers
{
public:
    ObjectBuffers();
    ~ObjectBuffers();

    std::vector<Vertex> vertices;
    VkBuffer vertexBuffer;
```

```
        VkDeviceMemory vertexBufferMemory;

        std::vector<uint32_t> indices;
        VkBuffer indexBuffer;
        VkDeviceMemory indexBufferMemory;

        VkBuffer uniformBuffers;
        VkDeviceMemory uniformBuffersMemory;

        void createVertexIndexUniformsBuffers(MeshType modelType);
        void destroy();

    private:
        void createVertexBuffer();
        void createIndexBuffer();
        void createUniformBuffers();

    };
```

Next, let's move on to the `ObjectBuffers.cpp` file. In this file, we include the headers and create the constructor and destructor:

```
    #include "ObjectBuffers.h"
    #include "Tools.h"
    #include "VulkanContext.h"

    ObjectBuffers::ObjectBuffers(){}

    ObjectBuffers::~ObjectBuffers(){}
```

`Tools.h` is included as we will be adding some more functionality to it that we will use. Next, we will create the `createVertexIndexUniformBuffers` function:

```
    void ObjectBuffers::createVertexIndexUniformsBuffers(MeshType modelType){
        switch (modelType) {

            case kTriangle: Mesh::setTriData(vertices, indices); break;
            case kQuad: Mesh::setQuadData(vertices, indices); break;
            case kCube: Mesh::setCubeData(vertices, indices); break;
            case kSphere: Mesh::setSphereData(vertices, indices); break;

        }

        createVertexBuffer();
        createIndexBuffer();
        createUniformBuffers();

    }
```

Similar to the OpenGL project, we will add a `switch` statement to set the vertex and index data depending on the mesh type. Then we call the `createVertexBuffer`, `createIndexBuffer`, and `createUniformBuffers` functions to set the respective buffers. We will create the `createVertexBuffer` function first.

To create the vertex buffer, it is better if we create the buffer on the device that is on the GPU itself. Now, the **GPU** has two types of memories: **HOST VISIBLE** and **DEVICE LOCAL**. **HOST VISIBLE** is a part of the GPU memory that the CPU has access to. This memory is not very large, so it is used for storing up to 250 MB of data.

For larger chunks of data, such as vertex and index data, it is better to use the **DEVICE LOCAL** memory, which the CPU doesn't have access to.

So, how do you transfer data to the `DEVICE LOCAL` memory? Well, we first have to copy the data to the **HOST VISIBLE** section on the **GPU**, and then copy it to the **DEVICE LOCAL** memory. So, we first create what is called a staging buffer, copy the vertex data into it, and then copy the staging buffer to the actual vertex buffer:

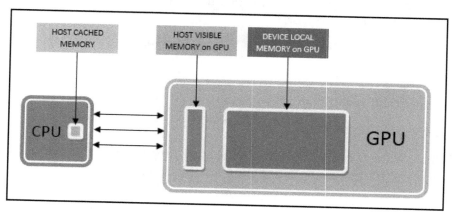

(Source: `https://www.youtube.com/watch?v=rXSdDE7NWmA`)

Let's add functionality into the `VkTool` file to create the different kinds of buffers. With this, we can create both the staging buffer and vertex buffer itself. So, in the `VkTools.h` file in the `vkTools` namespace, add a new function called `createBuffer`. This function takes in five parameters:

- The first is `VkDeviceSize`, which is the size of the data for which the buffer is to be created.
- The second is the `usage` flag, which tells us what the buffer is going to be used for.

- The third is the memory properties where we want to create the buffer; this is where we will specify whether we want it in the HOST VISIBLE section or the DEVICE LOCAL area.
- The fourth is the buffer itself.
- The fifth is the buffer memory to bind the buffer to the following:

```
namespace vkTools {

    VkImageView createImageView(VkImage image,
            VkFormat format,
            VkImageAspectFlags aspectFlags);

    void createBuffer(VkDeviceSize size,
            VkBufferUsageFlags usage,
            VkMemoryPropertyFlags properties,
            VkBuffer &buffer,
            VkDeviceMemory& bufferMemory);

}
```

In the `VKTools.cpp` file, we add the functionality for creating the buffer and binding it to `bufferMemory`. In the namespace, add the new function:

```
void createBuffer(VkDeviceSize size,
        VkBufferUsageFlags usage,
        VkMemoryPropertyFlags properties,
        VkBuffer &buffer, // output
        VkDeviceMemory& bufferMemory) {

// code
}
```

Before binding the buffer, we create the buffer itself. Hence, we populate the `VkBufferCreateInfo` struct as follows:

```
VkBufferCreateInfo bufferInfo = {};
bufferInfo.sType = VK_STRUCTURE_TYPE_BUFFER_CREATE_INFO;
bufferInfo.size = size;
bufferInfo.usage = usage;
bufferInfo.sharingMode = VK_SHARING_MODE_EXCLUSIVE;

if (vkCreateBuffer(VulkanContext::getInstance()->
    getDevice()->logicalDevice, &bufferInfo,
    nullptr, &buffer) != VK_SUCCESS) {

        throw std::runtime_error(" failed to create
          vertex buffer ");
}
```

The struct takes the usual type first, and then we set the buffer size and usage. We also need to specify the buffer sharing mode, because a buffer can be shared between queues, such as graphics and compute, or could be exclusive to one queue. So, here we specify that the buffer is exclusive to the current queue.

Then, the buffer is created by calling `vkCreateBuffer` and passing in `logicalDevice` and `bufferInfo`. Next, to bind the buffer, we have to get the suitable memory type for our specific use of the buffer. So, first we have to get the memory requirements for the kind of buffer we are creating. The requisite memory requirement is received by calling the `vkGetBUfferMemoryRequirements` function, which takes in the logical device, the buffer, and the memory requirements get stored in a variable type called `VkMemoryRequirements`.

We get the memory requirements as follows:

```
VkMemoryRequirements memrequirements;
vkGetBufferMemoryRequirements(VulkanContext::getInstance()->getDevice()->
    logicalDevice, buffer, &memrequirements);
```

To bind memory, we have to populate the `VkMemoryAllocateInfo` struct. It requires the allocation size and the memory index of the type of memory. Each GPU has a different memory type index, with a different heap index and memory type. These are the corresponding values for 1080Ti:

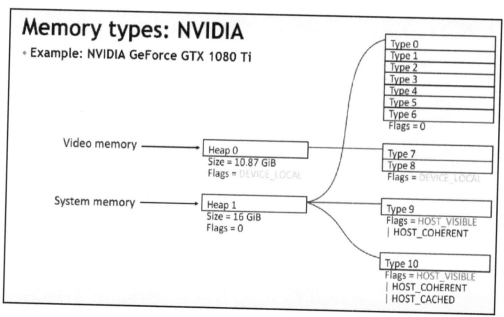

We will now add a new function in VkTools to get the correct kind of memory index for our buffer usage. So, add a new function in VkTool.h under the vkTools namespace, called findMemoryTypeIndex:

```
uint32_t findMemoryTypeIndex(uint32_t typeFilter, VkMemoryPropertyFlags
    properties);
```

It takes two parameters, which are the memory type bits available and the memory properties that we need. Add the implementation for the findMemoryTypeIndex function to the VkTools.cpp file. Under the namespace, add the following function:

```
uint32_t findMemoryTypeIndex(uint32_t typeFilter, VkMemoryPropertyFlags
properties) {

    //-- Properties has two arrays -- memory types and memory heaps
    VkPhysicalDeviceMemoryProperties memProperties;
      vkGetPhysicalDeviceMemoryProperties(VulkanContext::
      getInstance()->getDevice()->physicalDevice,
      &memProperties);

    for (uint32_t i = 0; i < memProperties.memoryTypeCount; i++) {

        if ((typeFilter & (1 << i)) &&
            (memProperties.memoryTypes[i].propertyFlags &
            properties) == properties) {

                return i;
        }
    }

    throw std::runtime_error("failed to find
        suitable memory type!");
}
```

This function gets the device's memory properties using the vkGetPhysicalDeviceMemoryProperties function, and populates the memory properties of the physical device.

The memory properties get information regarding the memory heap and memory type for each index. From all the available indices, we choose what is required for our purposes and return the values. Once the function has been created, we can go back to binding the buffer. So, continuing with our createBuffer function, add the following to it in order to bind the buffer to the memory:

```
VkMemoryAllocateInfo allocInfo = {};
allocInfo.sType = VK_STRUCTURE_TYPE_MEMORY_ALLOCATE_INFO;
```

```
allocInfo.allocationSize = memrequirements.size;
allocInfo.memoryTypeIndex = findMemoryTypeIndex(memrequirements.
                            memoryTypeBits, properties);


if (vkAllocateMemory(VulkanContext::getInstance()->
    getDevice()->logicalDevice, &allocInfo, nullptr,
    &bufferMemory) != VK_SUCCESS) {

        throw std::runtime_error("failed to allocate
           vertex buffer memory");
}

vkBindBufferMemory(VulkanContext::getInstance()->
    getDevice()->logicalDevice, buffer,
    bufferMemory, 0);
```

After all that, we can go back to `ObjectBuffers` to actually create the `createVertexBuffers` function. So, create the function as follows:

```
void ObjectBuffers::createVertexBuffer() {
// code
}
```

In it, we will create the staging buffer first, copy the vertex data into it, and then copy the staging buffer into the vertex buffer. In the function, we first get the total buffer size, which is the number of vertices and the size of the data stored per vertex:

```
VkDeviceSize bufferSize = sizeof(vertices[0]) * vertices.size();
```

Next, we create the staging buffer and `stagingBufferMemory` to bind the staging buffer to it:

```
VkBuffer stagingBuffer;
VkDeviceMemory stagingBufferMemory;
```

And then we call the newly created `createBuffer` in `vkTools` to create the buffer:

```
vkTools::createBuffer(bufferSize,
    VK_BUFFER_USAGE_TRANSFER_SRC_BIT,
    VK_MEMORY_PROPERTY_HOST_VISIBLE_BIT |
    VK_MEMORY_PROPERTY_HOST_COHERENT_BIT,
    stagingBuffer, stagingBufferMemory);
```

In it, we pass in the size, usage, memory type we want, and the buffer and buffer memory. VK_BUFFER_USAGE_TRANSFER_SRC_BIT indicates that the buffer is going to be used as part of a source transfer command when data is transferred.

VK_MEMORY_PROPERTY_HOST_VISIBLE_BIT specifies that we want this to be allocated in the host-visible (CPU) memory space on the GPU.

VK_MEMORY_PROPERTY_HOST_COHERENT_BIT means that CPU cache management is not done by us, but by the system. This will make sure the mapped memory matches the allocated memory. Next, we use vkMapMemory to get a host pointer to the staging buffer and create a void pointer called data. Then, call vkMapMemory to get the pointer to the mapped memory:

```
void* data;

vkMapMemory(VulkanContext::getInstance()->getDevice()->
    logicalDevice, stagingBufferMemory,
        0, // offet
        bufferSize,// size
        0,// flag
        &data);
```

VkMapMemory takes the logical device, the staging buffer binding, we specify 0 for the offset, and pass the buffer size. There are no special flags, so we pass in 0 and get the pointer to the mapped memory. We use memcpy to copy the vertex data to the data pointer:

```
memcpy(data, vertices.data(), (size_t)bufferSize);
```

We unmap the staging memory once host access to it is no longer required:

```
vkUnmapMemory(VulkanContext::getInstance()->getDevice()->logicalDevice,
    stagingBufferMemory);
```

Now that the data is stored in the staging buffer, let's next create the vertex buffer and bind it to vertexBufferMemory:

```
// Create Vertex Buffer
    vkTools::createBuffer(bufferSize,
            VK_BUFFER_USAGE_TRANSFER_DST_BIT |
            VK_BUFFER_USAGE_VERTEX_BUFFER_BIT,
            VK_MEMORY_PROPERTY_DEVICE_LOCAL_BIT,
            vertexBuffer,
            vertexBufferMemory);
```

We use the `createBuffer` function to create the vertex buffer. We pass in the buffer size. For the buffer usage, we specify that it is used as the destination of the transfer command when we transfer the staging buffer to it, and it will be used as the vertex buffer. For the memory property, we want this to be created in `DEVICE_LOCAL` for the best performance. Pass the vertex buffer and vertex buffer memory to bind the buffer to the memory. Now, we have to copy the staging buffer to the vertex buffer.

Copying buffers on the GPU has to be done using transfer queues and command buffers. We could get the transfer queue to do the transfer in the same way as we retrieved the graphics and presentation queues. The good news is that we don't need to, because all graphics and compute queues also support transfer functionality, so we will use the graphics queue for it.

We will create two helper functions in the `vkTools` namespace for creating and destroying temporary command buffers. So, in the `VkTools.h` file, add two functions in the namespace for the beginning and ending single-time commands:

```
VkCommandBuffer beginSingleTimeCommands(VkCommandPool commandPool);
    void endSingleTimeCommands(VkCommandBuffer commandBuffer,
VkCommandPool commandPool);
```

Basically, `beginSingleTimeCommands` returns a command buffer for us to use, and `endSingleTimeCommands` destroys the command buffer. In the `VkTools.cpp` file, under the namespace, add these two functions:

```
VkCommandBuffer beginSingleTimeCommands(VkCommandPool commandPool) {

    //-- Alloc Command buffer
    VkCommandBufferAllocateInfo allocInfo = {};

    allocInfo.sType = VK_STRUCTURE_TYPE_COMMANDBUFFER
                      ALLOCATE_INFO;
    allocInfo.level = VK_COMMAND_BUFFER_LEVEL_PRIMARY;
    allocInfo.commandPool = commandPool;
    allocInfo.commandBufferCount = 1;

    VkCommandBuffer commandBuffer;
    vkAllocateCommandBuffers(VulkanContext::getInstance()->
      getDevice()->logicalDevice,
      &allocInfo, &commandBuffer);

    //-- Record command buffer

    VkCommandBufferBeginInfo beginInfo = {};
    beginInfo.sType = VK_STRUCTURE_TYPE_COMMAND_BUFFER_BEGIN_INFO;
    beginInfo.flags = VK_COMMAND_BUFFER_USAGE_ONE_TIME_SUBMIT_BIT;
```

```
        //start recording
        vkBeginCommandBuffer(commandBuffer, &beginInfo);

        return commandBuffer;

    }


void endSingleTimeCommands(VkCommandBuffer commandBuffer,
    VkCommandPool commandPool) {

        //-- End recording
        vkEndCommandBuffer(commandBuffer);

        //-- Execute the Command Buffer to complete the transfer
        VkSubmitInfo submitInfo = {};
        submitInfo.sType = VK_STRUCTURE_TYPE_SUBMIT_INFO;
        submitInfo.commandBufferCount = 1;
        submitInfo.pCommandBuffers = &commandBuffer;

        vkQueueSubmit(VulkanContext::getInstance()->
            getDevice()->graphicsQueue, 1, &submitInfo,
            VK_NULL_HANDLE);
        vkQueueWaitIdle(VulkanContext::getInstance()->
            getDevice()->graphicsQueue);

        vkFreeCommandBuffers(VulkanContext::getInstance()->
            getDevice()->logicalDevice, commandPool, 1,
            &commandBuffer);

    }
```

We have already looked at how to create and destroy command buffers. If you have any questions, you can refer to `Chapter 11`, *Preparing the Clear Screen*. Next, in the `Vktools.h` file, we will add the functionality to copy a buffer. Add a new function under the namespace:

```
VkCommandBuffer beginSingleTimeCommands(VkCommandPool commandPool);
void endSingleTimeCommands(VkCommandBuffer commandBuffer,
    VkCommandPool commandPool);

void copyBuffer(VkBuffer srcBuffer,
        VkBuffer dstBuffer,
        VkDeviceSize size);
```

The `copyBuffer` function takes a source buffer, a destination buffer, and the buffer size as input. Now, add this new function to the `VkTools.cpp` file:

```cpp
void copyBuffer(VkBuffer srcBuffer,
        VkBuffer dstBuffer,
        VkDeviceSize size) {

QueueFamilyIndices qFamilyIndices = VulkanContext::getInstance()->
    getDevice()->getQueueFamiliesIndicesOfCurrentDevice();


    // Create Command Pool
    VkCommandPool commandPool;

    VkCommandPoolCreateInfo cpInfo = {};

    cpInfo.sType = VK_STRUCTURE_TYPE_COMMAND_POOL_CREATE_INFO;
    cpInfo.queueFamilyIndex = qFamilyIndices.graphicsFamily;
    cpInfo.flags = 0;

    if (vkCreateCommandPool(VulkanContext::getInstance()->
        getDevice()->logicalDevice, &cpInfo, nullptr, &commandPool) !=
        VK_SUCCESS) {
            throw std::runtime_error(" failed to create
                command pool !!");
    }


    // Allocate command buffer and start recording
    VkCommandBuffer commandBuffer = beginSingleTimeCommands(commandPool);

    //-- Copy the buffer
    VkBufferCopy copyregion = {};
    copyregion.srcOffset = 0;
    copyregion.dstOffset = 0;
    copyregion.size = size;
    vkCmdCopyBuffer(commandBuffer, srcBuffer, dstBuffer,
        1, &copyregion);

    // End recording and Execute command buffer and free command buffer
    endSingleTimeCommands(commandBuffer, commandPool);

    vkDestroyCommandPool(VulkanContext::getInstance()->
        getDevice()->logicalDevice, commandPool,
        nullptr);

}
```

In the function, we first get the queue family indices from the device. We then create a new command pool, and then we create a new command buffer using the `beginSingleTimeCommands` function. To copy the buffer, we create the `VkBufferCopy` struct. We set the source and destination offset to be 0 and set the buffer size.

To actually copy the buffers, we call the `vlCmdCopyBuffer` function, which takes in a command buffer, the source command buffer, the destination command buffer, the copy region count (which is 1 in this case), and the copy region struct. Once the buffers are copied, we call `endSingleTimeCommands` to destroy the command buffer and call `vkDestroyCommandPool` to destroy the command pool itself.

Now, we can go back to the `createVertexBuffers` function in `ObjectsBuffers` and copy the staging buffer to the vertex buffer. We also destroy the staging buffer and the buffer memory:

```
vkTools::copyBuffer(stagingBuffer,
        vertexBuffer,
        bufferSize);

vkDestroyBuffer(VulkanContext::getInstance()->
    getDevice()->logicalDevice, stagingBuffer, nullptr);
vkFreeMemory(VulkanContext::getInstance()->
    getDevice()->logicalDevice, stagingBufferMemory, nullptr);
```

The index buffers are created the same way, using the `createIndexBuffer` function:

```
void ObjectBuffers::createIndexBuffer() {

    VkDeviceSize bufferSize = sizeof(indices[0]) * indices.size();

    VkBuffer stagingBuffer;
    VkDeviceMemory stagingBufferMemory;

    vkTools::createBuffer(bufferSize,
        VK_BUFFER_USAGE_TRANSFER_SRC_BIT,
        VK_MEMORY_PROPERTY_HOST_VISIBLE_BIT |
        VK_MEMORY_PROPERTY_HOST_COHERENT_BIT,
        stagingBuffer, stagingBufferMemory);

    void* data;
    vkMapMemory(VulkanContext::getInstance()->
        getDevice()->logicalDevice, stagingBufferMemory,
        0, bufferSize, 0, &data);
    memcpy(data, indices.data(), (size_t)bufferSize);
    vkUnmapMemory(VulkanContext::getInstance()->
```

```
        getDevice()->logicalDevice, stagingBufferMemory);

    vkTools::createBuffer(bufferSize,
            VK_BUFFER_USAGE_TRANSFER_DST_BIT |
            VK_BUFFER_USAGE_INDEX_BUFFER_BIT,
            VK_MEMORY_PROPERTY_DEVICE_LOCAL_BIT,
            indexBuffer,
            indexBufferMemory);

    vkTools::copyBuffer(stagingBuffer,
            indexBuffer,
            bufferSize);

    vkDestroyBuffer(VulkanContext::getInstance()->
        getDevice()->logicalDevice,
        stagingBuffer, nullptr);
    vkFreeMemory(VulkanContext::getInstance()->
        getDevice()->logicalDevice,
        stagingBufferMemory, nullptr);

}
```

Creating `UniformBuffer` is easier, because we will just be using the `HOST_VISIBLE` GPU memory, so staging buffers are not required:

```
void ObjectBuffers::createUniformBuffers() {

    VkDeviceSize bufferSize = sizeof(UniformBufferObject);

    vkTools::createBuffer(bufferSize,
            VK_BUFFER_USAGE_UNIFORM_BUFFER_BIT,
            VK_MEMORY_PROPERTY_HOST_VISIBLE_BIT |
            VK_MEMORY_PROPERTY_HOST_COHERENT_BIT,
            uniformBuffers, uniformBuffersMemory);

}
```

Finally, we destroy the buffers and memories in the `destroy` function:

```
void ObjectBuffers::destroy(){

    vkDestroyBuffer(VulkanContext::getInstance()->
        getDevice()->logicalDevice, uniformBuffers, nullptr);
    vkFreeMemory(VulkanContext::getInstance()->
        getDevice()->logicalDevice, uniformBuffersMemory,
        nullptr);
```

```
vkDestroyBuffer(VulkanContext::getInstance()->
    getDevice()->logicalDevice, indexBuffer, nullptr);
vkFreeMemory(VulkanContext::getInstance()->
    getDevice()->logicalDevice, indexBufferMemory,
    nullptr);

vkDestroyBuffer(VulkanContext::getInstance()->
    getDevice()->logicalDevice, vertexBuffer, nullptr);
vkFreeMemory(VulkanContext::getInstance()->
    getDevice()->logicalDevice, vertexBufferMemory, nullptr);


}
```

Creating the Descriptor class

Unlike OpenGL, where we had uniform buffers to pass in the model, view, projection, and other kinds of data, Vulkan has descriptors. In descriptors, we have to first specify the layout of the buffer, as well as the binding location, count, type of descriptor, and the shader stage it is associated with.

Once the descriptor layout is created with the different types of descriptors, we have to create a descriptor pool for the number-swapchain image count because the uniform buffer will be set for each time per frame.

After that, we can allocate and populate the descriptor sets for both the frames. The allocation of data will be done from the pool.

We will create a new class for creating the descriptor set, layout binding, pool, and allocating and populating the descriptor sets. Create a new class called Descriptor. In the Descriptor.h file, add the following code:

```
#pragma once
#include <vulkan\vulkan.h>
#include <vector>

class Descriptor
{
public:
    Descriptor();
    ~Descriptor();

    // all the descriptor bindings are combined into a single layout

    VkDescriptorSetLayout descriptorSetLayout;
```

```
    VkDescriptorPool descriptorPool;
    VkDescriptorSet descriptorSet;

    void createDescriptorLayoutSetPoolAndAllocate(uint32_t
        _swapChainImageCount);
    void populateDescriptorSets(uint32_t _swapChainImageCount,
        VkBuffer uniformBuffers);

    void destroy();

  private:

    void createDescriptorSetLayout();
    void createDescriptorPoolAndAllocateSets(uint32_t
        _swapChainImageCount);

};
```

We include the usual `Vulkan.h` and vector. In the public section, we create the class with the constructor and the destructor. We also create three variables, called `descriptorSetLayout`, `descriptorPool`, and `descriptorSets`, of the `VkDescriptorSetLayout`, `VkDescriptorPool`, and `VkDescriptorSet` types for easy access to the set. The `createDescriptorLayoutSetPoolAndAllocate` function will call the private `createDescriptorSetLayout` and `createDescriptorPoolAndAllocateSets` functions, which will create the layout set and then create the descriptor pool and allocate to it. The `populateDescriptorSets` function will be called when we set the uniform buffer to populate the sets with the data.

We also have a `destroy` function to destroy the Vulkan objects that have been created. In the `Descriptor.cpp` file, we will add the implementations of the functions. Add the necessary includes first, and then add the constructor, destructor, and the `createDescriptorLayoutAndPool` function:

```
#include "Descriptor.h"

#include<array>
#include "VulkanContext.h"

#include "Mesh.h"

Descriptor::Descriptor(){

}
Descriptor::~Descriptor(){
```

```
}

void Descriptor::createDescriptorLayoutSetPoolAndAllocate(uint32_t
    _swapChainImageCount) {

    createDescriptorSetLayout();
    createDescriptorPoolAndAllocateSets(_swapChainImageCount);


}
```

The `createDescriptorLayoutSetPoolAndAllocate` function calls the `createDescriptorSetLayout` and `createDescriptorPoolAndAllocateSets` functions. Let's now add the `createDescriptorSetLayout` function:

```
void Descriptor::createDescriptorSetLayout() {

    VkDescriptorSetLayoutBinding uboLayoutBinding = {};
    uboLayoutBinding.binding = 0;// binding location
    uboLayoutBinding.descriptorCount = 1;
    uboLayoutBinding.descriptorType = VK_DESCRIPTOR_TYPE_UNIFORM_BUFFER;
    uboLayoutBinding.stageFlags = VK_SHADER_STAGE_VERTEX_BIT;
    std::array<VkDescriptorSetLayoutBinding, 1>
        layoutBindings = { uboLayoutBinding };

    VkDescriptorSetLayoutCreateInfo layoutCreateInfo = {};
    layoutCreateInfo.sType = VK_STRUCTURE_TYPE_DESCRIPTORSET
                        LAYOUT_CREATE_INFO;
    layoutCreateInfo.bindingCount = static_cast<uint32_t>
                            (layoutBindings.size());
    layoutCreateInfo.pBindings = layoutBindings.data();

    if (vkCreateDescriptorSetLayout(VulkanContext::getInstance()->
        getDevice()->logicalDevice, &layoutCreateInfo, nullptr,
        &descriptorSetLayout) != VK_SUCCESS) {

            throw std::runtime_error("failed to create
                descriptor set layout");
    }
}
```

For our project, the layout set will just have one layout binding, which is the one struct with the model, view, and projection matrix information.

We have to populate the `VkDescriptorSetLayout` struct and specify the binding location index, the count, the type of information we will be passing in, and the shader stage to which the uniform buffer will be sent. After creating the set layout, we populate `VkDescriptorSetLayoutCreateInfo`, in which we specify the binding count and the bindings itself.

Then, we call the `vkCreateDescriptorSetLayout` function to create the descriptor set layout by passing in the logical device and the layout creation info. Next, we add the `createDescriptorPoolAndAllocateSets` function:

```cpp
void Descriptor::createDescriptorPoolAndAllocateSets(uint32_t
    _swapChainImageCount) {

    // create pool
    std::array<VkDescriptorPoolSize, 1> poolSizes = {};

    poolSizes[0].type = VK_DESCRIPTOR_TYPE_UNIFORM_BUFFER;
    poolSizes[0].descriptorCount = _swapChainImageCount;


    VkDescriptorPoolCreateInfo poolInfo = {};
    poolInfo.sType = VK_STRUCTURE_TYPE_DESCRIPTOR_POOL_CREATE_INFO;
    poolInfo.poolSizeCount = static_cast<uint32_t>(poolSizes.size());
    poolInfo.pPoolSizes = poolSizes.data();

    poolInfo.maxSets = _swapChainImageCount;

    if (vkCreateDescriptorPool(VulkanContext::getInstance()->
        getDevice()->logicalDevice, &poolInfo, nullptr,
        &descriptorPool) != VK_SUCCESS) {

        throw std::runtime_error("failed to create descriptor pool ");
    }


    // allocate
    std::vector<VkDescriptorSetLayout> layouts(_swapChainImageCount,
        descriptorSetLayout);

    VkDescriptorSetAllocateInfo allocInfo = {};
    allocInfo.sType = VK_STRUCTURE_TYPE_DESCRIPTOR_SET_ALLOCATE_INFO;
    allocInfo.descriptorPool = descriptorPool;
    allocInfo.descriptorSetCount = _swapChainImageCount;
    allocInfo.pSetLayouts = layouts.data();

    if (vkAllocateDescriptorSets(VulkanContext::getInstance()->
        getDevice()->logicalDevice, &allocInfo, &descriptorSet)
```

```
        != VK_SUCCESS) {

            throw std::runtime_error("failed to allocate descriptor
                sets ! ");
    }
}
```

To create the descriptor pool, we have to specify the pool size using `VkDescriptorPoolSize`. We create an array of it and call it `poolSizes`. Since, in the layout set, we just have the uniform buffer, we set its type and set the count equal to the swap-chain-image count. To create the descriptor pool, we have to specify the type, pool-size count, and the pool-size data. We also have to set the maxsets, which is the maximum number of sets that can be allocated from the pool, which is equal to the swap-chain-image count. We create the descriptor pool by calling `vkCreateDescriptorPool` and passing in the logical device and the pool-creation info. Next, we have to specify allocation parameters for the description sets.

We create a vector of the descriptor set layout. Then, we create the `VkDescriptionAllocationInfo` struct to populate it. We pass in the description pool, the descriptor set count (which is equal to the swap-chain-images count), and pass in the layout data. Then, we allocate the descriptor sets by calling `vkAllocateDescriptorSets` and passing in the logical device and the create info struct.

Finally, we will add the `populateDescriptorSets` function, as follows:

```
void Descriptor::populateDescriptorSets(uint32_t _swapChainImageCount,
    VkBuffer uniformBuffers) {

    for (size_t i = 0; i < _swapChainImageCount; i++) {

        // Uniform buffer info

        VkDescriptorBufferInfo uboBufferDescInfo = {};
        uboBufferDescInfo.buffer = uniformBuffers;
        uboBufferDescInfo.offset = 0;
        uboBufferDescInfo.range = sizeof(UniformBufferObject);

        VkWriteDescriptorSet uboDescWrites;
        uboDescWrites.sType = VK_STRUCTURE_TYPE_WRITE_DESCRIPTOR_SET;
        uboDescWrites.pNext = NULL;
        uboDescWrites.dstSet = descriptorSet;
        uboDescWrites.dstBinding = 0; // binding index of 0
        uboDescWrites.dstArrayElement = 0;
        uboDescWrites.descriptorType = VK_DESCRIPTOR_TYPE_UNIFORM_BUFFER;
        uboDescWrites.descriptorCount = 1;
        uboDescWrites.pBufferInfo = &uboBufferDescInfo; // uniforms
```

```
                                                              buffers
    uboDescWrites.pImageInfo = nullptr;
    uboDescWrites.pTexelBufferView = nullptr;


    std::array<VkWriteDescriptorSet, 1> descWrites = { uboDescWrites};


    vkUpdateDescriptorSets(VulkanContext::getInstance()->
      getDevice()->logicalDevice, static_cast<uint32_t>
      (descWrites.size()), descWrites.data(), 0,
      nullptr);
  }


}
```

This function takes in the swapchain image count and the uniform buffer as parameters. For both the images of the swapchain, the configuration of the descriptor needs to be updated by calling `vkUpdateDescriptorSets`. This function takes in an array of `VkWriteDescriptorSet`. Now, `VkWriteDescriptorSet` takes in either a buffer, image struct, or `texelBufferView` as a parameter. Since we are going to use the uniform buffer, we will have to create it and pass it in. `VkdescriptorBufferInfo` takes in a buffer (which will be the uniform buffer we created), takes an offset (which is none in this case), and then takes the range (which is the size of the buffer itself).

After creating it, we can start specifying `VkWriteDescriptorSet`. This takes in the type, `descriptorSet`, and the binding location (which is the 0th index). It has no array elements in it, and it takes the descriptor type (which is the uniform buffer type); the descriptor count is 1, and we pass in the buffer info struct. For the image info and the texel buffer view, we specify none, as it is not being used.

We then create an array of `VkWriteDescriptorSet` and add the uniform buffer descriptor writes info we created, called `uboDescWrites`, to it. We update the descriptor set by calling `vkUpdateDescriptorSets` and pass in the logical device, the descriptor writes size, and the data. That's it for the `populateDescriptorSets` function. We finally add the destroy function, which destroys the descriptor pool and the descriptor set layout. Add the function as follows:

```
void Descriptor::destroy(){

    vkDestroyDescriptorPool(VulkanContext::getInstance()->
      getDevice()->logicalDevice, descriptorPool, nullptr);
    vkDestroyDescriptorSetLayout(VulkanContext::getInstance()->
      getDevice()->logicalDevice, descriptorSetLayout, nullptr);
}
```

Creating the SPIR-V shader binary

Unlike OpenGL, which takes in GLSL (OpenGL Shading Language) human-readable files for shaders, Vulkan takes in shaders in binary or byte code format. All shaders, whether vertex, fragment, or compute, have to be in byte code format.

SPIR-V is also good for cross-compilation, making porting shader files a lot easier. If you have a Direct3D HLSL shader code, it can be compiled to SPIR-V format and can be used in a Vulkan application, making it very easy to port Direct3D games to Vulkan. The shader is initially written in GLSL, with some minor changes to how we wrote it for OpenGL. A compiler is provided, which compiles the code from GLSL to SPIR-V format. The compiler is included with the Vulkan SDK installation. The basic vertex-shader GLSL code is as follows:

```
#version 450
#extension GL_ARB_separate_shader_objects : enable

layout (binding = 0) uniform UniformBufferOBject{

mat4 model;
mat4 view;
mat4 proj;

} ubo;

layout(location = 0) in vec3 inPosition;
layout(location = 1) in vec3 inNormal;
layout(location = 2) in vec3 inColor;
layout(location = 3) in vec2 inTexCoord;

layout(location = 0) out vec3 fragColor;


void main() {
    gl_Position = ubo.proj * ubo.view * ubo.model * vec4(inPosition, 1.0);
    fragColor = inColor;
}
```

The shader should look very familiar, with some minor changes. For example, the GLSL version is still specified at the top. In this case, it is #version 450. But we also see new things, such as #extension GL_ARB_seperate_shader_objects: enable. This specifies the extension that the shader uses. In this case, an old extension is needed, which basically lets us use vertex and fragment shaders as separate files. Extensions need to be approved by the **Architecture Review Board (ARB).**

Apart from the inclusion of the extension, you may have noticed that there is a location layout specified for all data types. And you may have noticed that when creating vertex and uniform buffers, we had to specify the binding index for the buffers. In Vulkan, there is no equivalent to GLgetUniformLocation to get the location index of a uniform buffer. This is because it takes quite a bit of system resources to get the location. Instead, we specify and sort of hardcode the value of the index. The uniform buffers, as well as the in and out buffer can all be assigned an index of 0 as they are of different data types. Since the uniform buffer will be sent as a st ruct with model, view, and projection matrices, a similar struct is created in the shader and assigned to the 0th index of the uniform layout.

All four attributes are also assigned a layout index 0, 1, 2, and 3, as specified in the Mesh.h file under the Vertex struct when setting the VkVertexInputAttributeDescription for the four attributes. The out is also assigned a layout location index of 0, and the data type is specified as vec3. Then, in the main function of the shader, we set the gl_Position value by multiplying the local coordinate of the object by the model, view, and projection matrix received from the uniform buffer struct. Furthermore, outColor is set as inColor received.

The fragment shader is as follows: open a .txt file, add the shader code to it, and name the file basic. Also, change the extension to *.vert from *.txt:

```
#version 450
#extension GL_ARB_separate_shader_objects : enable

layout(location = 0) in vec3 fragColor;

layout(location = 0) out vec4 outColor;

void main() {

    outColor = vec4(fragColor, 1.0f);
}
```

Here, we specify the GLSL version and the extension to use. There are in and out, both of which have a location layout of 0. Note that in is a vec3 called fragColor, which is what we sent out of the vertex shader, and that outColor is a vec4. In the main function of the shader file, we convert vec3 to vec4 and set the resultant color to outColor. Add the fragment shader to a file called basic.frag. In the VulkanProject root directory, create a new folder called shaders and add the two shader files to it:

Create a new folder called SPIRV, as this is where we will put the compiled SPIRV bytecode file. To compile the .glsl files, we will use the glslValidator.exe file, which was installed when we installed the Vulkan SDK. Now, to compile the code, we can use the following command:

```
glslangValidator.exe -V basic.frag -o basic.frag.spv
```

Hold *Shift* on the keyboard, right-click in the shaders folder, and click the Open PowerShell window here:

In PowerShell, type in the following command:

```
\VulkanProject\shaders> glslangValidator.exe -V basic.frag -o basic.frag.spv
```

Make sure the *V* is capitalized and the *o* is lowercase, otherwise, it will give compile errors. This will create a new spirv file in the folder. Change frag to vert to compile the SPIRV vertex shader:

```
\VulkanProject\shaders> glslangValidator.exe -V basic.frag -o basic.frag.spv
\VulkanProject\shaders> glslangValidator.exe -V basic.vert -o basic.vert.spv
```

This will create the vertex and fragment shader SPIRV binaries in the folder:

Name	Date modified	Type	Size
SPIRV	3/18/2019 5:12 PM	File folder	
basic.frag	3/18/2019 5:16 PM	FRAG File	1 KB
basic.frag.spv	4/1/2019 2:34 PM	SPV File	1 KB
basic.vert	3/18/2019 5:12 PM	VERT File	1 KB
basic.vert.spv	4/1/2019 2:34 PM	SPV File	3 KB

Instead of compiling the code manually each time, we can create a `.bat` file that can do this for us, and put the compiled SPIRV binaries in the `SPIRV` folder. In the `shaders` folder, create a new `.txt` file and name it `glsl_spirv_compiler.bat`.

In the `.bat` file, add the following:

```
@echo off
echo compiling glsl shaders to spirv
for /r %%i in (*.vert;*.frag) do %VULKAN_SDK%\Bin32\glslangValidator.exe -V
"%%i" -o  "%%~dpiSPIRV\%%~nxi".spv
```

Save and close the file. Now double-click on the `.bat` file to execute it. This will compile the shaders and place the compiled binary in the SPIRV shader files:

You can delete the SPIRV files in the `shaders` folder that we compiled earlier using the console command because we will be using the shader files in the `SPIRV` subfolder.

Summary

In this chapter, we created all the resources required to render the geometry. First of all, we added the Mesh class, which has vertex and index information for all the mesh types, including triangle, quad, cube, and sphere. Then, we created the ObjectBuffers class, which was used to store and bind the buffers to the GPU memory using the VkTool file. We also created a separate descriptor class, which has our descriptor set layout and pool. In addition, we created descriptor sets. Finally, we created the SPIRV bytecode shader files, which were compiled from the GLSL shader.

In the next chapter, we will use the resources we created here to draw our first colored geometry.

12
Drawing Vulkan Objects

In the previous chapter, we created all the resources that were required for an object to be drawn. In this chapter, we will create the `ObjectRenderer` class, which will draw an object on the viewport. This class is used so that we have an actual geometric object to draw and view alongside our awesome purple viewport.

We will also learn how to synchronize CPU and GPU operations at the end of the chapter, which will remove the validation error that we got in Chapter 11, *Creating Object Resources*.

Before we set the scene up for rendering, we have to prepare one last thing for the geometry render; that is, the graphics pipeline. We will begin setting this up next.

In this chapter, we will cover the following topics:

- Preparing the `GraphicsPipeline` class
- The `ObjectRenderer` class
- Changes to the `VulkanContext` class
- The `Camera` class
- Drawing an object
- Synchronizing an object

Preparing the GraphicsPipeline class

The graphics pipeline defines the pipeline an object should follow when it is drawn. As we discovered in Chapter 2, *Mathematics and Graphics Concepts,* there is a series of steps that we need to follow to draw an object:

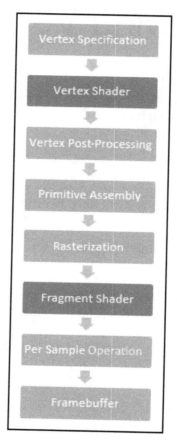

In OpenGL, pipeline states can be changed at any time, just like we enabled and disabled blending when drawing text in Chapter 8, *Enhancing Your Game with Collision, Loop, and Lighting.* However, changing states takes up a lot of system resources, which is why Vulkan discourages you from changing states at will. Therefore, you will have to set the pipeline states in advance for each object. Before you create a pipeline's state, you also need to create a pipeline layout that takes the descriptor set layout we created in the previous chapter. So, we will create the pipeline layout first.

Then, we also need to provide the shader SPIR-V files, which will have to be read to understand how to create the shader modules. So, add the functionality to the class. We then populate the graphics pipeline info, which will use the different shader modules that we created. We also specify the vertex input state, which will have information regarding the buffer's bindings and attributes, which we created earlier when defining the vertex struct.

The input assembly state also needs to be specified, which describes the kind of geometry to be drawn with the vertices. Note that we can draw points, lines, or triangles with the given set of vertices.

Additionally, we need to specify the viewport state, which describes the region of the framebuffer that will be rendered, as we can display part of the framebuffer to the viewport if necessary. In our case, we will be displaying the whole region to the viewport. We specify the rasterization state, which will perform depth testing and back-face culling, and convert the geometry to rasterized lines – which will be colored, as specified in the fragment shader.

The multisampling state will specify whether you want to enable multisampling to enable anti-aliasing. The depth and stencil states specify whether the depth and stencil tests are enabled and are to be performed on the object. The color blending state specifies whether blending is enabled or not. Finally, the dynamic state enables us to change some pipeline states dynamically without creating the pipeline again. We won't be using dynamic states for our implementation. With all this set, we can create the graphics pipeline for the object.

Let's begin by creating a new class for the graphics pipeline. In the `GraphicsPipeline.h` file, add the following:

```
#include <vulkan\vulkan.h>
#include <vector>

#include <fstream>

class GraphicsPipeline
{
public:
    GraphicsPipeline();
    ~GraphicsPipeline();

    VkPipelineLayout pipelineLayout;
    VkPipeline graphicsPipeline;

    void createGraphicsPipelineLayoutAndPipeline(VkExtent2D
        swapChainImageExtent, VkDescriptorSetLayout descriptorSetLayout,
        VkRenderPass renderPass);
```

```
    void destroy();

private:

    std::vector<char> readfile(const std::string& filename);
    VkShaderModule createShaderModule(const std::vector<char> & code);

    void createGraphicsPipelineLayout(VkDescriptorSetLayout
        descriptorSetLayout);
    void createGraphicsPipeline(VkExtent2D swapChainImageExtent,
        VkRenderPass renderPass);

};
```

We include the usual headers and also fstream, because we will need it for reading the shader files. We then create the class itself. In the public section, we will add the constructor and destructor. We create objects for storing the pipelineLayout and graphicsPipeline of the VkPipelineLayout and VkPipeline types respectively.

We create a new function called createGraphicsPipelineLayoutAndPipeline, which takes VkExtent2D, VkDesriptorSetLayout, and VkRenderPass, as this is required for creating both the layout and the actual pipeline itself. The function will internally be calling createGraphicsPipelineLayout and createGraphicsPipeline, which will create the layout and the pipeline respectively. These functions are added to the private section.

In the public section, we also have a function called destroy, which will destroy all the created resources. In the private section, we also have two more functions. The first is the readFile function, which reads the SPIR-V file, and the second is createShaderModule, which will create the shader module from the read shader file. Let's now move on to the GraphicsPipeline.cpp file:

```
#include "GraphicsPipeline.h"

#include "VulkanContext.h"
#include "Mesh.h"

GraphicsPipeline::GraphicsPipeline(){}

GraphicsPipeline::~GraphicsPipeline(){}
```

In the preceding code block, we include the GraphicsPipeline.h, VulkanContext.h, and Mesh.h files because they are required. We also add the implementation for the constructor and the destructor.

We then add the `createGraphicsPipelineLayoutAndPipeline` function, as follows:

```
void GraphicsPipeline::createGraphicsPipelineLayoutAndPipeline(VkExtent2D
   swapChainImageExtent, VkDescriptorSetLayout descriptorSetLayout,
VkRenderPass renderPass){

   createGraphicsPipelineLayout(descriptorSetLayout);
   createGraphicsPipeline(swapChainImageExtent, renderPass);

}
```

The `createPipelineLayout` function is created as follows. We have to create a `createInfo` struct with the structure type, set the `descriptorLayout` and count, and then create the pipeline layout using the `vkCreatePipelineLayout` function:

```
void GraphicsPipeline::createGraphicsPipelineLayout(VkDescriptorSetLayout
   descriptorSetLayout){

   VkPipelineLayoutCreateInfo pipelineLayoutInfo = {};
   pipelineLayoutInfo.sType = VK_STRUCTURE_TYPEPIPELINE_
                              LAYOUT_CREATE_INFO;

// used for passing uniform objects and images to the shader
pipelineLayoutInfo.setLayoutCount = 1;
   pipelineLayoutInfo.pSetLayouts = &descriptorSetLayout;


   if (vkCreatePipelineLayout(VulkanContext::getInstance()->
      getDevice()->logicalDevice, &pipelineLayoutInfo, nullptr,
      &pipelineLayout) != VK_SUCCESS) {

         throw std::runtime_error(" failed to create pieline
            layout !");
   }

}
```

Before we add the create pipeline function, we will add the `readFile` and `createShaderModule` functions:

```
std::vector<char> GraphicsPipeline::readfile(const std::string& filename) {

   std::ifstream file(filename, std::ios::ate | std::ios::binary);

   if (!file.is_open()) {
```

```
                    throw std::runtime_error(" failed to open shader file");
        }
        size_t filesize = (size_t)file.tellg();
        std::vector<char> buffer(filesize);

        file.seekg(0);
        file.read(buffer.data(), filesize);

        file.close();

        return buffer;

    }
```

readFile takes a SPIR-V code file, opens and reads it, saves the contents of the file into a vector of char called buffer, and then returns it. We then add the createShaderModule function, as follows:

```
VkShaderModule GraphicsPipeline::createShaderModule(const std::vector<char>
& code) {

    VkShaderModuleCreateInfo cInfo = {};

    cInfo.sType = VK_STRUCTURE_TYPE_SHADER_MODULE_CREATE_INFO;
    cInfo.codeSize = code.size();
    cInfo.pCode = reinterpret_cast<const uint32_t*>(code.data());

    VkShaderModule shaderModule;
    if (vkCreateShaderModule(VulkanContext::getInstance()->getDevice()->
        logicalDevice, &cInfo, nullptr, &shaderModule) != VK_SUCCESS) {
        throw std::runtime_error(" failed to create shader module !");
    }

    return shaderModule;
}
```

To create the shader module, which is required for ShaderStageCreateInfo to create the pipeline, we need to populate the ShaderModuleCreateInfo, which takes the code and the size from the buffer to create the shader module. The shader module is created using the vkCreateShaderModule function, which takes the device and the CreateInfo. Once the shader module is created, it is returned. To create the pipeline, we have to create the following info structs: the shader stage info, the vertex input info, the input assembly struct, the viewport info struct, the rasterization info struct, the multisample state struct, the depth stencil struct (if required), the color blending struct, and the dynamic state struct.

So, let's create each, one after the other, starting with the shader stage struct. Add the `createGraphicsPipeline` function, and in it, we will create the pipeline:

```
void GraphicsPipeline::createGraphicsPipeline(VkExtent2D
swapChainImageExtent,  VkRenderPass renderPass) {

...

}
```

In this function, we will now add the following, which will create the graphics pipeline.

ShaderStageCreateInfo

To create the vertex shader, `ShaderStageCreateInfo`, we need to read the shader code first and create the shader module for it:

```
auto vertexShaderCode = readfile("shaders/SPIRV/basic.vert.spv");

VkShaderModule vertexShadeModule = createShaderModule(vertexShaderCode);
```

To read the shader file, we pass in the location of the shader file. Then, we pass the read code into the `createShaderModule` function, which will give us `vertexShaderModule`. We create the shader stage info struct for the vertex shader and pass in the stage, the shader module, and the name of the function to be used in the shader, which is `main`, in our case:

```
VkPipelineShaderStageCreateInfo vertShaderStageCreateInfo = {};
vertShaderStageCreateInfo.sType = VK_STRUCTURE_TYPE_PIPELINE_SHADER
                                  _STAGE_CREATE_INFO;
vertShaderStageCreateInfo.stage = VK_SHADER_STAGE_VERTEX_BIT;
vertShaderStageCreateInfo.module = vertexShadeModule;
vertShaderStageCreateInfo.pName = "main";
```

Similarly, we will create the `ShaderStageCreateInfo` struct for the fragment shader:

```
auto fragmentShaderCode = readfile("shaders/SPIRV/basic.frag.spv");
VkShaderModule fragShaderModule = createShaderModule
                                  (fragmentShaderCode);

VkPipelineShaderStageCreateInfo fragShaderStageCreateInfo = {};

fragShaderStageCreateInfo.sType = VK_STRUCTURE_TYPE_PIPELINESHADER_
                                  STAGE_CREATE_INFO;
fragShaderStageCreateInfo.stage = VK_SHADER_STAGE_FRAGMENT_BIT;
fragShaderStageCreateInfo.module = fragShaderModule;
fragShaderStageCreateInfo.pName = "main";
```

Note that the shader stage is set to `VK_SHADER_STAGE_FRAGMENT_BIT` to show that this is the fragment shader, and we also pass in `basic.frag.spv` as the file to read, which is the fragment shader file. We then create an array of `shaderStageCreateInfo` and add the two shaders to it for convenience:

```
VkPipelineShaderStageCreateInfo shaderStages[] = {
    vertShaderStageCreateInfo, fragShaderStageCreateInfo };
```

VertexInputStateCreateInfo

In this info, we specify the input buffer binding and the attribute description:

```
auto bindingDescription = Vertex::getBindingDescription();
auto attribiteDescriptions = Vertex::getAttributeDescriptions();

VkPipelineVertexInputStateCreateInfo vertexInputInfo = {};
vertexInputInfo.sType = VK_STRUCTURE_TYPEPIPELINE
                        VERTEX_INPUT_STATE_CREATE_INFO;
// initially was 0 as vertex data was hardcoded in the shader
vertexInputInfo.vertexBindingDescriptionCount = 1;
vertexInputInfo.pVertexBindingDescriptions = &bindingDescription;

vertexInputInfo.vertexAttributeDescriptionCount = static_cast<uint32_t>
(attribiteDescriptions.size());
vertexInputInfo.pVertexAttributeDescriptions = attribiteDescriptions
                                               .data();
```

This is specified in the `Mesh.h` file under the vertex struct.

InputAssemblyStateCreateInfo

Here, we specify the geometry we want to create, which is a triangle list. Add it as follows:

```
VkPipelineInputAssemblyStateCreateInfo inputAssemblyInfo = {};
inputAssemblyInfo.sType = VK_STRUCTURE_TYPE_PIPELINEINPUT
                          ASSEMBLY_STATE_CREATE_INFO;
inputAssemblyInfo.topology = VK_PRIMITIVE_TOPOLOGY_TRIANGLE_LIST;
inputAssemblyInfo.primitiveRestartEnable = VK_FALSE;
```

RasterizationStateCreateInfo

In this struct, we specify that depth clamping is enabled, which, instead of discarding the fragments if they are beyond the near and far planes, still keeps the value of that fragment and sets it equal to the near or far plane, even if that pixel is beyond either of these planes.

Discard the pixel in the rasterization stage by setting the value of rasterizerDiscardEnable to true or false. Set the polygon mode to either VK_POLYGON_MODE_FILL or VK_POLYGON_MODE_LINE. If it is set to line, then only a wireframe will be drawn; otherwise, the insides are also rasterized.

We can set the line width with the lineWidth parameter. Additionally, we can enable or disable back-face culling and then set the order of the front face winding by setting the cullMode and frontFace parameters.

We can alter the depth value by enabling it and adding a constant value to the depth, clamping it, or adding a slope factor. Depth biases are used in shadow maps, which we won't be using, so we won't enable depth bias. Add the struct and populate it as follows:

```
VkPipelineRasterizationStateCreateInfo rastStateCreateInfo = {};
rastStateCreateInfo.sType = VK_STRUCTURE_TYPE_PIPELINE_RASTERIZATION
                            STATE_CREATE_INFO;
rastStateCreateInfo.depthClampEnable = VK_FALSE;
rastStateCreateInfo.rasterizerDiscardEnable = VK_FALSE;
rastStateCreateInfo.polygonMode = VK_POLYGON_MODE_FILL;
rastStateCreateInfo.lineWidth = 1.0f;
rastStateCreateInfo.cullMode = VK_CULL_MODE_BACK_BIT;
rastStateCreateInfo.frontFace = VK_FRONT_FACE_CLOCKWISE;
rastStateCreateInfo.depthBiasEnable = VK_FALSE;
rastStateCreateInfo.depthBiasConstantFactor = 0.0f;
rastStateCreateInfo.depthBiasClamp = 0.0f;
rastStateCreateInfo.depthBiasSlopeFactor = 0.0f;
```

MultisampleStateCreateInfo

For our project, we won't be enabling multisampling for anti-aliasing. However, we will still need to create the struct:

```
VkPipelineMultisampleStateCreateInfo msStateInfo = {};
msStateInfo.sType = VK_STRUCTURE_TYPE_PIPELINEMULTISAMPLE
                    STATE_CREATE_INFO;
msStateInfo.sampleShadingEnable = VK_FALSE;
msStateInfo.rasterizationSamples = VK_SAMPLE_COUNT_1_BIT;
```

We disable it by setting `sampleShadingEnable` to false and setting the sample count to 1.

Depth and stencil create info

Since we don't have a depth or stencil buffer, we don't need to create it. But when you have a depth buffer, you will need to add it to use the depth texture.

ColorBlendStateCreateInfo

We set the color blending to false because it is not required for our project. To populate it, we have to first create the `ColorBlend` attachment state, which contains the configuration of each `ColorBlend` in each attachment. Then, we create `ColorBlendStateInfo`, which contains the overall blend state.

Create the `ColorBlendAttachment` state as follows. In this, we still specify the color write mask, which is the red, green, blue, and alpha bits, and set the attachment state to false, which disables blending for the framebuffer attachment:

```
VkPipelineColorBlendAttachmentState  cbAttach = {};
cbAttach.colorWriteMask = VK_COLOR_COMPONENT_R_BIT |
                          VK_COLOR_COMPONENT_G_BIT |
                          VK_COLOR_COMPONENT_B_BIT |
                          VK_COLOR_COMPONENT_A_BIT;
cbAttach.blendEnable = VK_FALSE;
```

We create the actual blend struct, which takes the blend attachment info created, and we set the attachment count to 1 because we have a single attachment:

```
cbCreateInfo.sType = VK_STRUCTURE_TYPE_PIPELINE_COLORBLEND_
                     STATE_CREATE_INFO;
cbCreateInfo.attachmentCount = 1;
cbCreateInfo.pAttachments = &cbAttach;
```

Dynamic state info

Since we don't have any dynamic states, this is not created.

ViewportStateCreateInfo

In `ViewportStateCreateInfo`, we can specify the region of the framebuffer in which the output will be rendered to the viewport. So, we can render the scene but then only show some of it to the viewport. We can also specify a scissor rectangle, which will discard the pixels being rendered to the viewport.

However, we won't be doing anything fancy like that because we will render the whole scene to the viewport as it is. To define the viewport size and scissor size, we have to create the respective structs, as follows:

```
VkViewport viewport = {};
viewport.x = 0;
viewport.y = 0;
viewport.width = (float)swapChainImageExtent.width;
viewport.height = (float)swapChainImageExtent.height;
viewport.minDepth = 0.0f;
viewport.maxDepth = 1.0f;

VkRect2D scissor = {};
scissor.offset = { 0,0 };
scissor.extent = swapChainImageExtent;
```

For the viewport size and extent, we set them to the size of the `swapChain` image size in terms of width and height, starting from `(0, 0)`. We also set the minimum and maximum depth, which is normally between 0 and 1.

For the scissor, since we want to show the whole viewport, we set the offset to `(0, 0)`, which indicates that we don't want the offset to start from where the viewport starts. Accordingly, we set the `scissor.extent` to the size of the `swapChain` image.

Now we can create `ViewportStateCreateInfo` function, as follows:

```
VkPipelineViewportStateCreateInfo vpStateInfo = {};
vpStateInfo.sType = VK_STRUCTURE_TYPE_PIPELINEVIEWPORT
                    STATE_CREATE_INFO;
vpStateInfo.viewportCount = 1;
vpStateInfo.pViewports = &viewport;
vpStateInfo.scissorCount = 1;
vpStateInfo.pScissors = &scissor;
```

GraphicsPipelineCreateInfo

To create the graphics pipeline, we have to create the final `Info` struct, which we will populate with the `Info` structs we have created so far. So, add the struct as follows:

```
VkGraphicsPipelineCreateInfo gpInfo = {};
gpInfo.sType = VK_STRUCTURE_TYPE_GRAPHICS_PIPELINE_CREATE_INFO;
gpInfo.stageCount = 2;
gpInfo.pStages = shaderStages;
gpInfo.pVertexInputState = &vertexInputInfo;
gpInfo.pInputAssemblyState = &inputAssemblyInfo;
gpInfo.pRasterizationState = &rastStateCreateInfo;
gpInfo.pMultisampleState = &msStateInfo;
gpInfo.pDepthStencilState = nullptr;
gpInfo.pColorBlendState = &cbCreateInfo;
gpInfo.pDynamicState = nullptr;

gpInfo.pViewportState = &vpStateInfo;
```

We also need to pass in the pipeline layout, render the pass, and specify whether there are any subpasses:

```
gpInfo.layout = pipelineLayout;
gpInfo.renderPass = renderPass;
gpInfo.subpass = 0;
```

Now we can create the pipeline, as follows:

```
if (vkCreateGraphicsPipelines(VulkanContext::getInstance()->
   getDevice()->logicalDevice, VK_NULL_HANDLE, 1, &gpInfo, nullptr,
   &graphicsPipeline) != VK_SUCCESS) {
      throw std::runtime_error("failed to create graphics pipeline !!");
}
```

Additionally, make sure that you destroy the shader modules, as they are no longer required:

```
vkDestroyShaderModule(VulkanContext::getInstance()->
   getDevice()->logicalDevice, vertexShadeModule, nullptr);
vkDestroyShaderModule(VulkanContext::getInstance()->
   getDevice()->logicalDevice, fragShaderModule, nullptr);
```

And that is all for the `createGraphicsPipeline` function. Finally, add the `destroy` function, which will destroy the pipeline and the layout:

```
void GraphicsPipeline::destroy(){

   vkDestroyPipeline(VulkanContext::getInstance()->
```

```
        getDevice()->logicalDevice, graphicsPipeline, nullptr);
    vkDestroyPipelineLayout(VulkanContext::getInstance()->
        getDevice()->logicalDevice, pipelineLayout, nullptr);


}
```

The ObjectRenderer class

With all the necessary classes created, we can finally create our ObjectRenderer class, which will render the mesh object to the scene.

Let's create a new class called ObjectRenderer. In ObjectRenderer.h, add the following:

```
#include "GraphicsPipeline.h"
#include "ObjectBuffers.h"
#include "Descriptor.h"

#include "Camera.h"

class ObjectRenderer
{
public:
    void createObjectRenderer(MeshType modelType, glm::vec3 _position,
        glm::vec3 _scale);
    void updateUniformBuffer(Camera camera);

    void draw();

    void destroy();

private:

    GraphicsPipeline gPipeline;
    ObjectBuffers objBuffers;
    Descriptor descriptor;

    glm::vec3 position;
    glm::vec3 scale;

};
```

We will include the descriptor, pipeline, and object buffer headers because they are required for the class. In the `public` section of the class, we will add objects of the three classes to define the pipeline, object buffers, and descriptors. We add four functions:

- The first one is the `createObjectRenderer` function, which takes the model type, the position in which the object needs to be created, and the scale of the object.
- Then, we have `updateUniformBuffer`, which will update the uniform buffer at every different frame and pass it to the shader. This takes the camera as a parameter because it is needed to get the view and perspective matrices. So, include the camera header as well.
- We then have the `draw` function, which will be used to bind the pipeline, vertex, index, and descriptors to make the draw call.
- We also have a `destroy` function to call the `destroy` functions of the pipeline, descriptors, and object buffers.

In the object's `Renderer.cpp` file, add the following `include` and the `createObjectRenderer` function:

```cpp
#include "ObjectRenderer.h"
#include "VulkanContext.h"
void ObjectRenderer::createObjectRenderer(MeshType modelType, glm::vec3
_position, glm::vec3 _scale){

uint32_t swapChainImageCount = VulkanContext::getInstance()->
                               getSwapChain()->swapChainImages.size();

VkExtent2D swapChainImageExtent = VulkanContext::getInstance()->
                                  getSwapChain()->swapChainImageExtent;

    // Create Vertex, Index and Uniforms Buffer;
    objBuffers.createVertexIndexUniformsBuffers(modelType);

    // CreateDescriptorSetLayout
      descriptor.createDescriptorLayoutSetPoolAndAllocate
      (swapChainImageCount);
      descriptor.populateDescriptorSets(swapChainImageCount,
      objBuffers.uniformBuffers);

    // CreateGraphicsPipeline
    gPipeline.createGraphicsPipelineLayoutAndPipeline(
        swapChainImageExtent,
        descriptor.descriptorSetLayout,
        VulkanContext::getInstance()->getRenderpass()->renderPass);
```

```
        position = _position;
        scale = _scale;
    }
```

We get the number of swap buffer images and their extents. Then, we create the vertex index and uniform buffers, we create and populate the descriptor set layout and sets, and then we create the graphics pipeline itself. Finally, we set the position and scale of the current object. Then, we add the `updateUniformBuffer` function. To get access to `SwapChain` and `RenderPass`, we will make some changes to the `VulkanContext` class:

```cpp
void ObjectRenderer::updateUniformBuffer(Camera camera){

    UniformBufferObject ubo = {};

    glm::mat4 scaleMatrix = glm::mat4(1.0f);
    glm::mat4 rotMatrix = glm::mat4(1.0f);
    glm::mat4 transMatrix = glm::mat4(1.0f);

    scaleMatrix = glm::scale(glm::mat4(1.0f), scale);
    transMatrix = glm::translate(glm::mat4(1.0f), position);

    ubo.model = transMatrix * rotMatrix * scaleMatrix;

    ubo.view = camera.viewMatrix

    ubo.proj = camera.getprojectionMatrix

    ubo.proj[1][1] *= -1; // invert Y, in Opengl it is inverted to
                          begin with

    void* data;
    vkMapMemory(VulkanContext::getInstance()->getDevice()->
        logicalDevice, objBuffers.uniformBuffersMemory, 0,
        sizeof(ubo), 0, &data);

    memcpy(data, &ubo, sizeof(ubo));

    vkUnmapMemory(VulkanContext::getInstance()->getDevice()->
        logicalDevice, objBuffers.uniformBuffersMemory);

}
```

Here, we create a new `UniformBufferObject` struct called `ubo`. To do so, initialize the translation, rotation, and scale matrices. We then assign values for the scale and rotation matrices. After multiplying the scale, rotation, and translation matrices together, assign the result to the model matrix. From the `camera` class, we assign the view and projection matrices to `ubo.view` and `ubo.proj`. Then, we have to invert the y axis in the projection space because, in OpenGL, the y axis is already inverted. We now copy the updated `ubo` struct to the uniform buffer memory.

Next is the `draw` function:

```
void ObjectRenderer::draw(){

    VkCommandBuffer cBuffer = VulkanContext::getInstance()->
                            getCurrentCommandBuffer();

    // Bind the pipeline
    vkCmdBindPipeline(cBuffer, VK_PIPELINE_BIND_POINT_GRAPHICS,
      gPipeline.graphicsPipeline);

    // Bind vertex buffer to command buffer
    VkBuffer vertexBuffers[] = { objBuffers.vertexBuffer };
    VkDeviceSize offsets[] = { 0 };

    vkCmdBindVertexBuffers(cBuffer,
        0, // first binding index
        1, // binding count
        vertexBuffers,
        offsets);

    // Bind index buffer to the command buffer
    vkCmdBindIndexBuffer(cBuffer,
        objBuffers.indexBuffer,
        0,
        VK_INDEX_TYPE_UINT32);

    //    Bind uniform buffer using descriptorSets
    vkCmdBindDescriptorSets(cBuffer,
        VK_PIPELINE_BIND_POINT_GRAPHICS,
        gPipeline.pipelineLayout,
        0,
        1,
        &descriptor.descriptorSet, 0, nullptr);

    vkCmdDrawIndexed(cBuffer,
        static_cast<uint32_t>(objBuffers.indices.size()), // no of indices
        1, // instance count -- just the 1
        0, // first index -- start at 0th index
```

```
        0, // vertex offset -- any offsets to add
        0);// first instance -- since no instancing, is set to 0

}
```

Before we actually make the draw call, we have to bind the graphics pipeline and pass in the vertex, index, and descriptor using the command buffer. To do this, we get the current command buffer and pass the commands through it. We will make changes to the VulkanContext class to get access to it as well.

We make the draw call using vkCmdDrawIndexed, in which we pass in the current command buffer, the index size, the instance count, the start of the index (which is 0), the vertex offset (which is again 0), and the location of the first index (which is 0). Then, we add the destroy function, which basically just calls the destroy function of the pipeline, the descriptor, and the object buffer:

```
    void ObjectRenderer::destroy() {

        gPipeline.destroy();
        descriptor.destroy();
        objBuffers.destroy();


    }
```

Changes to the VulkanContext class

To get access to SwapChain, RenderPass, and the current command buffer, we will add the following functions to the VulkanContext.h file under the VulkanContext class in the public section:

```
        void drawBegin();
        void drawEnd();
        void cleanup();

        SwapChain* getSwapChain();
        Renderpass* getRenderpass();
        VkCommandBuffer getCurrentCommandBuffer();
```

Then, in the VulkanContext.cpp file, add the implementation for accessing the values:

```
    SwapChain * VulkanContext::getSwapChain() {

        return swapChain;
    }
```

```
Renderpass * VulkanContext::getRenderpass() {

    return renderPass;
}

VkCommandBuffer VulkanContext::getCurrentCommandBuffer() {

    return curentCommandBuffer;
}
```

The Camera class

We will create a basic camera class so that we can set the camera's position and set the view and projection matrices. This class will be very similar to the camera class created for the OpenGL project. The camera.h file is as follows:

```
#pragma once

#define GLM_FORCE_RADIAN
#include <glm\glm.hpp>
#include <glm\gtc\matrix_transform.hpp>

class Camera
{
public:
    void init(float FOV, float width, float height, float nearplane,
        float farPlane);
    void setCameraPosition(glm::vec3 position);
    glm::mat4 getViewMatrix();
    glm::mat4 getprojectionMatrix();

private:

    glm::mat4 projectionMatrix;
    glm::mat4 viewMatrix;
    glm::vec3 cameraPos;

};
```

It has an init function, which takes the FOV, width, and height of the viewport, and the near and far planes to construct the projection matrix. We have a setCameraPosition function, which sets the location of the camera and two getter functions to get the camera view and projection matrices. In the private section, we have three local variables: two are for storing the projection and view matrices, and the third is a vec3 for storing the camera's position.

The `Camera.cpp` file is as follows:

```cpp
#include "Camera.h"

void Camera::init(float FOV, float width, float height, float nearplane,
    float farPlane) {

    cameraPos = glm::vec3(0.0f, 0.0f, 4.0f);
    glm::vec3 cameraFront = glm::vec3(0.0f, 0.0f, 0.0f);
    glm::vec3 cameraUp = glm::vec3(0.0f, 1.0f, 0.0f);

    viewMatrix = glm::mat4(1.0f);
    projectionMatrix = glm::mat4(1.0f);

    projectionMatrix = glm::perspective(FOV, width / height, nearplane,
                       farPlane);
    viewMatrix = glm::lookAt(cameraPos, cameraFront, cameraUp);

}

glm::mat4 Camera::getViewMatrix(){

    return viewMatrix;

}
glm::mat4 Camera::getprojectionMatrix(){

    return projectionMatrix;
}

void Camera::setCameraPosition(glm::vec3 position){

    cameraPos = position;
}
```

In the `init` function, we set the view and projection matrices, and then we add two getter functions and the `setCameraPosition` function.

Drawing the object

Now that we have completed the prerequisites, let's draw a triangle:

1. In `source.cpp`, include `Camera.h` and `ObjectRenderer.h`:

```cpp
#define GLFW_INCLUDE_VULKAN
#include<GLFW/glfw3.h>
```

```
#include "VulkanContext.h"

#include "Camera.h"
#include "ObjectRenderer.h"
```

2. In the `main` function, after initializing `VulkanContext`, create a new camera and an object to render, as follows:

```
int main() {

    glfwInit();

    glfwWindowHint(GLFW_CLIENT_API, GLFW_NO_API);
    glfwWindowHint(GLFW_RESIZABLE, GLFW_FALSE);

    GLFWwindow* window = glfwCreateWindow(1280, 720,
                        "HELLO VULKAN ", nullptr, nullptr);

    VulkanContext::getInstance()->initVulkan(window);

    Camera camera;
    camera.init(45.0f, 1280.0f, 720.0f, 0.1f, 10000.0f);
    camera.setCameraPosition(glm::vec3(0.0f, 0.0f, 4.0f));

    ObjectRenderer object;
    object.createObjectRenderer(MeshType::kTriangle,
            glm::vec3(0.0f, 0.0f, 0.0f),
            glm::vec3(0.5f));
```

3. In the `while` loop, update the object's buffer and call the `object.draw` function:

```
    while (!glfwWindowShouldClose(window)) {

        VulkanContext::getInstance()->drawBegin();

        object.updateUniformBuffer(camera);
        object.draw();

        VulkanContext::getInstance()->drawEnd();

        glfwPollEvents();
    }
```

4. When the program is done, call the `object.destroy` function:

```
    object.destroy();

    VulkanContext::getInstance()->cleanup();
```

```
        glfwDestroyWindow(window);
        glfwTerminate();

        return 0;
    }
```

5. Run the application and see a glorious triangle, as follows:

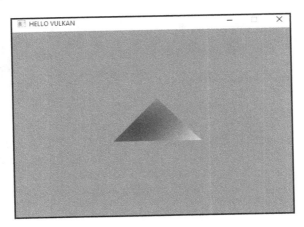

Woohoo! Finally, we have a triangle. Well, we are still not quite done yet. Remember the annoying **validation layer** error that we keep getting? Take a look:

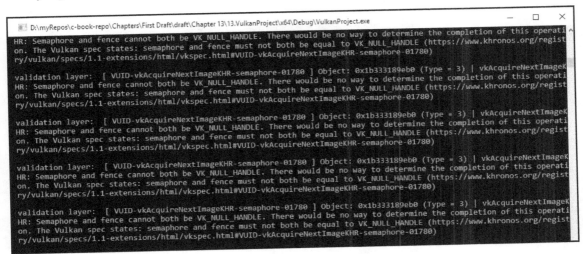

It is time to understand why we are getting this error and what it actually means. This leads us to our final topic of this book: synchronization.

Synchronizing the object

The process of drawing is actually asynchronous, meaning that the GPU might have to wait until the CPU has finished its current job. For example, using the constant buffer, we send instructions to the GPU to update each frame of the model view projection matrix. Now, if the GPU doesn't wait for the CPU to get the uniform buffer for the current frame, then the object would not be rendered correctly.

To make sure that the GPU only executes when the CPU has done its work, we need to synchronize the CPU and GPU. This can be done using two types synchronization objects:

- The first is fences. Fences are synchronization objects that synchronize CPU and GPU operations.

- We have a second kind of synchronization object, called semaphores. Semaphore objects synchronize GPU queues. In the current scene of one triangle that we are rendering, the graphics queue submits all the graphics commands, and then the presentation queue takes the image and presents it to the viewport. Of course, even this needs to be synchronized; otherwise, we will see scenes that haven't been fully rendered.

There are also events and barriers, which are other types of synchronization objects used for synchronizing work within a command buffer or a sequence of command buffers.

Since we haven't used any synchronization objects, the Vulkan validation layer is throwing errors and telling us that when we acquire an image from the SwapChain, we need to either use a fence or a semaphore to synchronize it.

In VulkanContext.h, in the private section, we will add the synchronization objects to be created, as follows:

```
const int MAX_FRAMES_IN_FLIGHT = 2;
VkSemaphore imageAvailableSemaphore;
VkSemaphore renderFinishedSemaphore;
std::vector<VkFence> inFlightFences;
```

We have created two semaphores: one semaphore to signal when an image is available for us to render into, and another to signal when the rendering of the image has finished. We also created two fences to synchronize the two frames. In VulkanContext.cpp, under the initVulkan function, create the Synchronization object after the DrawCommandBuffer object:

```
drawComBuffer = new DrawCommandBuffer();
drawComBuffer->createCommandPoolAndBuffer(swapChain->
```

```
        swapChainImages.size());


    // Synchronization

    VkSemaphoreCreateInfo semaphoreInfo = {};
    semaphoreInfo.sType = VK_STRUCTURE_TYPE_SEMAPHORE_CREATE_INFO;

    vkCreateSemaphore(device->logicalDevice,  &semaphoreInfo,
        nullptr, &imageAvailableSemaphore);
    vkCreateSemaphore(device->logicalDevice,  &semaphoreInfo,
        nullptr, &renderFinishedSemaphore);


    inFlightFences.resize(MAX_FRAMES_IN_FLIGHT);

    VkFenceCreateInfo fenceCreateInfo = {};
    fenceCreateInfo.sType = VK_STRUCTURE_TYPE_FENCE_CREATE_INFO;
    fenceCreateInfo.flags = VK_FENCE_CREATE_SIGNALED_BIT;


    for (size_t i = 0; i < MAX_FRAMES_IN_FLIGHT; i++) {

        if (vkCreateFence(device->logicalDevice, &fenceCreateInfo,
            nullptr, &inFlightFences[i]) != VK_SUCCESS) {

        throw std::runtime_error(" failed to create synchronization
            objects per frame !!");
        }
    }
```

We created the semaphore first using the semaphoreCreatInfo struct. We just have to set the struct type; we can create it using the vkCreateSemaphore function and pass in the logical device and the info struct.

Next, we create our fences. We resize the vector with the number of frames in flight, which is 2. Then, we create the fenceCreateInfo struct and set the type of the struct. We now also signal the fences so that they are ready to be rendered. Then, we create the fences using vkCreateFence and pass in the logical device and the create fence info using a for loop. In the DrawBegin function, when we acquire the image, we pass in the imageAvailable semaphore to the function so that the semaphore will be signaled when the image is available for us to render into:

```
        vkAcquireNextImageKHR(device->logicalDevice,
            swapChain->swapChain,
            std::numeric_limits<uint64_t>::max(),
            imageAvailableSemaphore, // is  signaled
```

```
            VK_NULL_HANDLE,
            &imageIndex);
```

Once an image is available to render into, we wait for the fence to be signaled so that we can start writing our command buffers:

```
vkWaitForFences(device->logicalDevice, 1, &inFlightFences[imageIndex],
    VK_TRUE, std::numeric_limits<uint64_t>::max());
```

We wait for the fence by calling `vkWaitForFences` and pass in the logical device, the fence count (which is 1), and the fence itself. Then, we pass TRUE to wait for all fences, and pass in a timeout. Once the fence is available, we set it to unsignaled by calling `vkResetFence`, and then pass in the logical device, the fence count, and the fence:

```
vkResetFences(device->logicalDevice, 1, &inFlightFences[imageIndex]);
```

The reset of the `DrawBegin` function remains the same so that we can begin recording the command buffer. Now, in the `DrawEnd` function, when it is time to submit the command buffer, we set the pipeline stage for `imageAvailableSemaphore` to wait on and set `imageAvailableSemaphore` to wait. We will set `renderFinishedSemaphore` to be signaled.

The `submitInfo` struct is changed accordingly:

```
// submit command buffer
VkSubmitInfo submitInfo = {};
submitInfo.sType = VK_STRUCTURE_TYPE_SUBMIT_INFO;
submitInfo.commandBufferCount = 1;
submitInfo.pCommandBuffers = &currentCommandBuffer;

// Wait for the stage that writes to color attachment
VkPipelineStageFlags waitStages[] = { VK_PIPELINESTAGECOLOR_
                                      ATTACHMENT_OUTPUT_BIT };
// Which stage of the pipeline to wait
submitInfo.pWaitDstStageMask = waitStages;

// Semaphore to wait on before submit command execution begins
submitInfo.waitSemaphoreCount = 1;
submitInfo.pWaitSemaphores = &imageAvailableSemaphore;

// Semaphore to be signaled when command buffers have completed
submitInfo.signalSemaphoreCount = 1;
submitInfo.pSignalSemaphores = &renderFinishedSemaphore;
```

The stage to wait on is `VK_PIPELINE_STAGE_COLOR_ATTACHMENT_OUTPUT_BIT` for `imageAvailableSemaphore` to go from unsignaled to signaled. This will be signaled when the color buffer is written to. We then set `renderFinishedSemaphore` to be signaled so that the image will be ready for presenting. Submit the command and pass in the fence to show that the submission has been done:

```
vkQueueSubmit(device->graphicsQueue, 1, &submitInfo,
inFlightFences[imageIndex]);
```

Once the submission is done, we can present the image. In the `presentInfo` struct, we set `renderFinishedSemaphore` to wait to go from an unsignaled state to a signaled state. We do this because, when the semaphore is signaled, the image will be ready for presentation:

```
// Present frame
VkPresentInfoKHR presentInfo = {};
presentInfo.sType = VK_STRUCTURE_TYPE_PRESENT_INFO_KHR;

presentInfo.waitSemaphoreCount = 1;
presentInfo.pWaitSemaphores = &renderFinishedSemaphore;

presentInfo.swapchainCount = 1;
presentInfo.pSwapchains = &swapChain->swapChain;
presentInfo.pImageIndices = &imageIndex;

vkQueuePresentKHR(device->presentQueue, &presentInfo);
vkQueueWaitIdle(device->presentQueue);
```

In the `cleanup` function in `VulkanContext`, make sure that you destroy the semaphores and fences, as follows:

```
void VulkanContext::cleanup() {


    vkDeviceWaitIdle(device->logicalDevice);

    vkDestroySemaphore(device->logicalDevice,
        renderFinishedSemaphore, nullptr);
    vkDestroySemaphore(device->logicalDevice,
        imageAvailableSemaphore, nullptr);

    // Fences and Semaphores
    for (size_t i = 0; i < MAX_FRAMES_IN_FLIGHT; i++) {

        vkDestroyFence(device->logicalDevice, inFlightFences[i], nullptr);

    }

    drawComBuffer->destroy();
```

```
    renderTarget->destroy();
    renderPass->destroy();
    swapChain->destroy();

    device->destroy();


    valLayersAndExt->destroy(vInstance->vkInstance,
  isValidationLayersEnabled);

    vkDestroySurfaceKHR(vInstance->vkInstance, surface, nullptr);
    vkDestroyInstance(vInstance->vkInstance, nullptr);

}
```

Now build and run the application in debug mode and see that the validation layer has stopped complaining:

Now draw other objects as well, such as a quad, cube, and sphere, by changing the
`source.cpp` file as follows:

```cpp
#define GLFW_INCLUDE_VULKAN
#include<GLFW/glfw3.h>
#include "VulkanContext.h"
#include "Camera.h"
#include "ObjectRenderer.h"
int main() {

glfwInit();

glfwWindowHint(GLFW_CLIENT_API, GLFW_NO_API);
glfwWindowHint(GLFW_RESIZABLE, GLFW_FALSE);

GLFWwindow* window = glfwCreateWindow(1280, 720, "HELLO VULKAN ",
                    nullptr, nullptr);
VulkanContext::getInstance()->initVulkan(window);

Camera camera;
camera.init(45.0f, 1280.0f, 720.0f, 0.1f, 10000.0f);
camera.setCameraPosition(glm::vec3(0.0f, 0.0f, 4.0f));
ObjectRenderer tri;
tri.createObjectRenderer(MeshType::kTriangle,
glm::vec3(-1.0f, 1.0f, 0.0f),
glm::vec3(0.5f));

ObjectRenderer quad;
quad.createObjectRenderer(MeshType::kQuad,
glm::vec3(1.0f, 1.0f, 0.0f),
glm::vec3(0.5f));

ObjectRenderer cube;
cube.createObjectRenderer(MeshType::kCube,
glm::vec3(-1.0f, -1.0f, 0.0f),
glm::vec3(0.5f));

ObjectRenderer sphere;
sphere.createObjectRenderer(MeshType::kSphere,
glm::vec3(1.0f, -1.0f, 0.0f),
glm::vec3(0.5f));

while (!glfwWindowShouldClose(window)) {

VulkanContext::getInstance()->drawBegin();

// updatetri.updateUniformBuffer(camera);
quad.updateUniformBuffer(camera);
```

```
    cube.updateUniformBuffer(camera);
    sphere.updateUniformBuffer(camera);

    // draw command
    tri.draw();
    quad.draw();
    cube.draw();
    sphere.draw();
    VulkanContext::getInstance()->drawEnd();
    glfwPollEvents();
    }
    tri.destroy();
    quad.destroy();
    cube.destroy();
    sphere.destroy();
    VulkanContext::getInstance()->cleanup();
    glfwDestroyWindow(window);
    glfwTerminate();
    return 0;
    }
```

And this should be the final output, with all the objects rendered:

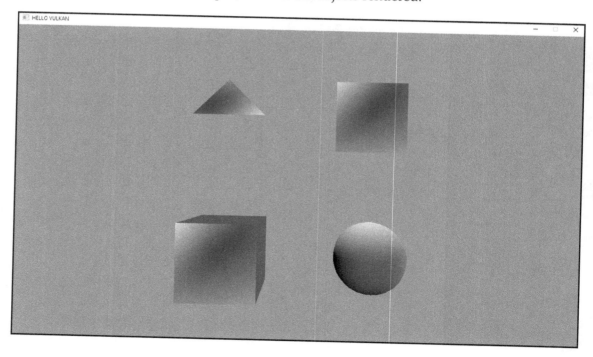

You can also add custom geometries that can be loaded from a file.

In addition to this, now that you have different shapes to render, you can add physics and try to replicate the physics game made in OpenGL, and port the game to use the Vulkan rendering API.

Furthermore, the code can be extended to include the depth buffer, adding textures to the object, and more.

Summary

So, this is the final summary of this book. In this book, we journeyed from creating a basic game in Simple and Fast Multimedia Library (SFML), which uses OpenGL for rendering, to showing how a rendering API fits into the whole scheme when making a game.

We then created a complete physics-based game from the ground up, using our own mini game engine. Apart from just drawing objects using the high-level OpenGL graphics API, we also added bullet physics to take care of game physics and contact detection between game objects. We also added some text rendering to make the score visible to the player, and we also learned about basic lighting to do lighting calculations for our small scene in order to make the scene a little more interesting.

Finally, we moved on to the Vulkan rendering API, which is a low-level graphics library. In comparison to OpenGL, which we used to make a small game by the end of Chapter 3, *Setting Up Your Game*, in Vulkan, at the end of four chapters, we were able to render a basic geometric objects. However, with Vulkan, we have complete access to the GPU, which gives us more freedom to tailor the engine based on the game's requirements.

If you have come this far, then congratulations! I hope you enjoyed going through this book and that you will continue to expand your knowledge of the SFML, OpenGL, and Vulkan projects.

Best wishes.

Further Reading

To learn more, I wholeheartedly recommend the Vulkan tutorial website: `https://vulkan-tutorial.com/`. The tutorial also covers how to add textures, depth buffers, model loading, and mipmaps. The code for the book is based on this tutorial, so it should be easy to follow and should help you take the Vulkan code base in the book further:

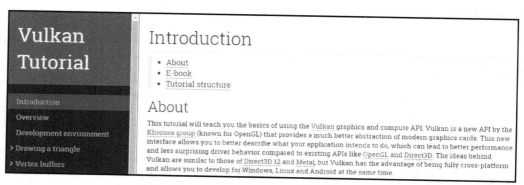

The source code for the Doom 3 Vulkan renderer is available at `https://github.com/DustinHLand/vkDOOM3`—it is fun to see the code in practice:

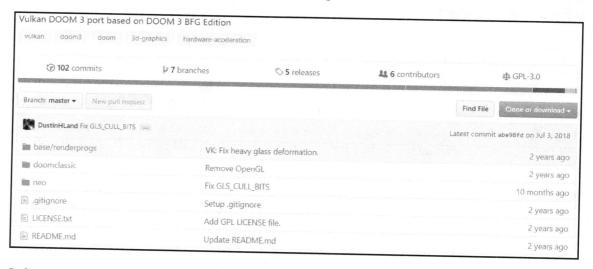

I also recommend reading the blog at `https://www.fasterthan.life/blog`, as it goes through the journey of porting the Doom 3 OpenGL code to Vulkan. In this book, we let Vulkan allocate and deallocate resources. This blog goes into detail about how memory management is done in Vulkan.

Other Books You May Enjoy

If you enjoyed this book, you may be interested in these other books by Packt:

Unreal Engine 4.x Scripting with C++ Cookbook - Second Edition
John P. Doran

ISBN: 9781789809503

- Create C++ classes and structs that integrate well with UE4 and the Blueprints editor
- Discover how to work with various APIs that Unreal Engine already contains
- Utilize advanced concepts such as events, delegates, and interfaces in your UE4 projects
- Build user interfaces using Canvas and UMG through C++
- Extend the Unreal Editor by creating custom windows and editors
- Implement AI tasks and services using C++, Blackboard, and Behavior Trees
- Write C++ code with networking in mind and replicate properties and functions

Qt5 C++ GUI Programming Cookbook - Second Edition
Lee Zhi Eng

ISBN: 9781789803822

- Animate GUI elements using Qt5's built-in animation system
- Draw shapes and 2D images using Qt5's powerful rendering system
- Implement an industry-standard OpenGL library in your project
- Build a mobile app that supports touch events and exports it onto devices
- Parse and extract data from an XML file and present it on your GUI
- Interact with web content by calling JavaScript functions from C++
- Access MySQL and SQLite databases to retrieve data and display it on your GUI

Leave a review - let other readers know what you think

Please share your thoughts on this book with others by leaving a review on the site that you bought it from. If you purchased the book from Amazon, please leave us an honest review on this book's Amazon page. This is vital so that other potential readers can see and use your unbiased opinion to make purchasing decisions, we can understand what our customers think about our products, and our authors can see your feedback on the title that they have worked with Packt to create. It will only take a few minutes of your time, but is valuable to other potential customers, our authors, and Packt. Thank you!

Index